FROM

GRASSLAND TO GLACIER

THE NATURAL HISTORY OF COLORADO AND THE SURROUNDING REGION

CORNELIA FLEISCHER MUTEL AND JOHN C. EMERICK

Johnson Books: Boulder

Cover design: Robert Schram

Second Edition
    2   3   4   5   6   7   8   9

ISBN 1-55566-089-4
LCCCN 84-80539

Printed in the United States of America by
Johnson Printing
1880 South 57th Court
Boulder, Colorado 80301

Contents

Foreword   v
Preface to the First Edition   ix
Preface to the Second Edition   xii
  1. Colorado's Environment   1
  2. Plains Grasslands   27
  3. Mountain Grasslands and Meadows   45
  4. Lowland Riparian Ecosystems   59
  5. Mountain Riparian Ecosystems   71
  6. Shrublands   87
  7. Piñon Pine–Juniper Woodlands   107
  8. Ponderosa Pine Forests   119
  9. Douglas Fir Forests   133
 10. Aspen Groves   141
 11. Lodgepole Pine Forests   153
 12. Limber Pine and Bristlecone Pine Woodlands   161
 13. Engelmann Spruce–Subalpine Fir Forests   169
 14. The Forest–Tundra Transition   181
 15. Alpine Tundra   189
 16. Aquatic Ecosystems   205
Epilogue   227
Self-Guided Tours to Regional Ecosystems   229
Key to Common Native Tree Species   267
Glossary   275
Suggested Reading List   279
Index   287

Dedicated to wild lands and to future generations of people who will treasure the beauty and serenity of such places as we do.

Foreword

The Natural History of Colorado—what does it mean? Why is it important? How to justify this book? For a start, natural history is history in an old-time sense, not history as chronology but history as stories, in this case natural stories, the stories of nature mostly and not stories about people and their artifacts.

Natural history has a history; at the present time, it is maturing to become ecology. Ecology is—in the apt if expansive phrase of one of the greatest of ecologists, G. E. Hutchinson—the study of the Universe. Natural history gave to ecology its starting point, the notion that everything is connected to everything else. Earth and Life are connected in a mutual dynamic powered by the sun, a dynamic of which we humans are an increasingly influential part. This is a book about dynamic connections. That alone would make it important.

Connections define Colorado. The very name, Colorado, evokes contrast, diversity, pattern. The connections cannot be known in a lifetime. They cannot be expressed in the mere two dimensions of print. Philosopher Alfred North Whitehead once observed that "art is the imposing of a pattern on experience." So is science. But there is more to understand of the natural history of Colorado than poet and scientist together can tell. This book is an invitation, but it cannot convey all there is to know. Only experience can teach the best of Colorado.

The Rocky Mountains are the ruling motif in Colorado, the dominating presence, the driving force. Mountains are central to the state's diversity. Visitors and residents alike are drawn almost instinctively to the mountains. Mountains are fundamental to local ecology. They allow a diversity of landscapes greater than any other inland state. The mighty ridge of the Rockies is highest here and stands farthest east. Here it rises most abruptly from plains and canyons and plateaus. High relief dictates a wide range of physical conditions which provide a wide range of opportunity. Colorado is built of recycled mountains. The eastern plains are bits of mountain worn by the ages and integrated by life into ecosystems. The western valleys are carved by mountain water through sediments derived from generations of Rocky Mountains long past.

We are drawn naturally to the mountains, their magnificent scale, their commanding presence. Most human intervention leaves mountains fundamentally unscathed. To really know Colorado, however, we have to look close. At smaller scales, human impact can be greater, human interaction more moving. Look, live, and know it better. Know it better to be the more tenacious in your grip on its wonders, its opportunities for enrichment.

Know Colorado beyond science. Know the damp, musty cool of a spruce forest in thaw, the mournful soliloquy of the hermit thrush through a subalpine fog. Breathe the richness of the sagebrush somewhere west of Maybell. Watch and wonder at the aerobatic flight of pelicans over an oxbow lake along the Platte, coursing as one, disappearing into the noonday sun, to reappear as magically as they had vanished. Hear a coyote howling to his colleagues and a frosty October moon. Delight in a beetle's mechanical tracks in the sand in Glade Park. Watch beavers pushing through the Yampa, working hard to change the course of history. Know spring's first sun climbing resolutely up Green Ridge, illuminating new opportunity in a tender land, tamed by generations of loving hands but not subjugated. Feel dew on the grass on Wilson Mesa changing through frost to steam at dawn. Know a meadowlark calling to a prairie dawn at Pawnee Buttes, a great blue heron plodding homeward, tired but honest, to his half-dead cottonwood, a harrier hovering over a North Park marsh.

Colorado is as icy harsh as wind-driven snow flailing the last heads of grama on a prairie rise, as gentle as the freshness of air after a "one-inch rain"—flat sweet drops an inch across and an inch apart—settles the red dust in the rabbitbrush out beyond Rifle. Colorado is as bright as the Sand Dunes under a full moon, as bright as snowflakes against a late-lying drift of precious winter moisture, as dark as bats working Deep Canyon at dusk, as dark as a moonless prairie night after the lightning has gone.

The images that inspire us to cherish this place are but superficial glimpses, momentary cross-sections through processes of Life and Earth. Know them to keep them steady and whole.

Colorado first was occupied by humans some 10,000 years ago. The last century—just 1 percent of the total tenure of humans here—has been particularly influential. We have changed the color of the sky and made water flow uphill. We have paved and plowed and fouled our nest in myriad ways. But some things still are right. We have a fair measure of wilderness left. There are pronghorn out at the Plains Conservation Center keeping a wary eye on the expanding megalopolis that is the "Queen City of the Plains." Prairie dogs burrow up through the new asphalt of a pretentious but plastic shopping mall. A wily and playful marten follows a right-minded backpacker through the subalpine forest. Can it wonder, I wonder, why all people cannot walk lightly on Earth? Our remaining wildlands have the capacity to lend perspective. Know them to keep them free.

Colorado is a stubborn land that has molded a stubborn and resilient life. Stubborn cattlemen (and women) on hardscrabble ranches and stubborn farmers on dryland farms; sheepherders, more stubborn still, Basque and Mexican, and Native American. Stubborn lichens taking on the Flatirons; stubborn piñons, squeezing a worthy life out of bare slickrock.

This book is an introduction to the ecology of Colorado. It also is an invitation to commitment. Most readers of this book will be latecomers to Colorado. Walk lightly here. Know as much as you can. Get as stubborn as the natives: the Utes, the bristlecone pine, imperious owl, imperial elk. Respect the genius of this place. Pass it on intact to enrich another generation.

David M. Armstrong
Boulder, Colorado
17 April 1984

Preface to the First Edition

Eight years ago, *From Grassland to Glacier* was first published and distributed throughout the Boulder area. Its purpose was to provide residents of Boulder County with a convenient guide to the natural history of that vicinity. The book's nontechnical description of ecological systems and processes was written for anyone wanting to increase his or her enjoyment of the out-of-doors. No other guidebook to the natural history of the Front Range existed, and it was widely used by land-use planners and as a textbook for high school, college, and adult education classes.

Although addressing one small region of Colorado, the book found acceptance by residents and educators up and down the Front Range and on Colorado's Western Slope as well. This widespread use was due in part to the fact that the natural history of the Boulder area closely resembles that of many other areas in the state.

Encouraged by this acceptance of *From Grassland to Glacier,* we have revised and expanded Cornelia Mutel's original version to serve as a guide to the natural history of the entire state of Colorado. John Emerick joined Mutel as a coauthor to assist in the preparation of this new edition, since Cornelia now lives in Iowa. John modified all of the original chapters to include statewide environmental features and added much new information, including discussions of mountain grasslands, piñon pine–juniper woodlands, bristlecone pine forests, and shrubland types that do not occur in Boulder County.

The book's format remains largely that of the original edition, with each of the major ecosystem units being described in terms of its physical appearance, location, site characteristics, dominant plants and animals, ecological processes, and use by humans. The book focuses on natural ecosystems, although modification of ecosystems through human activities is also discussed. While the text emphasizes the ecology of Colorado, it is applicable to other areas in surrounding states that have similar ecosystems. The size of the book was purposefully kept small so that it can be conveniently carried into the field. Several self-guided tours have been added as an aid to ecosystem identification, and we also have included a key to native Colorado tree species.

Scientific names have been excluded from the text but appear in the species lists at the end of each chapter. For the most part, common names of plants follow those used by W. A. Weber in *Rocky Mountain Flora*. Dr. Weber has reviewed the scientific names for all of the plant species, and we have accepted his suggestions regarding their nomenclature. Several field guides for the identification of plant and animal species have been included in the suggested reading list. Many of these guides will be a useful accompaniment to this book when traveling through Colorado's ecosystems. The species lists have been compiled to summarize in a general sense the organisms most common in, or most representative of, each ecosystem. The lists are not exhaustive, so one might see many species other than those listed while visiting a particular ecosystem. (This is especially true of riparian ecosystems.)

We hope that this expanded edition of *From Grassland to Glacier* will continue to meet the needs of residents and visitors to Colorado, as well as those of educators and land-use planners, and in this way will further the understanding and the wise use of Colorado's natural resources.

Many Boulder-area ecologists contributed ideas and expertise to the original edition; we once again extend thanks to Drs. David Armstrong, Jane Bunin, Joyce Greene, John Marr, and Olwen Williams. In addition, we wish to thank Drs. David Armstrong, Richard Beidleman, Joyce Greene, Diana Tomback, William Weber, and Beatrice Willard for their valuable comments on the manuscript of the revised edition. Nova Brown Young produced most of the plant and animal drawings, and Jan Logan constructed the maps and other diagrams. Photographs were provided by W. Perry Conway, Robert C. Farentinos, Lee Gregory, James C. Halfpenny, Stephen Jones, Leonard Lee Rue III and the National Park Service (special thanks to Glen Kaye and Michael Smithson, chief naturalist and naturalist, respectively, at Rocky Mountain National Park). Carse Pustmueller, director of the Colorado Natural Areas Program, William L. Baker of the Colorado Natural Heritage Inventory, and Tom Cardamone, director of the Aspen Center for Environmental Studies, all provided valuable information and other assistance related to the development of this new edition. Peter DeBrine, Shelley Emerick, DeForest Guertin, and Silver Miller assisted with recent field work, and Juanita Smith and Joanne Baer aided in the preparation of the manuscript. We extend our gratitude to all of these people for their contributions.

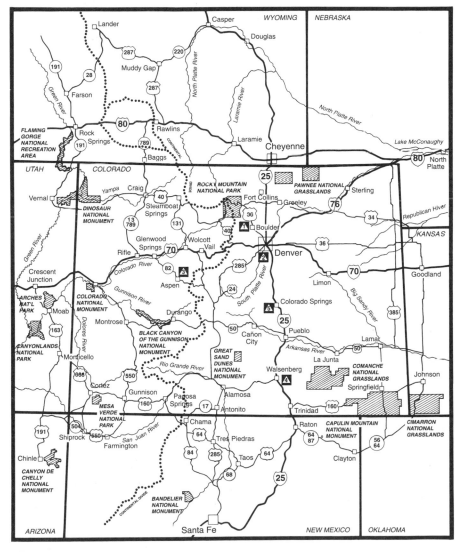

△ Self guided tour

Preface to the Second Edition

For eight years, *From Grassland to Glacier: The Natural History of Colorado* has provided a meaningful introduction to Colorado's ecosystems for students and visitors alike. Continued sales and use of the book by individuals and by classes have been especially gratifying in that the book enabled many people to combine enjoyment of Colorado's outdoors with a greater appreciation of the region's ecological systems and processes. Hopefully, increased sensitivity to the effects of human use has been a natural result.

Since publication of the first edition, new ecological information became available, interactions with book users have suggested possibilities for text improvement, and of course some of our own ideas have changed. Therefore a new edition seemed to be appropriate.

Our original goal of providing a non-technical guide to the region's natural ecosystems has not changed. The original format has been maintained, although we reordered the chapters to provide a better grouping of those describing similar ecosystems. New information was added to many of the chapters, old errors were corrected, and plants and animals lists were updated.

The book remains focused on Colorado, but the text was modified to include portions of adjoining states. The discussion of vegetation patterns in Chapter 1 was changed from a life-zone orientation to one based on major ecosystem types. This was done primarily because visitors recognize ecosystems more easily than life zones, especially in forested regions. Interaction with Denver Museum of Natural History staff members and other ecologists regarding interpretation of regional ecosystems added further impetus for the change. The major ecosystem classification presented in Chapter 1 is based on a system developed by Carron Meaney and David Cooper for the renovation of the Museum's Explore Colorado Hall.

As before, we express our appreciation to all those who, through their contributions of time and expertise, have helped make *From Grassland to Glacier* so successful. In particular, for this edition, we thank Dr. David Armstrong, Hugh Kingery, and Dr. William Weber for their review of species lists, and Carron Meaney of the Denver Museum of Natural History for her review of the first chapter. Greg Policky and John Woodling of the Colorado Division of Wildlife, Dr. James Ward of Colorado State University, and Craig Severn were particularly helpful in assisting with the aquatic ecosystem chapter. Deep appreciation is given to Tom Cardamone and the staff of the Aspen Center for Environmental Studies, who provided assistance as well as a peaceful place for John Emerick to prepare the manuscript for this edition during his sabbatical year.

·1·

Colorado's Environment

The Great Plains roll westward for hundreds of miles across the central United States, ending abruptly at the base of the Rocky Mountains. There landforms change dramatically. Within thirty-five miles of Denver, the mountains rise more than 8,000 feet to the lofty peaks of the Continental Divide. Steeply tilted slabs of sedimentary rock form long, narrow hogbacks along the mountain base, and ravines with nearly vertical sides cut through the foothills behind the hogbacks. West of the Divide, the Rockies descend to a country of plateaus and mesas that have been dissected by the Colorado River and its tributaries. These broad tablelands, interrupted by rocky canyons and arid valleys, extend far into Utah, New Mexico, and Arizona, where they meet the southwestern deserts.

This dramatic change in topography within a few hundred miles results in a diverse array of plant communities. Colorado and the surrounding region boast expansive prairies, moist coniferous forests, hot semidesert shrublands, broad-leaved deciduous forests, alpine tundra, and a correspondingly rich host of animal species.

Although complex, the arrangement of these plant and animal communities is not haphazard. The plants grow in predictable patterns determined by climate, topography, and soils. With a little experience, visitors to the region's wild lands can learn to

A thunderstorm brewing over Mt. Sopris. *J.C. Emerick.*

recognize the major plant communities and understand some of the reasons for their occurrence in each location. Because birds, mammals, and other animals are often dependent upon specific types of vegetation for shelter and food, the observant visitor can anticipate the kinds of animals that may be seen in each type of vegetation.

The plant and animal communities occupying a given locality, along with their physical environment (climate, soil, geologic features, and the like) can be considered as a single interacting unit, called an ecosystem. Since plants are the most conspicuous and sedentary ecosystem component, ecosystems are named for the dominant plants—those that occupy the most space (for example, piñon pine–juniper ecosystems).

The distribution of ecosystems in the region occupied by Colorado and much of her neighboring states can be best understood by first examining topography and climate. The combined effect of these factors produces striking and easily recognized changes in ecosystems as one ascends from lowlands to the mountaintops. This chapter first explores these physical elements, and then gives an overview of the regional plant and animal life.

The Shape of the Land

Travelers in the southern Rocky Mountain west are greeted by a kaleidoscope of scenery, from snow-covered mountains to deep gorges and expansive prairies. The topography is diverse and often characterized by strong vertical relief. Five natural regions, called physiographic provinces, make up most of the landscape. The most prominent are the Southern Rocky Mountains, Great Plains, and Colorado Plateau provinces. Two other provinces, the Middle Rocky Mountains and the Wyoming Basin, are also represented in the northwestern part of the region.

The Southern Rocky Mountains bisect the region from north to south and dominate its topography. These high and rugged peaks contain the oldest rocks in the region, some formed over a billion years ago from ancient sediments and transformed into metamorphic rocks (gneisses and schists). The Southern Rockies are the highest part of the Rocky Mountain chain in the United States, with fifty-three peaks over 14,000 feet high. Some of the most prominent are Long's Peak (14,255 feet), Gray's Peak

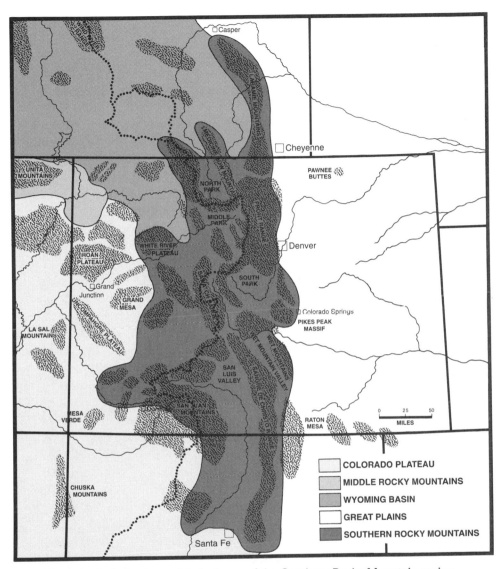

The principal physiographic features of the Southern Rocky Mountain region.
Shaded patches depict major mountain ranges, plateaus, and mesas.

(14,270 feet), and Mount Elbert (14,433 feet), the highest in the Southern Rockies. Pike's Peak, perhaps the most famous, is a mere 14,110 feet. Historically, the Southern Rockies have been a principal barrier to travel, as they can be crossed only through high passes, all above 9,000 feet and some much higher.

The Rocky Mountains form the Continental Divide, a major hydrographic feature of the continent. In Colorado, waters on the Western Slope of the Divide flow into the Colorado River and its tributaries, eventually entering the Gulf of California. Eastern Slope waters flow into the Rio Grande, North and South Platte, and Arkansas River drainages, and ultimately enter the Gulf of Mexico. The cordillera of the Southern Rocky Mountains comprises numerous mountain ranges and high intervening valleys. The Continental Divide follows a winding course from north to south, passing through many of these ranges.

The geologic history of the Southern Rocky Mountains is long and complex. It is characterized by several alternating periods of mountain uplift and erosion during the past several hundred million years. The region acquired its present shape during the last 70 million years, when the most recent episodes of uplift, volcanism, erosion, and sedimentation occurred. Much of the terrain we see in the higher mountains today resulted from Ice Age activity of the past two million years. Four, five, or more sets of major valley glaciers have extended down to elevations as low as 8,500 feet. The glaciers formed huge bowls called cirques at the heads of valleys and widened the valley bottoms. They carved pockets that now form lakes; and rocks were deposited in ridges, called moraines, and over much of the ground surface in valleys. Small glaciers remain in the Front Range west of Denver. The Arapahoe Glacier, Isabelle Glacier, St. Vrain Glaciers, and glaciers in Rocky Mountain National Park are barely able to survive today's climate.

High-altitude unglaciated uplands were also affected during the Ice Ages when land was cyclically frozen and thawed, breaking rocks and churning the soil. These freeze-thaw processes created patterns on the ground—stripes and polygons of sorted rocks. Saturated soils slid down hillsides, changing smooth slopes into lobes and terraces. The patterns can still be readily seen, although processes that formed the patterns are rarely active today.

The Great Plains province extends eastward from the Southern Rocky Mountains, occupying a broad belt in the central United

Deep, glacially carved valleys and rugged peaks of the San Juan Mountains, part of the Southern Rocky Mountain province. *J.C. Emerick.*

States from Texas to the Dakotas, and covering approximately 40 percent of Colorado. Much of this province consists of flat terrain or gently rolling hills, but it is by no means featureless. From the Rockies, the plains slope gently downward to the east, a fact realized when one considers that Kansas City is 4000 feet lower in elevation than Denver. Two major drainages flow eastward across the plains from the Southern Rockies: the North and South Platte in the northeastern section of Colorado and the Arkansas River to the southeast. Along the northern border of Colorado, the plains are interrupted by steep escarpments and buttes. In southeastern Colorado and northeastern New Mexico, the province is characterized by many mesas and volcanic formations. The latter includes the Spanish Peaks near Trinidad and caps of volcanic rock on Raton Mesa and Mesa de Maya. This southern region is dissected by shallow canyons, cut chiefly by the Purgatoire River and its tributaries.

Between Denver and Colorado Springs, a wide, cool highland known as the Palmer, or Arkansas, Divide extends eastward, separating the drainages of the Arkansas and South Platte Rivers. Its westward end, where it intersects the mountain foothills, is high enough to locally affect climatic patterns and to carry a finger of forest ecosystems eastward into the prairie.

The Great Plains and Southern Rocky Mountains meet at the western edge of the Great Plains province, causing an abrupt change in topography. Topographic relief is increased by a number of mesas and hills. Behind these rise the hogbacks, a discontinuous series of narrow ridges formed by sedimentary rock formations that were steeply tilted during mountain uplift.

To the west of the Continental Divide, the Southern Rockies grade more gradually into the third physiographic province, the Colorado Plateau. This gradual grade occurs because the Plateau province is somewhat dish shaped, with the plateaus around its edge being higher than those toward the center. Grand Mesa and Battlement Mesa both have elevations exceeding 10,000 feet, while farther west the Roan and Uncompahgre plateaus are several hundred to over a thousand feet lower. Their margins have been dissected extensively by steep canyons of the Colorado River and its tributaries. Their relatively high elevations allow a

In this section of the Great Plains province near Pawnee Buttes in northeastern Colorado, high sedimentary cliffs provide numerous nesting sites for hawks, eagles, and other raptors that hunt over the surrounding grasslands. *J.C. Emerick.*

The transition between the Great Plains and the Southern Rocky Mountains is particularly abrupt along the eastern slope of the Front Range near Boulder, where the high peaks along the Continental Divide are less than twenty miles from the edge of the grasslands. *J.C. Emerick.*

considerable westward extension of lower mountain environments, which contrast sharply with desert-like conditions at the bases of the plateaus, often several thousand feet below.

The tablelands of the Colorado Plateau province are made up of nearly horizontal sedimentary formations that can be seen at numerous locations where deep canyons cut through the various layers. These formations are evident almost anywhere alongside the Colorado River east of Rifle, Colorado, and are particularly impressive south of Grand Junction in Unaweep Canyon (along Colorado 141). They can be seen at their best west of Colorado in the Canyonlands area of Utah and in the Grand Canyon in Arizona. Sparse vegetation stemming from the relatively arid climate has permitted rapid erosion by wind and water which has led to the formation of these canyons as well as to the sculpting of many natural arches and other unique rock forms. The spectacular scenery in this region, with its red and yellow hues, would not have occurred if it were not for the aridity.

The Climate

The region's climate is as varied as its topography and is strongly influenced by the mountains. Only a few climatic generalizations are true. The climate is sunny, with warm summers and cool winters. The weather is marked by extreme variations in temperature and precipitation from year to year, season to season, day to night, and even hour to hour. Clear skies can change within an hour to a rainstorm or blizzard and the weather can clear up equally fast. These variations occur because the climate is not moderated by a large body of water; the region, in the center of North America, has a continental climate. Local climate is affected by elevation and position of mountain ranges or valleys.

Wide climatic variations occur within short distances. The difference in average annual temperature between the summit of Pikes Peak and Las Animas, Colorado, 115 miles to the southeast, is about 35°F. This is comparable to the difference between southern Florida and Iceland. Manassa in the San Luis Valley is one of the driest areas in Colorado, averaging only about seven inches of precipitation per year. Yet Cumbres, less than thirty

Exposed horizontal sedimentary beds typify much of the Colorado Plateau as seen here at Dolores Canyon. *Lee Gregory.*

miles away, is one of the wettest areas, receiving about thirty-six inches of annual precipitation.

In general air temperature decreases with increasing altitude at the rate of about 3°F for each thousand feet of elevation gain. Higher elevations therefore usually have cooler average temperatures than lower elevations, but this pattern is disrupted by cold air drainage. Mountain valleys, such as North Park, Middle Park, South Park, and the San Luis Valley, are much colder during the winter months than are surrounding higher areas because the dense, cold air sinks into valley bottoms from adjacent slopes. The entrapment of cold air by surrounding mountains results in air stagnation and prolongs cold temperatures. Even during the summer, nighttime temperatures may drop below freezing. Because of these features, valley climates are distinctive.

As a result of high elevations in the Rockies, the air is "thinner," or less dense, than it is at a lower altitude. The thin air and intense solar radiation mean that air heats and cools more rapidly than it does at lower altitudes. This rapid heating and cooling of air in early morning and evening is felt more intensely than under a thicker blanket of air. Skin sunburns rapidly since the ultraviolet wavelengths are not filtered out as effectively as at lower elevations.

Precipitation patterns are as profoundly influenced by the mountains as are temperatures. Air masses are forced to rise as they encounter mountains. The air chills as it rises, and water vapor condenses to form rain or snow that falls to earth. This is called orographic precipitation and usually comes from eastward moving Pacific air masses. Much of the air masses' original moisture is lost as they pass over mountains in Washington, Oregon, California, Nevada, and Utah. More moisture is lost as the air masses rise over the western mountains of Colorado, and by the time the air masses reach the Front Range, most of the Pacific moisture has been lost. This explains why Colorado's western ranges usually have more snow (and better skiing) than does the Front Range, which is on the eastern edge of the Southern Rockies. It also explains why the plains east of the Rockies have low annual precipitation.

In general, average annual precipitation increases with altitude. The alpine tundra receives two to three times as much precipitation as the plains, but much of the tundra's snowfall is blown into forests just below timberline, causing the effective maximum precipitation to occur in the upper coniferous forests. The length of the frost-free season decreases as temperature decreases and altitude increases. High altitude plants must produce seed and nutrients for the following year's growth in two months or less. Thus the advantages of abundant moisture at high altitudes are offset by the disadvantages of low temperature.

During the spring and fall, warm, moist air masses from the Gulf of Mexico move northward, often causing large amounts of precipitation. When warm gulf moisture collides with frigid arctic air masses, heavy snowfalls occur on the plains and foothills. Occasionally gulf moisture is pushed up against the Eastern Slope, resulting in so-called upslope precipitation. This precipitation may extend upward to the mountain tops, although it usually decreases at higher elevations. The movement of moist gulf air into eastern Colorado and New Mexico provides significant additional moisture to this part of the region.

Precipitation west of the Continental Divide comes mostly during the winter months as a result of orographic activity. Thus lower elevations receive little moisture during the growing season, with June being the driest month. This is in contrast with the precipitation pattern on the eastern plains, which receive most of their moisture during the spring, largely as a result of upslope activity, and in the summer during thunderstorms. Higher forests have a less pronounced seasonal difference in precipitation distribution and receive more of their moisture as snow. The alpine tundra receives most of its precipitation as winter snow, although much of it is removed by wind; summer convective storms provide most of the effective precipitation for plants. The driest period in the tundra occurs in the fall.

Convective storms result when air warmed by the earth's surface rises rapidly, causing moisture to condense. This type of storm is frequent during the warmer months at all elevations, particularly when monsoon flow sweeps moist air from the equatorial Pacific and Gulf of California over the southwestern states and into the southern Rocky Mountain region. Convective storms that begin forming along the Continental Divide in late morning continue to intensify during the day as they drift eastward with the prevailing winds over the plains. Often they become violent thunderstorms, shedding large amounts of rain and hail and occasionally developing into tornados.

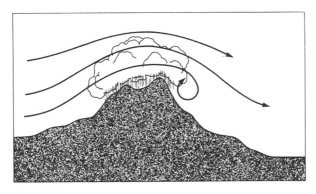

Orographic precipitation from Pacific air masses moving eastward over the Rockies. Much of this precipitation falls over the mountains as snow during the wintertime.

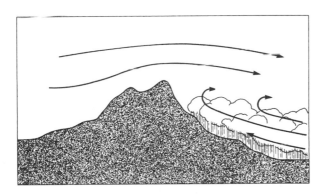

Upslope circulation of moist air masses from the Gulf of Mexico brings precipitation to the eastern side of the Rocky Mountains during spring and fall.

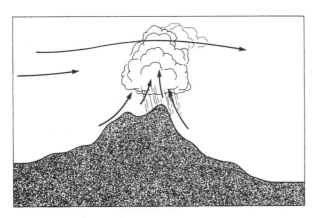

Rising air warmed by land surfaces leads to the generation of convective storms, most prevalent during summer afternoons.

Average wind velocities in the mountains generally increase with an increase in elevation. The treeless tundra regions on mountain tops are the windiest sites, and wind gusts exceeding 100 miles per hour are not uncommon during the winter. One wind study measured a gust of 201 miles per hour on top of Long's Peak in January of 1981. High wind gusts approaching ninety miles per hour also are common along the eastern foot of the Front Range from November through March. Here the Continental Divide bows toward the east, forming a giant funnel that channels winds over the Front Range and down valleys and canyons of the Eastern Slope. Winds near Boulder, Colorado, often exceed 120 miles per hour, and are intensively studied by a number of research organizations. These warm, dry winds are called chinooks, and they often displace cold arctic air masses, causing a temperature increase of 50° or more in just a few hours. Even during the summer, higher elevations are windy places. The average wind speed measured at one tundra location in Rocky Mountain National Park during June, July, and August of 1980 was 20 miles per hour, with higher gusts of nearly 80 miles per hour.

While the prevailing winds along mountain ridges are generally from the west, canyons and valleys may alter their direction by channeling them along drainages. A phenomenon known as the valley wind may also change the direction of air movement. On sunny afternoons, air heated by warm ground surfaces rises and moves up-valley as a gentle breeze. At night the ground surfaces lose their heat and cool the surrounding air, which becomes more dense. This results in a breeze blowing down-valley in the early morning hours.

On the plains and in some large mountain valleys, prevailing surface wind directions are so variable that generalization is difficult. In eastern Colorado near Akron, extensive sand dunes cover the ground. The prevailing wind direction is toward the southeast and the dunes are aligned in that direction. Winds of the San Luis Valley, in contrast, have blown toward the northeast for thousands of years, picking up sand from the floor of this large, arid basin. As the sediment laden air reaches the mountain slopes at the valley's edge and begins its ascent over the Sangre de Cristos, its velocity drops, releasing the sand and forming the Great Sand Dunes in the northeastern part of the valley. They are about 700 feet high and cover nearly forty square miles.

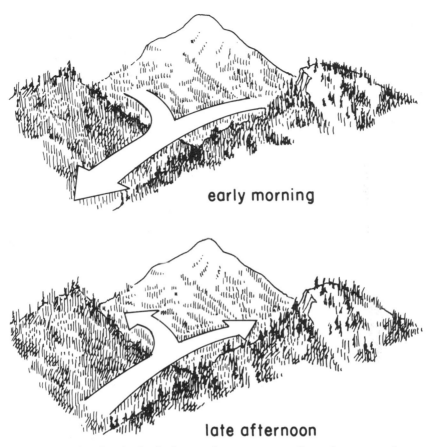

early morning

late afternoon

Valley winds. Cool air drainage from surrounding slopes produces down-valley air movement during the early morning. As mountainsides become warmer during the day, air begins to rise, creating an up-valley movement during the afternoon.

The Arkansas Divide south of Denver rises some 2000 feet above the elevation of Denver and Colorado Springs, and has a profound effect on the local climate along that part of the mountain front. Both summer and winter temperatures are lower than those of areas immediately to the north or south, and the frost-free season is shorter by several weeks. This divide is also characterized by many violent thunderstorms and by a marked rise in annual precipitation, at least four inches greater than Denver's. Because of these climatic anomalies, the Arkansas Divide marks the north-south distributional limits of some species found along the foothills.

Vegetation Patterns

Through the millennia plant species have moved into the region from all over the northern hemisphere. Plains grasslands contain species both of the Great Plains and of tall grass prairies to the east. Trees typical of deciduous forests of the eastern United States also grow in moist ravines in the mountains at lower elevations. Most alpine tundra species are related to tundra plants of the Arctic and Asia. Close relatives of other tundra species grow in southwestern deserts of the United States. Numerous plants migrated to the Rocky Mountains when the climatic regime differed greatly from that found here today. Other plants evolved in the Rocky Mountains, and still others have been accidentally or purposefully introduced by people in the last 120 years.

The combination of migration, evolution, and introduction has resulted in a great diversity of plant species. An estimated 1500 species of ferns, conifers, and flowering plants grow in the Front Range vicinity alone, along with four to five hundred species of lichens and two to three hundred species of mosses and liverworts. Considering the tremendous variation in climate and topography, this should not be surprising. The greatest plant diversity occurs in the low foothills where the mountains rise steeply, furnishing an especially great topographic diversity and numerous variations in site moisture.

The most visible trait of vegetation is the natural domination of highest and lowest elevations by herbs and grasses; forests cover the mountains only between 5600 and 11,000 feet. Thus there is both an upper and lower treeline. In simple terms trees are excluded from the highest elevations by cold, drought, and wind, and from the lowest elevations by drought; these climatic conditions are better survived by herbs. Another obvious vegetational trait is the domination of forests by needle-leaved conifers. Other than mountainside groves of aspen, broad-leaved deciduous trees are limited to sites next to bodies of water.

Tree dominants of mountain forests change as altitude increases. For example, piñon pine is most common in the lowest, driest mountain forests; Douglas fir and ponderosa pine occupy middle elevations; and Engelmann spruce and subalpine fir characterize the highest, wettest forests.

The timing of plants' processes is also related to altitude. Spring comes later in the high mountains than at lower elevations. Herbs green up in waves, those on the plains producing flowers while higher areas are still under snow. Species with a wide altitudinal range, such as yarrow or stonecrop, flower first at low elevations. High-elevation flowers appear when low-elevation plants of the same species are already in fruit. The mountain grasses turn a dry, golden brown several weeks after their lower-altitude relatives change color. But leaves of trees and shrubs turn yellow first at high altitudes, marking the early onset of autumn and winter in the upper mountains.

Populations of plants, animals, and other types of organisms that exist in a particular area form biological communities. The members of a community are held together by site environmental conditions, feeding relationships, nesting or denning preferences, or other factors. An *ecosystem* includes not only the biological community of a particular area, but the nonliving components as well, such as the soil, rocks, water, air, and dead organic matter. The ecosystem concept also presumes that all of these components are linked or interact with one another. Therefore, ecosystems are to some degree always changing in response to alterations in their environment or to significant increases or decreases in the population of one or more species.

Plants and animals interact over time to modify site characteristics. Organisms remove or add nutrients to soil, decrease wind speed, and intercept precipitation and sunlight. If a site is altered to the point that its plants and animals can no longer survive, the ecosystem is successional and it is replaced by a different type of ecosystem. For example a mature lodgepole pine forest shades the forest floor so completely that its sunloving seedlings cannot survive. Species of tree seedlings that thrive in shade invade the dark forest and with time replace the lodgepole pine.

Eventually these successional changes result in a climax ecosystem. Such an ecosystem does not change its characteristics to the point at which another set of organisms is better able to survive. A climax ecosystem is in equilibrium century after century, remaining in an area as long as major fires, climatic changes, or other disturbances do not occur.

Since ecosystems include associations of species, each with its own set of requisites for survival, ecosystems are ordered in predictable patterns on the landscape. Each species can survive only within a given range of temperature, precipitation, growing-season length, and soil conditions. Species are further limited by competition to sites where they can best utilize local resources and, by doing so, exclude other species.

Many site characteristics are related to altitude, and thus ecosystems tend to change in a regular way from the lowlands to the mountaintops. For example, tree species in the highest mountain forests are adapted to survive a very short growing season. Tree species of lower forests have a growing season twice as long, but they are adapted to survive frequent drought. The abrupt altitudinal rise of the Rocky Mountains results in ecosystem changes that are much more sharply defined than those in most sections of the United States.

The limits of elevation of each type of ecosystem may vary considerably from place to place. In addition, as one travels northward, these limits are shifted progressively lower. In the Rocky Mountains the elevation of timberline decreases approximately 360 feet for every latitudinal degree northward. Stated another way, a climb of 1000 feet is roughly equivalent to a journey of 600 miles to the north. The altitudinal limits of certain ecosystems are also slightly higher on the western side of the mountains than they are on the eastern side. In northeastern Colorado the subalpine forest extends up to 11,000 feet; in the southwestern part of the state, it is found up to 12,000 feet.

Most of the terrestrial ecosystems found in the greater Rocky Mountain region can be classified into the following major ecosystem types: grasslands, shrublands, piñon–juniper woodlands, montane forests, subalpine forests, alpine tundra, and riparian ecosystems.

Grasslands ecosystems are devoid of trees except along watercourses, where riparian ecosystems are found. Occasionally shrubs flourish on sandy or alkaline soils. *Plains grasslands* are extensive at elevations below 5600 feet in the eastern part of Colorado, and in adjacent New Mexico, Kansas, Nebraska, and Wyoming. *Mountain grasslands and meadows* are found at higher elevations, interspersed among the various forest ecosystems.

Riparian ecosystems appear as narrow bands of distinctive vegetation along the margins of streams, rivers, ponds and lakes. They form more or less continuous ecosystems from the alpine tundra to the grasslands and deserts. *Mountain riparian ecosystems* are dominated at the highest elevations by shrub willows, which are joined by other shrub species as well as blue spruce, aspen and narrowleaf cottonwood, and other tree species as elevations decrease. Mountain riparian ecosystems grade into *lowland riparian ecosystems* when the watercourses reach the plains to the east or the low elevation valleys and canyons to the south and west. *Aquatic ecosystems* are closely tied to riparian areas.

Shrublands are a diverse group of ecosystems that also occupy a wide range of elevations. *Semidesert shrublands* consist of saltbush, shadscale, greasewood, and other drought- or salt-tolerant shrub species. These shrublands are typical of low-elevation mountain valleys in western Colorado, the San Luis Valley, and are extensive throughout the Colorado Plateau region in Utah, Arizona, and New Mexico. Semidesert shrublands typically are found below 6000 to 7000 feet, although in the San Luis Valley they are found at elevations as high as 8000 feet. Near their upper elevational limit, semidesert shrublands frequently border piñon pine–juniper woodlands. *Sagebrush shrublands* extend from lower elevations in the Great Basin and Wyoming Basin to as high as 10,000 feet in the Rockies. While there are changes in the species composition from lower semidesert sagebrush stands to higher montane sagebrush communities, their general appearance is similar, and they will be discussed together. *Montane shrublands* occupy elevations from approximately 5500 to 10,000 feet in the mountains, and are mainly characterized by Gambel oak, serviceberry, and mountain mahogany. In eastern Colorado, north of Colorado Springs, montane shrublands dominated by mountain mahogany form a thin transitional belt between the plains grasslands and the montane forests. Elsewhere, oak–serviceberry shrublands form a common mid-elevation plant community in southern and western Colorado, the Great Basin, and throughout the Southwest.

Piñon–juniper woodlands are dominated by piñon pine and tree juniper. These woodlands form the lowest elevation forests and are extensive in southern and western Colorado, New Mexico, Arizona, and throughout the Colorado Plateau and the Great Basin.

Montane forests, also of low to middle elevations from about 5500 to 9000 feet, consist primarily of *ponderosa pine forests* on

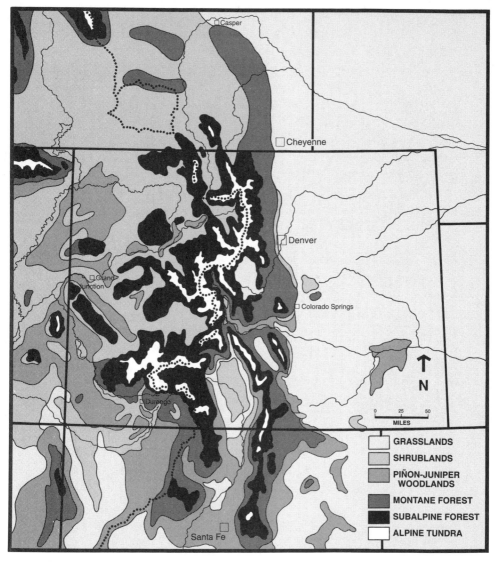

Distribution of major ecosystem types in the Southern Rocky Mountain region.

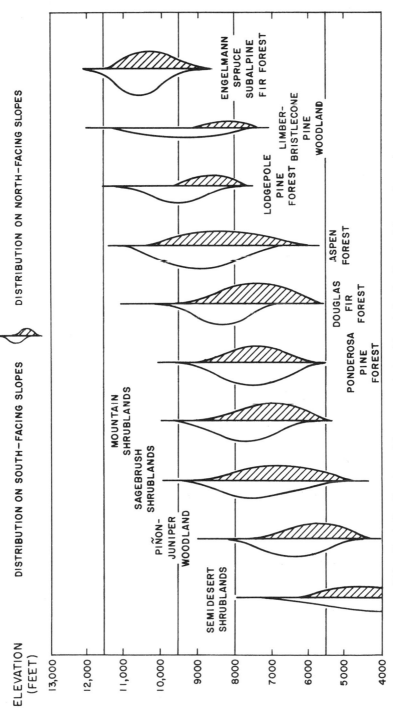

Altitudinal distribution of forests and shrublands in the Rocky Mountain region.

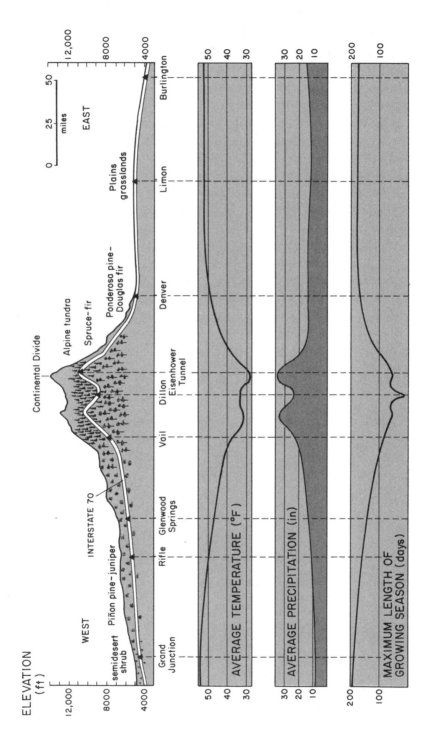

the warm south-facing slopes and *Douglas fir forests* on the cooler north-facing slopes. *Aspen groves* and *lodgepole pine forests* are common, and they mark sites of past disturbance. In the southern half of Colorado, and in New Mexico and Arizona, white fir forms stands in sheltered valleys and on lower slopes.

Subalpine forests occupy higher elevations from about 9000 feet up to timberline and are comprised mostly of dense, moist communities of *Engelmann spruce and subalpine fir* that are more homogeneous than forests of lower elevations. At their lower edge, spruce–fir forests are interrupted by lodgepole pine and aspen ecosystems, and at their upper limits or along exposed ridges, *limber and bristlecone pine woodlands* are often present (although this latter ecosystem occurs in montane forests as well). The upper forest edge consists of a band of wind-sculptured tree islands known as krummholz, which becomes smaller and more shrublike with increasing elevation, finally disappearing altogether.

Alpine tundra consists of low shrubs and herbaceous plants, and bears a superficial resemblance to the treeless plains grasslands. This highest ecosystem type is dominated by a cold, windy climate. Plants must survive a short growing season dur-

Climatic conditions and major vegetation patterns across the Southern Rockies in Colorado are illustrated by an east-west transect along Interstate 70. (Opposite page.) As the mountains are approached from either direction, the average annual temperature and the maximum reported length of the growing season (the number of summer days between 32°F frosts) declines as elevation increases, while average annual precipitation rises. Where cold air drains into mountain valley bottoms from surrounding slopes, summer frosts are frequent; the reported growing season length for Dillon is only six days. Westbound travelers pass through 150 miles of plains grasslands and agricultural lands before ascending the Eastern Slope of the Rockies, driving through Douglas fir and ponderosa pine forests in the lower mountains and dense subalpine forests of Engelmann spruce and subalpine fir at elevations above 9000 feet. Although the route of Interstate 70 does not cross alpine tundra, travelers can see this treeless region on the mountaintops above Eisenhower Tunnel at the Continental Divide. On the Western Slope, the highway descends from the spruce–fir forests, and again through warmer forests of Douglas fir mixed with a few ponderosa pine. Travelers pass through many miles of piñon pine–juniper woodlands as the interstate follows the Eagle and Colorado Rivers below Vail. West of Grand Junction, dry semidesert shrublands border the highway. Climate information is based on data reported by E.G. Siemer, *Colorado Climate*, published in 1977 by the Colorado Experiment Station, Colorado State University.

The difference in vegetation cover between north-facing and south-facing slopes is often distinct. Here in Clear Creek Canyon in the Front Range, north-facing slopes are forested with Douglas fir and ponderosa pine, while south-facing slopes on the opposite side of the canyon are sparsely covered with shrubs and a few Rocky Mountain juniper. *J.C. Emerick.*

ing which many species seem to bloom instantaneously, resulting in spectacular floral displays in late June and early July.

Boundaries between adjacent ecosystems are rarely distinct. There is usually a great deal of interfingering and mixing of species as one passes from one ecosystem to another. These transitional areas, called ecotones, are characterized by a mixture of plant species from two or more ecosystems. In some locations an isolated patch or stand of one plant community will be completely surrounded by a different type of ecosystem. This may indicate past disturbance or a difference in soils, but sometimes there seems to be no apparent reason for the isolated stand's occurrence.

Changes in local topography result in variations of ecosystem distribution similar to those variations produced by traveling from north to south. Slopes facing north receive considerably less direct sunlight than those facing south and accordingly are cooler and more humid. Northern exposures lose less water from evaporation, hold snow longer, and have a shorter frost-free season. These differences are great enough to change the types of ecosystems found on adjacent slopes with different exposures.

Since the climate of northern exposures is similar to that of higher altitudes, north-facing slopes typically are covered by ecosystems representative of higher elevations than those covering nearby south-facing slopes.

Patterns of Animal Distribution

Animals do not occur randomly in nature. Each species is adapted to use specific resources of the land, minimizing competition with other species and ensuring its own survival. Because an animal's requirements for food, shelter, and nesting or breeding sites are often specialized, many animal species occupy only those ecosystems that best satisfy their requirements. Locations that have a diversity of ecosystems, and thus have a variety of food and other resources, support diverse animal populations. The varied climate, topography, and vegetation, of the Southern Rocky Mountains and surrounding area support a relatively high number of animal species.

Colorado is a hub in which animals from several regions of North America meet: the fox squirrel and eastern cottontail from eastern deciduous forests, Nuttall's cottontail from the Great Basin to the west, the thirteen-lined ground squirrel typical of the Great Plains, and the snowshoe hare and pine squirrel of northern coniferous forests. Other native mammals are limited to the Rocky Mountains, or are widespread throughout North America.

The resident bird fauna is supplemented by large numbers of migratory birds—including species of sandpipers, ducks, and warblers—that fly northward along the base of the mountains in the spring, returning in the fall. Other birds spend only the summer or winter in the region, migrating south for winter or north to their breeding grounds. In addition to latitudinal migrations, many birds migrate altitudinally, breeding in the mountains and returning to the foothills or far out onto the plains in the winter.

Animal diversity is generally higher in the low foothills as a result of mild climate and abundance of food and cover. This is not universally true, however, for some insect groups such as ants, grasshoppers, and ground beetles are more diverse on the plains, with the number of species declining as elevations increase in the mountains.

Different kinds of animals respond to different altitudinal variables; few animals fit neatly into altitudinal zones. The distribution of grasshoppers is affected primarily by the length of the growing season. Mammalian distribution corresponds to distribution of the mammals' preferred food, cover, or denning sites, and in many cases is associated with certain ecosystem types. Bird distribution likewise is related to habitat preference. Ground beetles, whose distribution corresponds to the location of moist soil of the proper texture, sufficient cover, and food, form one of the few groups of animals with over half of the species limited to the plains grasslands.

The distribution of reptile and amphibian species is strongly influenced by climate. Most cannot live in a cold environment. Eighty percent of all reptile species and 70 percent of all amphibian species in the region are restricted to the lower, warmer elevations below 8000 feet. Because their eggs must be deposited in water, most amphibians are found in or near aquatic environments.

Nuttall's, or mountain, cottontail occurs in forested ecosystems throughout the mountains although it prefers shrubby forest edges. It is the only cottontail seen at elevations above 8000 feet. *James C. Halfpenny.*

Several factors obscure distributional patterns. Besides birds migrating with the seasons, many large mammals such as elk, mule deer, and coyote return to low elevations to winter. Many more species move among ecosystems and altitudinal ranges on a time scale of days to weeks, using one area for feeding and another for reproduction. The distribution of some species is correlated with ecosystem characteristics that do not change much with elevation. For example, the dipper, a small slate-colored bird, is found along streams from plains to timberline, as are beavers.

Elevation has definite effects on animal activities as well as on patterns of distribution. For example, a rodent that produces two summer litters of young on the plains may produce only one high in the mountains. Insect larvae on the tundra may require two or more years to mature, although they would need only one year at low altitudes. And animal activities start later in the summer as one proceeds higher into the mountains. Hikers may escape May ticks in the foothills, only to encounter July ticks in a subalpine meadow.

The Southern Rocky Mountains retain much of the wild character of animal life that has disappeared from more developed sections of the nation. Although the fauna has been disturbed by elimination of some native animals and introduction of other species, native animals still dominate the mountains and portions of the plains. Herds of elk and mule deer roam the woodlands. Mountain lions and black bears are sighted occasionally, as are bobcats and foxes. Golden eagles, as well as a host of other birds of prey, nest in many areas.

The following chapters describe the most prevalent ecosystems of the Southern Rockies and surrounding lowlands. It is important to remember that several of the ecosystem types, as well as a number of animal species that occur in them, occupy a relatively broad range of elevation. The best way to recognize the ecosystems is by their dominant plant species. Plants reveal much about the characteristics of the site and often are good predictors of what animal species may be present.

·2·
Plains Grasslands

When the first pioneers came to the region, grasslands extended eastward from the base of the mountains for hundreds of miles, interrupted only along permanent streams by lines of cottonwoods and willows. Over much of the land, grasses formed compact, short mats that were interspersed with bunches of taller grasses. Grasses were green only during the warm, moist spring and early summer. Late summer drought turned the plains golden brown as the grasses became dormant until the arrival of spring rains the following year. The large number of forb species became obvious when bright sunflowers, prairie-clovers, and goldenrods bloomed. Herds of pronghorn and bison were hunted by gray wolves and Indians.

Today much of the natural vegetation has been replaced by extensive croplands, and other areas have been used for grazing, with cattle superseding their bison relatives. Some of these grazed areas closely resemble the earlier prairies, although many of the native grasses have been replaced by introduced species. Along the Front Range, extensive urbanization has dramatically changed the character of the grasslands, which have been supplanted by cities, highways, reservoirs, and cultivated trees. In spite of this, some unplowed mesa tops, steep hillsides, and floodplains retain native grasses, although predisturbance plant communities are rare.

J.C. Emerick.

Location

Remnants of plains grassland ecosystems occur on the uplands and drier river bottoms of the eastern third of Colorado. The grasslands blend with ponderosa pine ecosystems, piñon pine–juniper woodlands, or shrublands at the base of the mountains. To the east they roll across Colorado and the Great Plains into the Midwest, the height and lushness of grasses increasing and species composition changing as moisture increases. Plains grassland ecosystems have been preserved in some old cemeteries and along railroad tracks, sites that have remained undisturbed for many decades. A few relatively well-preserved grass communities still exist where grazing has been minimal. Pawnee National Grasslands in northeastern Colorado and Comanche National Grasslands in southeastern Colorado contain grassland ecosystems that retain many of their natural characteristics.

Pronghorn. These large herbivores are found throughout the plains grasslands as well as in some large mountain parks and in open shrublands.

Site Characteristics

The climate of plains grassland ecosystems is dry, warm, and sunny during summer, and cold in winter. Rainfall is below twenty inches a year, less than in the mountains, with most of the precipitation coming in the spring and summer. Temperatures are higher than in the mountains, the annual average being around 50°F with changes of up to 40°F occurring between night and day. The frost-free season can exceed 150 days. Wind speeds are high, and their drying effects, coupled with high temperatures, cause summer drought. During the winter winds produce blizzard conditions during snowstorms and pile snows into deep drifts. Seasonal and annual climatic variations are great and are marked by changes in plant lushness.

Soils vary from well-developed, old, fine-textured clays and rich loams to young, sandy, or cobbly soils. They have developed primarily from materials washed or blown down from the mountains. The soils are drier than those of plains riparian ecosystems but vary in their ability to retain moisture. Because of the low precipitation, salts are not leached downward to great depths in the soil. Thus a layer called hardpan, made up of calcium carbonate, is deposited at the depth of leaching, below the soil's surface. In some places, such as in shallow basins, salt accumulations occur on the ground surface, resulting in highly alkaline soils.

Plains grassland ecosystems cover a variety of landforms—flat plains, rolling hillsides, flat-topped steep-sided mesas, and alluvial-capped isolated prominences. As in the mountains, climate and soil characteristics change locally as altitude, exposure, and geologic history change. Mesas for example are often warmer than surrounding lowlands chilled by cold air drainage. These conditions control the types of plant communities that occupy a given site.

Plant Characteristics

Grassland species are well adapted to the dry climate. In relatively undisturbed sites, most species are perennials, plants that live for many years. Perennial grassland plants typically have most of their structure below the surface of the soil. The subterranean plant parts include extensive root systems and reproductive structures, such as bulbs and underground horizontal stems called rhizomes. Although most of the roots of prairie grasses are in the upper six inches of soil, they may extend downward to ten feet in some species. Extensive root systems are essential for vigorous growth. Shallow roots absorb moisture from brief prairie rainstorms, while deeper roots can reach water during times of drought. The roots store food and allow the plant to survive during poor growth conditions. Root development is severely retarded on overgrazed plants, leading to lower forage production and a decreased ability to withstand harsh climatic conditions.

The above-ground shoots of most grassland plants are characterized by narrow or finely divided leaves. This is an apparent adaptation to increase air movement and cooling of leaves during warm midday temperatures. The nearly vertical arrangement of grass blades maximizes light absorption during cooler parts of the day while minimizing the heating effects of the sun when it is directly overhead.

Blue grama.

Buffalograss.

Most prairie species are either drought tolerant or avoid drought altogether by becoming dormant. Many grass species, such as Junegrass and western wheatgrass, are cool-season grasses that grow rapidly on the heels of spring rainstorms and complete their growth before the summer drought arrives. They may have a second period of growth in the fall if sufficient moisture permits. Warm-season grasses such as blue grama and little bluestem begin growth in the spring but are slower to mature. They commonly possess deeper roots and bloom later in the summer than cool-season grasses.

Prairie fires once were an important component of grassland ecosystems. Fires occurred during the seasonal drought and did not damage the already dormant grasses. Overwintering buds of the perennial grasses are at or below the soil surface, a growth habit that protects them from fire as well as from drought and cold. Plants with other growth forms, such as shrubs, are more susceptible to fire damage, and their populations were to some extent controlled by periodic fires. If they are not too frequent, fires stimulate the growth of some grasses and perennial herbs by reducing competition from other species and by removing dead plant material.

Plains grasslands of eastern Colorado are dominated by a mixture of blue grama and buffalograss. These are perennial, sod-forming grasses with short, curly leaves three to five inches tall. Interspersed are occasional shrubs and bright flowered forbs, most of which are members of the pea and sunflower families. The number of plant species is lower than in midwestern prairie grasslands and mountain meadows.

Taller grass species cover 10 to 25 percent of the ground of little-grazed, moist sites, increasing in wet years and in very moist areas such as river bottoms. Most are perennial bunch-grasses up to three feet tall. Needle-and-thread, sand dropseed, side-oats grama, western wheatgrass, Junegrass, and red three-awn are common species. Big and little bluestem, grasses characteristic of eastern tall grass prairies, grow sparingly on very moist sites.

Grassland communities are strongly affected by their proximity to the mountains and the consequent variations in site characteristics. Buffalograss is widespread across the plains in Colorado, but it is absent from many areas near the base of the mountains. In contrast blue grama is abundant and also is an important component of meadow ecosystems in the foothills. Because of greater moisture near the mountains, tall grasses are more abundant than farther to the east. Some mountain-front communities are highly diverse, with well over 100 species of vascular plants in a plot of less than an acre. The diversity is partially due to mixing of mountain meadow species (such as yarrow, common lupine, mountain muhly) and plains forbs (sunflowers, Kansas gayfeather, snow-on-the-mountain) with various grasses. In addition these areas have been used primarily for grazing and are less disturbed than plowed areas east of the mesas. The mountain-front communities described below are now present only in small patches.

Communities of nearly pure western wheatgrass are found on deep, fine-grained, well-developed soils such as accumulations in depressions and at the base of mesa slopes. An understory of blue grama and scattering of forbs or shrubs may be present. This community used to be extensive in a band a few miles wide just east of the foothills.

Tall grass communities resembling those of the prairies of mid-western states are found on upland, cobbly soils with intermixed sands and clays. These soils provide moisture throughout the summer, absorbing greater quantities of rain and releasing it to plants more readily than do clay soils. Big bluestem may form

Sandhill prairie in southeastern Colorado. The dominant shrub is sand sagebrush. *J.C. Emerick.*

nearly pure communities, or big and little bluestem may mix with other tall grass species such as Indiangrass, prairie dropseed, and switchgrass. When mountain meadow species are present, the communities contain twice as many plant species as those of drier sites. These moist communities may be remnants from ten thousand years ago, when the mountains were heavily glaciated and the entire West was cooler and wetter.

In contrast, those upland soils that are composed of a high percentage of clays derived from shale bedrock are not moist through the summer. These soils are covered with communities resembling the short and mixed grass plains of eastern Colorado, communities that require high moisture in spring but dry up during summer. Junegrass, little bluestem, and species of needle-grass or bluegrass form pure communities, or mix with one another, blue grama, and mountain forbs and shrubs. These communities extend from the mesas up into the foothills, and down onto nearby alluvial terraces.

On very dry sterile soils, such as gravels and compacted shales on southern mesa exposures, plant cover is sparse. Here grow species of three-awn, sometimes mixing with Junegrass and blue grama or pasture sagebrush, gilia, mountain bladderpod, and species of sunflower and milk vetch.

Farther east the grassland communities lose the mountain species, and short grass prairies dominate the landscape. Topographical features cause variations in soils and plant communities. Moist bottomlands often support stands of taller grasses and sedges, while well-drained alkaline soils in depressions may contain shrub communities of four-winged saltbush and winterfat. In moderately loose, deep soils, the taller bunchgrasses are found where their deep roots can take advantage of moisture unavailable to plants with shallower roots. In more compacted, disturbed soils, shrubs such as rabbitbrush and broom snakeweed are common. Buffalograss and grama grow in shallower loamy soils, although these species also are found where taller grasses have been grazed extensively.

Sandhills are scattered across many areas in eastern Colorado, Kansas, and Nebraska. Vegetation differs markedly from that of surrounding prairies, especially where the sand has not been sta-

Burrowing owls. These small raptors nest in abandoned prairie dog tunnels. *Stephen Jones*.

bilized. Sandhill muhly, blowout grass, and heliotrope first invade loose sand. Later other species such as red three-awn, western wheatgrass, sand bluestem, and yucca become established. Wherever the soil is sandy, one is likely to find sand sagebrush, a widespread dominant shrub.

One is reminded of the arid climate by the common presence of cacti. Prickly pear and pincushion cacti are especially abundant. The candelabra cactus imparts a distinctive New Mexican flavor to the southern portion of Colorado's grasslands. The erect, shrublike form of this cactus can attain a height of six feet, and its bright purple blossoms impart a flush of color to the browning grasses of July.

Mesas and portions of lower grasslands have been used for grazing, a use that does not remove the original plant cover but can alter it dramatically. Cattle preferentially remove tall grasses and native forbs, reducing plant cover to short grass species that survive trampling and flourish in intense sunlight. This conversion has occurred on thousands of square miles of grassland. Further grazing pressures cause an increase in the numbers of weedy and drought-resistant species such as cacti and yucca. Loss of plant cover by grazing has also decreased the incidence of prairie fires in some areas, which might additionally contribute to the successful expansion of these weedy plant populations. Wind and water erosion of soil increases, and annual grasses eventually replace native perennial grasses.

Natural disturbances such as the burrowing of pocket gophers and prairie dogs, construction of ant hills, and severe drought have effects that are similar to overgrazing. Such disturbances create pebble-covered mounds nearly a foot tall and three to six feet in diameter. Although surrounded by mixed and tall grass communities, the mounds themselves are covered with weeds such as cheatgrass and ragweed.

Since plains grasslands have been altered through human use, all except a few small, relict sites are theoretically successional. Natural succession is being prevented by continued land use. Grazing maintains some areas in short grass or short grass-and-weed communities. Weedy ecosystems and cropland communities are maintained by repeated overturning of the soil by farmers.

Abandoned wagon roads and cultivated fields are initially invaded by weedy forbs such as Russian thistle, pigweed, and amaranth, which in turn are invaded by two or three types of grass communities including foxtail barley, cheatgrass, squirreltail, and tumble-grass. Return to climax grassland communities requires a minimum of twenty to forty years, and often much longer.

Animal Characteristics

Grasslands are noted for their large numbers of plant-eating animals, or herbivores, which include many insect, bird, and mammal species. Among the large variety of herbivorous insects, grasshoppers and ants are the most important. Grasshoppers can occur in enormous populations and are capable of completely denuding the landscape. Even grasshopper numbers as low as three per square yard can consume half of the vegetation in a relatively unproductive prairie. Ants destroy vegetation through their leaf-cutting and seed-gathering activities and may remove all plants in the vicinity of their nests. However, because they move large quantities of nutrients and organic material into the ground and also mix the soil, improving its quality, they are considered to be beneficial in the long run.

Many of the familiar songbirds of the grasslands are herbivorous, although most eat insects as well. These birds include Colorado's state bird, the lark bunting, and others such as the western meadowlark, McCown's longspur, vesper sparrow, and the horned lark. Prairie chickens and sharp-tailed grouse were once common on the prairie, but extensive cultivation and habitat destruction have drastically reduced their numbers. Their spectacular mating displays can still be observed on a few remaining strutting grounds.

Large numbers of small rodents make their home in the grasslands. These include pocket gophers, harvest mice, pocket mice, deer mice, and kangaroo rats. Black-tailed prairie dogs live wherever there is suitable soil for burrowing; their high pitched "yips" can be heard from vacant fields even in urban areas. Pronghorn and mule deer are the only large native herbivores that are still common on the prairies. Once millions of bison traveling in enormous herds dominated the plains, but these were hunted to near extinction, and by the turn of the century less than a thousand remained in the United States. Numerous elk also wintered in the grasslands near the mountains; now they rarely are seen below the foothills.

Grassland carnivores include many bird and mammal species, as well as all of the reptiles and amphibians. For the most part these prey upon the abundant rodents and insects, as well as jackrabbits and cottontail rabbits. Soaring raptors are conspicuous in prairie skies; they include golden eagles and red-tailed, ferruginous, and Swainson's hawks. Prairie falcons and American kestrels are a common sight as they hunt on rapidly beating wings, their flight contrasting with the low, languid glide of the northern harriers (marsh hawks).

The largest predator on the grasslands today is the coyote, although the gray wolf roamed the prairies until the late 1800s. Other carnivorous mammals include the swift fox, badger, and the endangered black-footed ferret. The northern grasshopper mouse is primarily an insect eater, but many other small rodents supplement their diets with insects, spiders, worms, and other invertebrates.

The warm prairie environment supports a larger number of reptile species than do environments at higher elevations. The more common reptiles include the short-horned lizard, lesser earless lizard, western box turtle, coachwhip, and bullsnake. Two rattlesnakes are found on the plains of the region, the widespread western rattlesnake and the massasauga of southeastern Colorado and eastern New Mexico.

Many grassland animals live in burrows, where they can retreat from the summer's midday heat and the winter's coldest temperatures. This habit also enables them to escape from some predators, but not all. Badgers are renowned for digging rodents from their burrows. Black-footed ferrets are small enough to follow prairie dogs into their burrows and undoubtedly were important predators of these rodents.

Although much reduced from their former numbers, prairie dogs still serve an important role in grassland ecosystems. They are gregarious animals that live in large underground communities, or prairie dog "towns," which in the past often covered several hundred acres or more and housed many thousands of animals. Prairie dogs consume large quantities of vegetation. Thus in earlier times these animals were instrumental in the development and maintenance of a short grass prairie, as they still

Black-tailed prairie dogs:
W. Perry Conway.

are on a much smaller scale. They are also an important prey for many predators, and their abandoned burrows are used by various other mammals, birds, and reptiles. Rattlesnakes hide in their burrows to escape the summer heat, and burrowing owls nest in the tunnels. Whether by coincidence or some other fate of nature, burrowing owl chicks produce a rattlesnake-like buzzing sound when disturbed, which wards off would-be predators.

Other prairie animals that do not burrow often use speed or camouflage to escape predators. Black-tailed jackrabbits and desert cottontails are capable of quick bursts of speed coupled with instantaneous changes in direction if necessary. The pronghorn is the swiftest North American mammal and can maintain speeds approaching sixty miles per hour for many miles to elude any coyote. In contrast the short-horned lizard is one of the slowest animals, but its protective coloration allows it to remain unnoticed. Grouse and many smaller prairie birds, especially the females, are similarly camouflaged.

During the last century cultivation, cattle grazing, and urbanization have brought many changes to grassland animal communities. Some of the large herbivores as well as some of the carnivores have disappeared. The ground-nesting songbirds suffered as the prairies were plowed. Butterflies of the natural plains plant communities, such as Riding's satyr and eyed brown, have largely been replaced by species that live on weeds and crops, the alfalfa butterfly and cabbage white.

Human actions created more favorable habitats for some animals, and these increased as a result. Raccoons fed on agricultural crops and the contents of city trash cans. The northern grasshopper mouse was favored by overgrazing and the consequent increase in the mouse's insect prey. Waterfowl and shorebirds increased locally as ponds and reservoirs were constructed. The Canada goose population has exploded in the past decade as nest boxes and protected nest areas were furnished.

Other species have established themselves on the plains as the result of purposeful introduction (for example, the ring-necked pheasant), natural expansion of range (the starling, a bird introduced to New York City from England in 1890 that now nests in the foothills and in suburban areas), or accidental introduction (the house mouse, which appeared in the United States about the time of the American Revolution and moved westward with early settlers). Thus, although the plains fauna has changed over the years and is no longer a balanced assemblage of native species, animal life is still abundant and diverse.

Human Use

The plains grasslands have been drastically altered by more than a century of agricultural and cattle-grazing practices. The combination of gentle topography, mild climate, and water from the mountains, as well as demand for more food for a growing population, has resulted in intensive use of the prairies. Unfortunately many of the farming and grazing policies, combined with natural climatic events, have produced large-scale deterioration of grassland ecosystems and widespread erosion.

Before settlers came to the region, native grasses intercepted the rain and broke the impact of prairie winds, protecting the soils from erosion. Although vast herds of bison roamed the grasslands, devastating much of the vegetation in their path, there were no fences and the herds moved on, permitting the plants to recover. The grassland ecosystems were adapted to this form of grazing and plant succession was relatively rapid: root systems were left intact, grasses quickly resprouted, and little soil damage occurred.

Intensive grazing and conventional farming practices removed the protective native grass cover and exposed prairie soils to wind and water erosion. In 1930 wheat prices dropped and many farmers abandoned their land. The drought of the mid-1930s accompanied by high winds caused great dust storms, removing soils from some areas and smothering vegetation in others. Many thousands of square miles of prairie were laid waste. When the drought ended, above-normal precipitation hastened the recovery of the vegetation, although many areas still have not returned to grassland.

We cannot prevent climatic fluctuations that produce wind and drought, but we can control short-sighted grazing and agricultural practices. In spite of the experience of the Dust Bowl era of the 1930s, large areas of the plains are exposed to erosion each year by plowing. Livestock are confined by fences, and where proper management principles are disregarded, destruction of the grass cover is evident. Grazing of cattle and other animals is compatible with maintenance of natural grassland ecosystems. Nearly all native grasses are palatable, and they provide excellent summer and winter forage. This is the only major land use that permits some native species to remain, protecting soil from wind and water erosion and feeding and sheltering native wildlife, as these ecosystems have done for centuries. Long-term productive cultivation is also possible in some areas if farming practices are carefully matched to soil and climatic conditions. During the last century the plains grasslands have been overused and misunderstood, yet they remain a valuable resource for our society. There are few other ecosystems in which the need for ecological knowledge to prevent further mistakes is more apparent.

Plants and Animals of Plains Grasslands

Species composition depends on local site characteristics and history of disturbance and may vary considerably from one place to another. Listed birds are mainly summer residents.

PLANTS

Shrubs

cactus, candelabra   *Cylindropuntia imbricata*
rabbitbrush   *Chrysothamnus nauseosus*
sagebrush, sand   *Oligosporus filifolius*
saltbush, four-winged   *Atriplex canescens*
winterfat   *Krascheninnikovia lanata*

Grasses

barley, foxtail   *Critesion jubatum*
bluegrass, Kentucky   *Poa pratensis*
bluestem, big   *Andropogon gerardii*
    little   *Schizachyrium scoparium*
    sand   *Andropogon hallii*
buffalograss   *Buchloe dactyloides*
cheatgrass   *Anisantha tectorum*
dropseed, prairie   *Sporobolus heterolepis*
    sand   *Sporobolus cryptandrus*
grama, **blue**   *Chondrosum gracile*
    side-oats   *Bouteloua curtipendula*
grass, blowout   *Redfieldia flexuosa*
Indiangrass   *Sorghastrum avenaceum*
Junegrass   *Koeleria macrantha*
muhly, sandhill   *Muhlenbergia pungens*
needle-and-thread   *Stipa comata*
needlegrass, green   *Stipa viridula*
squirreltail   *Elymus longifolius*
switchgrass   *Panuum virgatum*
three-awn, red   *Aristida purpurea*
tumblegrass   *Schedonnardus paniculatus*
wheatgrass, western   *Pascopyrum smithii*

Forbs

amaranth   *Amaranthus arenicola*
bee plant, Rocky Mountain   *Cleome serrulata*
bladderpod, mountain   *Lesquerella montana*
cactus, pincushion   *Coryphantha vivipara*
evening primrose, prairie   *Oenothera albicaulis*
    white stemless   *Oenothera caespitosa*
gayfeather, Kansas   *Liatris punctata*
goldenrod, smooth   *Solidago missouriensis*
gourd, wild *Cucurbita foetidissima*
heliotrope   *Euploca convolvulacea*
milk vetch   *Astragalus missouriensis*
pigweed, rough   *Amaranthus retroflexus*
prairie-clover   *Dalea candida*
prickly pear   *Opuntia polyacantha*
ragweed, western   *Ambrosia psilostachya*
Russian thistle   *Salsola australis*
sage, pasture   *Artemisia frigida*
snakeweed, broom   *Gutierrezia sarothrae*
snow-on-the-mountain   *Agaloma marginata*
sunflower, common   *Helianthus annuus*
yucca   *Yucca glauca*

ANIMALS

Reptiles and Amphibians
bullsnake *Pituophis melanoleucus*
coachwhip *Masticophis flagellum*
lizard, lesser earless *Holbrookia maculata*
short-horned *Phrynosoma douglassii*
● massasauga *Sistrurus catenatus*
rattlesnake, western *Crotalus viridis*
snake, plains garter *Thamnophis radix*
● toad, plains spadefoot *Scaphiopus bombifrons*
● turtle, western box *Terrapene ornata*

Birds
curlew, long-billed *Numenius americanus*
eagle, golden *Aquila chrysaetos*
falcon, prairie *Falco mexicanus*
harrier, northern *Circus cyaneus*
hawk, **ferruginous** *Buteo regalis*
    red-tailed *Buteo jamaicensis*
    Swainson's *Buteo swainsoni*
kestrel, American *Falco sparverius*
● **bunting, lark** *Calamospiza melanocorys*
lark, horned *Eremophila alpestris*
longspur, ● chestnut-collared *Calcarius ornatus*
    ● McCown's *Calcarius mccownii*
meadowlark, western *Sturnella neglecta*
nighthawk, common *Chordeiles minor*
● owl, burrowing *Athene cunicularia*
pheasant, ring-necked *Phasianus colchicus*

● plover, mountain* *Charadrius montanus*
prairie chicken, ● greater* *Tympanuchus cupido*
    ● lesser *Tympanuchus pallidicinctus*
sandpiper, upland* *Bartramia longicauda*
sparrow, Cassin's *Aimophila cassinii*
    ● grasshopper *Ammodramus savannarum*
    lark *Chondestes grammacus*
    vesper *Pooecetes gramineus*

Mammals
badger *Taxidea taxus*
bison* *Bison bison*
cottontail, desert *Sylvilagus audubonii*
coyote *Canis latrans*
deer, mule *Odocoileus hemionus*
elk* *Cervus elaphus*
ferret, black-footed* *Mustela nigripes*
● **fox, swift** *Vulpes velox*
ground squirrel, thirteen-lined *Spermophilus tridecemlineatus*
jackrabbit, black-tailed *Lepus californicus*
kangaroo rat, Ord's *Dipodomys ordii*
mouse, **deer** *Peromyscus maniculatus*
    ● hispid pocket *Chaetodipus hispidus*
    northern grasshopper *Onychomys leucogaster*
    plains harvest *Reithrodontomys montanus*
    silky pocket *Perognathus flavus*

Mammals (continued)
> **Western harvest**

Reithrodontomys megalotis

● **pocket gopher, plains** *Geomys*
  bursarius
● **prairie dog, black-tailed**
  Cynomys ludovicianus
pronghorn   *Antilocapra americana*
wolf, gray*   *Canis lupus*

● Breeds almost exclusively in the plains grasslands.
* Extirpated or greatly reduced in number and geographic distribution.
Species in bold-faced type are more abundant.

·3·
Mountain Grasslands and Meadows

Identifying Traits

Herbaceous vegetation dominates the region's highest and lowest elevations. Grasslands and pockets of meadow are also tucked into the mid-elevational forest belt. These latter ecosystems, discussed in this chapter, can be recognized by dominance of herbs as opposed to trees or shrubs, although widely scattered trees and shrubs may be present. Larger meadows and extensive mountain grasslands are called "parks," and many regional place names originate from these landscape features. Ryan Park, North Park, Middle Park, South Park, Park County, Bergen Park, and Estes Park are a few examples.

Natural dry meadows occur on very well-drained soils; *natural wet meadows and fens* occur on soils with a high water table. These types of meadows are the natural result of local soil and moisture conditions. *Successional meadows* are found on sites where tree cover has been destroyed but where trees will eventually return. They can be distinguished from natural meadows when charred logs, cut stumps, charcoal, rotted wood, and other

Beaver Meadows in Rocky Mountain National Park.
National Park Service.

such remnants of previous forests remain. Otherwise natural and successional meadows are not easy to distinguish from each other. *Mountain grasslands* are similar to natural dry meadows, except that they occupy much larger areas, up to several hundred square miles.

Location

Natural meadows are located throughout the forested mountains wherever gentle slopes or basins have accumulated deep, fine-textured soils that are very wet or very dry. The meadows decrease in abundance with increasing altitude. At the same time, the number of dry meadows decreases while that of wet meadows increases. Most natural meadows in the foothills are dry, those of intermediate elevations may be wet or dry, and most subalpine meadows are wet.

Natural meadows can be of any size, from small patches in a forest to entire ridges or hillsides. Wet meadows are usually smaller than dry meadows. Natural dry meadows are found on south-facing slopes where they are often interspersed with patches of ponderosa pine, on upper terraces of broad floodplains, and on ridge tops. Natural wet meadows and fens are interspersed with riparian ecosystems on low terraces. They also surround montane ponds and cover subalpine valleys where drainages have been blocked by glacial debris. Wet meadows and fens are occasionally found on hillside terraces where blocked drainages or seeps provide a high water table.

Successional meadows are interspersed throughout all forest ecosystems wherever the timber was destroyed, the area was invaded by dense herbs, and trees have not yet returned because of lack of a seed source, extreme moisture or climatic conditions, or herb competition. The size and environmental characteristics of these meadows are highly variable.

Mountain grasslands occur in intermountain basins where the combination of soil conditions, precipitation, and temperature is unsuitable for tree growth. They are located in the north-central, central, and south-central parts of the Rockies and include North Park (8000-9000 feet elevation), parts of Middle Park (7300-9000 feet elevation), South Park (9000-10,000 feet elevation), the Wet

Extensive mountain grasslands in the Wet Mountain Valley. *Lee Gregory.*

Mountain Valley (7500-8500 feet elevation), and a broad band of grassland (7500-9000 feet elevation) around the perimeter of the San Luis Valley.

Site Characteristics

Natural meadow soils are deep and fine textured. The correlation with soil depth and texture is obvious between the hogbacks and foothills along the base of the Front Range. Rocky upper slopes are covered with ponderosa pine and dry shrub ecosystems. Meadows fill the valleys where fine material from the surrounding slopes has accumulated to great depths.

Wet meadows actually may be of several types, depending on soil and nutrient conditions. True wet meadows are wet sites that have predominantly mineral soils. Other types of meadows that have been wet long enough to accumulate substantial amounts of organic matter are fens and bogs. Fens and bogs often are characterized by thick accumulations of peat, in some cases many thousands of years old. The main difference between fens and bogs is that fens receive nutrients in runoff from surrounding lands, whereas bogs receive their nutrients from rain and snow, and thus are relatively low in nutrients. There are few, if any, true bogs in the Rocky Mountain region, but lots of fens.

Soils of wet meadows and fens are saturated with water at least part of the year. The high water table rises and floods the ecosystems in late spring and early summer. In some locations, particularly where springs maintain a relatively high flow, soils may be saturated year-round. Well-drained soils of dry meadows, in contrast, are subject to periodic drought.

Successional meadows cover a variety of sites. It is likely that soils are not as wet or dry as those of natural climax meadows, although soils of successional meadows often appear to be coarse, rocky, and dry.

The climate of meadow ecosystems varies with altitude. In general, since meadows do not have the protection of large plants, they are exposed to the full forces of wind and solar radiation. Snow may accumulate along shaded edges, but large meadows are often snow-free when adjacent forest floors are covered.

Mountain grasslands abound wherever fine-grained soils, low precipitation, and cold temperatures discourage tree growth. The well-drained soils are deep and fine-textured, contrasting strongly with coarser, thinner soils of surrounding mountain slopes. Summer temperatures are generally cool because of the elevation, and winter temperatures are very cold due primarily to cold air drainage from adjacent mountains. In most of the large parks, annual precipitation is less than fifteen inches. These conditions are too dry for spruce and fir, and too cold for ponderosa pine. The few trees that are present occur on higher ground or rocky outcrops within the parks, where coarser soils favor tree establishment. The San Luis Valley differs from other mountain parklands in that summer drought conditions discourage tree growth. This valley is drier than other mountain areas and much warmer in the summer.

Plant Characteristics

A discussion of mountain grassland and meadow ecosystems is complex for numerous reasons. The potential number of plant

species and species associations in each area is large. There are
natural differences among these ecosystems, and nearly all show
signs of disturbance such as the presence of introduced species
and weeds (for example, Kentucky bluegrass and common dandelion). Species composition varies according to the type and extent of disturbance and the length of time since disturbance has
ceased. In addition species composition varies with altitude. Altitudinal variations are further confused by tundra herbs joining
subalpine species on ski runs and avalanche chutes below timberline and plains grassland species mixing into foothills meadows. Because of these variations, the following discussion must
be general.

Natural wet meadows and fens are dominated by moisture-loving species, primarily members of the sedge and rush families.
Spike-rush, sedges, Canadian reedgrass, and tufted hairgrass are
common. Clumps of willow, bog birch, and shrubby cinquefoil

Once nearly extirpated from the state, the elk, or wapiti, is now common
in mountain parks, meadows, and open forests. *W. Perry Conway.*

may be present. The number of species is low; often one species covers a large area. Different associations may encircle a pond or other site of maximum moisture, each circular zone being drier than its inner neighbor. Wet meadows may be pockets within dry meadows or forests. In the montane and subalpine, a border of quaking aspen with an understory of meadow species frequently lies between meadow and coniferous ecosystems. Subalpine fens include sedge and sphagnum moss mats with a thick, peaty substratum. The mats are often floating on ponds.

Natural wet meadows and fens, particularly those in the subalpine, have been less disturbed than the lower dry meadows. These meadows probably bear closer resemblance to climax ecosystems. Subalpine wet meadows often mark sites of deep snow that persists well into summer. Wet meadows may accumulate enough organic material in the soil to become fens if the source of moisture is dependable. Because of the water-absorbing and water-holding capacity of peat soils, fens may increase their size over time, invading adjacent wet meadows and forests. Freeze-thaw processes, differences in topography and moisture conditions, and other factors often produce a hummocky surface on fens. The tops of the hummocks have drier, better-aerated soils than in the intervening troughs, and often are invaded by willows, bog birch, and a variety of herbaceous species.

Natural dry meadows typically have more species than wet meadows and fens. Members of the grass family dominate. A large number of forb species is also present, but forbs do not form the lush growth common in undisturbed quaking aspen and mountain riparian ecosystems. Species associations are not arranged neatly in circular zones.

At low elevations bunchgrasses dominate. Needle-and-thread, mountain muhly, Junegrass, blue grama, and species of wheatgrass and bluegrass are common; some of these species extend higher into the mountains where they mix with timber danthonia and Thurber fescue. Weedy forbs like yarrow and pasture sage may be abundant. Isolated ponderosa pine and western red cedar are common at lower elevations. Scattered dry shrub clumps may indicate variations in local soils or ecosystem history.

Natural dry meadows frequently have young ponderosa or lodgepole pine around the edges. These trees are present because of overgrazing. Immediately after cattle are removed from

Mountain bluebird. These birds nest in tree cavities along forest borders and are most commonly seen perching on fences and power lines in meadows.

a meadow where little herb cover remains, pine seedlings successfully establish themselves because herb competition has been temporarily eliminated. The seedlings will live to maturity, but the forest will then be successional to meadow. Offspring of the invading pines will not survive competition from the herb turf once it has recovered from overgrazing.

Successional meadows contain a combination of weedy, introduced plants and plants typical of dry, rocky slopes, such as common dandelion, golden banner, Colorado locoweed, pussytoes, daisies, stonecrop, and some sedges. Montane successional meadows may include aster, bluegrass species, prairie and pasture sage, wild rose, and sticky cinquefoil. Shrubby cinquefoil and other shrubs are often scattered through the meadows. Wax currant usually indicates the previous presence of ponderosa pine, and pieces of rotted ponderosa can often be found at the shrub's base.

Successional meadows will eventually be invaded by the tree species that were originally present, although aspen or lodgepole pine may form intermediary forests. Aspen appear to be particularly able to invade herb turfs, probably because aspen suckers (young trees that have sprouted from the lateral roots of mature aspen) do not have to compete with herbs for water and soil nutrients. Tree invasion into successional meadows may be slow, especially near timberline where the climate becomes very severe once trees are removed.

Mountain grasslands have a similar plant species composition to dry meadows. Thurber fescue and mountain muhly were once the dominant grasses, but these have been largely replaced by blue grama, Canada bluegrass, foxtail barley, and other species as a result of grazing. In some areas, grazing has been very detrimental to the vegetation by decreasing plant vigor and cover, seed stalk production, and total herbage yield. Heavy grazing also impairs root development which delays growth in the spring and increases soil erosion. Weedy species such as Russian thistle and snakeweed increase, and bunchgrasses eventually are replaced by sod-forming species.

Animal Characteristics

Mountain meadows and grasslands are important foraging areas for mammals. The lush, diverse herb growth provides optimal summer range for elk, as it did in the past for bison. Pronghorn roam some mountain grassland areas.

Low elevation shrubby meadows on south-facing slopes that remain snow-free are used as winter range by mule deer. Smaller common herbivores include the Wyoming ground squirrel, the deer mouse, and the long-tailed vole. Wet meadows and fens also include shrews, montane voles, and species typical of riparian ecosystems. Badgers are most abundant in dry meadows where they prey on small mammals, serving the important function of mixing the soil while digging their meal. Several species of bats forage insects over meadows.

Northern pocket gophers, whose mounds of bare earth are conspicuous throughout dry meadows and grasslands, are reputed as the mountain mammals that have the most impact on ecosystems. They dig elaborate tunnel systems, feeding on roots as they move along. In winter, they tunnel through snow eating above-ground plant portions. They affect plant distribution and succession by creating large areas of bare, raised soil that are invaded by pioneer species. Their burrowing action also loosens and aerates the soil, exposes it to the wind, and increases its water-retaining capacity. In some areas, their tunnels become runoff channels during the spring, and the ensuing water erosion may form deep gullies. Their burrows are used by other small mammal species.

Domestic herbivores have replaced natural ungulates throughout much of the region. When cover and food are depleted by severe overgrazing, small mammal species also disappear. Only northern pocket gophers and omnipresent deer mice remain in any quantity.

In addition to their significance as foraging sites, mountain meadows are important because of border areas formed between meadows and adjacent forest ecosystems. The borders are typified by an increase in animal density and the number of animal

The golden-mantled ground squirrel is a conspicuous resident in relatively open woodlands and along forest edges. *James C. Halfpenny.*

species. They contain a distinctive fauna including the golden-mantled ground squirrel, least chipmunk, and Nuttall's cottontail. Edges are a good habitat for species that depend on forest plants for cover and on the meadow's lush herbs for food. These species include both carnivores, such as bobcat and coyote, and herbivores (mule deer and elk).

The number of bird species that nest in meadows is limited. In subalpine areas, white-crowned and Lincoln's sparrows nest in nearby shrubs, and dark-eyed juncos raise their broods on moist meadow edges. Other songbirds such as the mountain bluebird feed in meadows but nest in adjacent forests. Poor-wills and common nighthawks lay their eggs on the ground on nearby open, forested hillsides. Flocks of rosy finches feed in meadows in winter, returning to the tundra to nest in summer. Other birds include vesper sparrows, savannah sparrows, and at lower elevations, western meadowlarks.

Predatory birds nest in forests but use open meadows and grasslands as hunting grounds. Red-tailed hawks are common. Goshawks, Cooper's hawks, and sharp-shinned hawks, species that hunt in the forest in morning and evening, soar over meadows at midday. Early risers might see great horned owls finishing a night's hunt.

Shrubby meadows that invade burned forests often have more animal activity than other mountain sites. Food, cover, and nesting sites are abundant in dead standing trees and lush understory. The formation of these successional meadows also increases the number of forest–meadow borders.

Human Use

Mountain meadows and grasslands all have been extensively used. Early homesteaders probably cultivated most natural dry meadows, and stream-side parks were praised around the turn of the century for their excellent hay crops and pasturage. Early settlers frequently created meadows by removing ponderosa pine to increase herb production for cattle or increase cultivated acreage. The number of today's meadows that are the result of human action is not known. Today, livestock grazing is the principal use of most dry meadows and grasslands, and hay production is still important in moist areas or where water is available for irrigation. With high demands for beef, this probably will continue to be the case.

Many large fens have been excavated for peat, which has accumulated to depths of six feet or more in some areas. Large tracts in South Park and in other mountain valleys have been mined. The peat resource in the southern Rockies is limited, and there is concern that continued peat mining could threaten rare plant species.

Plants and Animals of Mountain Grasslands and Meadows

Species composition of mountain meadows and grasslands depends primarily on site moisture and history of disturbance. Some plant species have been introduced to improve range conditions for cattle grazing. Many of the listed animal species do not breed in these ecosystems, but rather nest or den in surrounding forests and move into the meadows on a regular basis for feeding or other purposes. Shrubs are an important component of some mountain meadows and grasslands, and where present will increase animal diversity. Listed birds are mainly summer residents.

PLANTS

Shrubs
birch, bog   *Betula glandulosa*
cinquefoil, shrubby   *Pentaphylloides floribunda*
currant, wax   *Ribes cereum*
rose, wild   *Rosa woodsii*
willows, shrub   *Salix* spp.

Grasses and Grasslike Plants
barley foxtail   *Critesion jubatum*
bluegrass, Canada   *Poa compressa*
cheatgrass   *Anisantha tectorum*
danthonia, timber   *Danthonia intermedia*
fescue, Idaho   *Festuca idahoensis*
   Thurber   *Festuca thurberi*
grama, blue   *Chondrosum gracile*
hairgrass, tufted   *Deschampsia cespitosa*
Junegrass   *Koeleria macrantha*
muhly, mountain   *Muhlenbergia montana*
needle-and-thread   *Stipa comata*
reedgrass, Canadian *Calamagrostis canadensis*
spike-rush   *Eleocharis palustris*
timothy   *Phleum pratense*
wheatgrass, slender   *Elymus trachycaulus*

Forbs
black-eyed susan   *Rudbeckia hirta*
blue-eyed grass   *Sisyrinchium montanum*
cinquefoil, sticky   *Drymocallis arguta*
daisy, showy   *Erigeron speciosus*
dandelion, common   *Taraxacum officinale*
geranium, white   *Geranium richardsonii*
golden banner   *Thermopsis divaricarpa*
harebell, common   *Campanula rotundifolia*
Iris, wild   *Iris missouriensis*
locoweed, Rocky Mountain   *Oxytropis sericea*
paintbrush, scarlet   *Castilleja miniata*
pussytoes, mountain   *Antennaria parvifolia*
rubber plant, Colorado   *Picradenia richardsonii*
sage, pasture   *Artemisia frigida*
   prairie   *Artemisia ludoviciana*
stonecrop   *Sedum lanceolatum*
strawberry, wild   *Fragaria virginiana*
yarrow   *Achillea lanulosa*

ANIMALS

Reptiles and Amphibians (restricted to moist locations)

frog, boreal chorus   *Pseudacris triseriata*

    northern leopard   *Rana pipiens*

salamander, tiger   *Ambystoma tigrinum*

snake, wandering garter   *Thamnophis elegans*

toad, boreal   *Bufo boreas*

Birds

blackbird, Brewer's   *Euphagus cyanocephalus*

bluebird, mountain   *Sialia currucoides*

falcon, prairie   *Falco mexicanus*

harrier, northern   *Circus cyaneus*

hawk, red-tailed   *Buteo jamaicensis*

hummingbird, broad-tailed   *Selasphorus platycercus*

kestrel, American   *Falco sparverius*

lark, horned   *Eremophila alpestris*

meadowlark, western   *Sturnella neglecta*

nighthawk, common   *Chordeiles minor*

sparrow, Lincoln's   *Melospiza lincolnii*

    savannah   *Passerculus sandwichensis*

    vesper   *Pooecetes gramineus*

Mammals

badger   *Taxidea taxus*

bat, western small-footed myotis   *Myotis ciliolabrum*

chipmunk, Colorado   *Tamias quadrivittatus*

    least   *Tamias minimus*

    Uinta   *Tamias umbrinus*

cottontail, Nuttall's   *Sylvilagus nuttallii*

coyote   *Canis latrans*

deer, mule   *Odocoileus hemionus*

elk   *Cervus elaphus*

ground squirrel, golden-mantled   *Spermophilus lateralis*

    Wyoming   *Spermophilus elegans*

jackrabbit, white-tailed   *Lepus townsendii*

marmot, yellow-bellied   *Marmota flaviventris*

mouse, deer   *Peromyscus maniculatus*

pocket gopher, northern   *Thomomys talpoides*

sheep, bighorn   *Ovis canadensis*

shrew, masked   *Sorex cinereus*

    montane   *Sorex monticolus*

skunk, striped   *Mephitis mephitis*

vole, long-tailed   *Microtus longicaudus*

    meadow   *Microtus pennsylvanicus*

weasel, long-tailed   *Mustela frenata*

Species in bold-faced type are more abundant.

·4·
Lowland Riparian Ecosystems

Identifying Traits

Riparian ecosystems occur along the banks of rivers, streams, and other bodies of water. They include floodplain woodlands and marshes with various associations of grasses, herbs, shrubs, and trees that depend on a more or less continuous and accessible water supply. These narrow ecosystems represent a transition zone between aquatic and terrestrial ecosystems but usually have distinct vegetation and soils. This chapter describes riparian ecosystems found on the plains east of the mountains and in semidesert lowlands to the south and west. At higher elevations, the character of riparian ecosystems changes, so mountain riparian ecosystems are discussed separately in the next chapter.

Early explorers on the plains found riparian ecosystems to be the only areas with deciduous trees. Large cottonwood trees and flowering shrubs formed groves and thickets of varying width and density bordering banks of streams. They were surrounded by rolling grasslands. Animal life was abundant, for the eco-

J.C. Emerick.

systems provided shelter from sun and wind and more abundant nest sites and food than the grasslands.

In the low semidesert valleys west of the mountains, groves of native cottonwoods and streamside shrubs provided moist and shady oases. As on the plains, these riparian ecosystems supported vegetation that was markedly different from that on surrounding land. However, in these near-desert regions, dry shrublands rather than grasslands bordered the riparian ecosystems.

Today riparian ecosystems rarely exist in a natural state. Many streams are flanked by cottonwoods or by no trees at all. Some introduced species have escaped cultivation and become established as common associates with the cottonwoods. Despite such alterations, riparian ecosystems differ greatly from their surroundings in their appearance, species composition, and ecological processes. They continue to be important to animal populations and support a diverse, often unique, fauna.

Location

Lowland riparian ecosystems border all major streams flowing out of the mountains and are the lowest-elevation ecosystems in the region. They join mountain riparian ecosystems at the base of the foothills.

Site Characteristics

Climate is generally similar to that of surrounding ecosystems, although the trees do moderate intense winds and sunlight. Riparian ecosystems may be colder than nearby uplands because of cold air drainage along rivers.

Soils are young and moist, with a high water table and poor drainage. They vary in depth and texture since they are formed from relatively recent deposits of coarse gravel, silt, and sand. Where streams remain unchanneled, flash floods are common during periods of intense rainfall.

Plant Characteristics

Several types of plant communities exist in lowland riparian zones. The most widespread, particularly along the South Platte

Plains cottonwood.

River, is the cottonwood community, dominated almost exclusively by plains cottonwood, with varying amounts of peach-leaved willow, a tree that grows up to fifty feet tall. Also present are several shrubs, such as wild plum, hawthorn, currant, wild rose, snowberry, and shrubby willows. Saltgrass and sand dropseed are the most common grasses. Plains cottonwoods are massive, broad-crowned trees with roughly triangular leaves and bark that is deeply fissured into long, vertical grooves. Trees grow rapidly, mature specimens being by far the largest (although not the oldest) trees in the region. "Cotton"—fluffy white fibers—surrounds the tiny tree seeds and allows the wind to carry these seeds long distances.

Cottonwood communities have been replaced in many areas along the South Platte and almost completely along the Arkansas River by a mixed community type. This consists of various combinations of cottonwood, peach-leaved willow, box elder, American elm, green ash, and Russian olive. Salt cedar (or tamarisk) commonly occurs in this community along the Arkansas River but is rare in South Platte riparian zones. This community type is a direct result of occupation by settlers, as the last four species listed above are all introduced plants.

In areas that are moist most of the year, sand willows form dense thickets along stream banks. In the Arkansas drainage these willows are mixed with, or replaced by, salt cedar. Uplands with lower soil moisture, which often are interspersed among the woody communities, support open parklands dominated by grasses such as western wheatgrass, foxtail barley, and sand dropseed, and forbs such as kochia, sunflower, poison ivy, and wild licorice.

Lowland riparian ecosystems on the Western Slope are similar to those in the eastern part of the region. Invasion by salt cedar is extensive along the Colorado and other rivers. Valley cottonwood usually is the dominant tree species and is accompanied by box elder, peach-leaved willow, and Russian olive.

Marshes and sloughs occur in shallow margins of streams and ponds and elsewhere where standing water remains during most of the year. Cat-tail, bulrush, and prairie cord-grass are conspicuous, and aquatic herbs such as pondweed, water-plantain, and arrowhead are common. This community type is perhaps the most productive found on the floodplain.

Riparian ecosystems are continually changing in response to the dynamic nature of the stream channel. As the stream meanders across the floodplain, sand is deposited in bars or along stream shores. The sand is invaded by species of sandbar willows, shrubs that guard against erosion while slowly building the soil. Eventually cottonwoods invade the willows. As this is occurring, other sections of the stream are undercutting mature cottonwood groves which, in time, collapse into the creek. Sand is deposited in collapsed areas, and the successional cycle begins again.

Occasionally streams shift their courses and start to flow through vegetated lowlands. The new watercourses are transformed into barren creek bottoms as water removes vegetation and soil. At the same time deserted oxbows form ponds that are invaded by aquatic plants which fill the ponds as they build the soil, and the area eventually is invaded by plants that require drier, better-developed soils.

Because of these processes, riparian ecosystems are composed of a mosaic of small plant communities, each community being in a different successional stage. The overall character of the total riparian area remains constant because young ecosystems are maturing while mature ecosystems are being destroyed.

Reports of early explorers tell us something about the appearance of riparian areas along the South Platte and Arkansas Rivers prior to settlement. The floodplain of the South Platte during the 1800s averaged a third of a mile in width as it crossed the plains west of Greeley, Colorado. Shrubs grew along the banks and on islands but apparently were sparse, and groves of cottonwoods were rare, often limited to only a few trees. The appearance of the South Platte today is much different. The floodplain is only a fifth as wide, due primarily to agriculture, and cottonwood groves and other riparian habitats are more widespread.

Zebulon Pike traveled up the Arkansas River in 1806 and reported continuous cottonwood forests along both sides of the river near the present town of Lamar. Cottonwoods were the only woody species he mentioned. In 1913 salt cedar was observed in the same area, and since then it has continued to spread to its present extensive distribution in the drainage.

White-tailed deer. The smaller antlers on the bucks, shorter ears, darker face, and longer tail with its conspicuous white fur are among the features that distinguish this species from the more widespread mule deer. *Leonard Lee Rue III.*

Lowland marshes and ponds support a diverse array of birds. Canada geese are a common nesting species. *Stephen Jones.*

Animal Characteristics

Lowland river bottoms and marshes are the most productive natural ecosystems in the region, both in terms of plants and the rich wildlife that abound here. In springtime, sunrise is greeted by the songs of dozens of birds. Colorful orioles fly through the trees, and the drumming of woodpeckers rattles through the forest. Along the plains to the east both mule deer and white-tailed deer live, and throughout the region the marsh waters teem with myriad insects and other aquatic life.

Many animals live here because of the lush forage, water, and abundant denning or nesting sites. In addition to the species that live exclusively along moist watercourses and marshes, animals from surrounding ecosystems take refuge in riparian ecosystems. Bison and wintering elk frequented cottonwood groves, as did pronghorn, which are still seen there today. Migrating birds use these ecosystems as resting places in the spring and fall, as do mixed flocks of small mountain birds (chickadees, brown creepers, nuthatches, pine siskins) during the winter.

Riparian forests provide protected migration routes along which species from eastern deciduous forests spread westward. Some of these species include the white-tailed deer, opossum, and fox squirrels, and birds such as the red-headed woodpecker and blue jay. The Rocky Mountains have been an effective barrier to migration; these species are rare in lowland riparian areas west of the Rockies.

Wildlife assemblages are characterized by large numbers of bird species, including waterfowl (such as geese, ducks, grebes), shorebirds (herons, egrets, rails), gulls, predators including owl and hawk species, woodpeckers, belted kingfishers, and songbirds (dippers, swallows, warblers, flycatchers, jays, wrens). Large flocks of great blue herons nest in rookeries in cottonwood groves in scattered locations.

Lowland riparian ecosystems harbor more species of reptiles and amphibians than do other ecosystems in the region. Summer temperatures are warm, there is abundant shelter, and large numbers of insects and other animals are available for food. Marshes and shallow portions of slow streams where rooted aquatic plants grow, as well as open cottonwood groves and meadows, are all important habitats. The more common reptiles and amphibians are tiger salamanders, leopard frogs, chorus frogs, Woodhouse's toads, painted turtles, various garter snakes, and bullsnakes. Many species, such as the Great Plains toad, plains leopard frog, snapping turtle, yellow mud turtle, six-lined racerunner, and the northern water snake, are restricted to the eastern side of the Rocky Mountains. Riparian wildlife has changed from what it was before human settlement. Some of the large herbivores and predators are gone as the result of hunting and poisoning. Raccoons, small songbirds, and other animals that can utilize the trees cultivated in cities and around farmhouses have flourished. Waterfowl populations have increased with the building of reservoirs, ponds, and irrigation ditches. Despite such changes, these ecosystems have not lost their importance to wildlife; the fauna is diverse and productive and provides us the opportunity to see many species that occur nowhere else in the region.

Human Use

Lowland riparian and wetland ecosystems are among the most heavily used and altered ecosystems in the region. Rocky deposits of ancient rivers have been mined for gravel. Cottonwoods have been cut for firewood and lumber. Housing developments have been built along stream sides, despite the dangers of flooding. Although high water tables discourage cultivation, the ecosystems have been heavily grazed by cattle, which congregate in the shade and trample young trees. Eventually the natural understory is destroyed and replaced by weedy species, and cottonwoods disappear since young trees cannot mature and replace old, dying trees. Streams have been artificially channelized, destroying oxbows and the natural mosaic of communities that is created by the simultaneous deposition and removal of soil and sand by free-running rivers.

At the same time human actions such as cultivation of trees and construction of artificial waterways have led to the relocation of riparian plants and animals. In short, human use has dramatically altered the location, species composition, and processes of lowland deciduous forests and wetlands, but has not eliminated these ecosystems. As urban and agricultural development progresses, changes to these ecosystems are likely to continue. Now as never before, careful planning is needed to balance human activities with the ecology of these environments, if the remaining natural qualities of these lands are to exist for future generations.

Plants and Animals of Lowland Riparian Ecosystems

Occurrence of each species depends on local site characteristics and history of disturbance, and may vary considerably from one place to another. (E) denotes species found only on the Eastern Slope and (W) denotes species found only on the Western Slope. Listed birds are mainly summer residents.

PLANTS

Trees

ash, green* *Fraxinus pennsylvanica*
box elder *Negundo aceroides*
cottonwood, plains (E) *Populus deltoidea* ssp. *occidentalis*
    valley (W) *Populus deltoidea* ssp. *wislizenii*
hackberry *Celtis reticulata*
Russian olive* *Elaeagnus angustifolia*
willow, peach-leaved *Salix amygdaloides*

Shrubs

currant, wax *Ribes cereum*
hawthorn *Crataegus* spp.
plum, wild *Prunus americana*
rose, wild *Rosa arkansana*
salt cedar* *Tamarix ramosissima*
snowberry *Symphoricarpos occidentalis*
willow, sandbar *Salix exigua*

Herbaceous plants

arrowhead *Sagittaria latifolia*
barley, foxtail *Critesion jubatum*
bulrush *Schoenoplectus lacustris*
cat-tail, broad-leaved *Typha latifolia*
cord-grass, prairie *Spartina pectinata*
dropseed, sand *Sporobolus cryptandrus*
kochia* *Kochia sieversiana*
licorice, wild *Glycyrrhiza lepidota*
poison ivy *Toxicodendron rydbergii*
pondweed *Potamogeton* spp.
saltgrass *Distichlis stricta*
sunflower *Helianthus nuttallii*
water-plantain *Alisma plantago-aquatica*
wheatgrass, western *Pascopyrum smithii*

ANIMALS

Reptiles and Amphibians
bullfrog* *Rana catesbeiana*
bullsnake *Pituophis melanoleucus*
frog, plains leopard (E) *Rana blairi*
   striped chorus *Pseudacris triseriata*
lizard, six-lined racerunner (E) *Cnemidophorus sexlineatus*
salamander, tiger *Ambystoma tigrinum*
snake, northern water (E) *Nerodia sipedon*
   plains garter (E) *Thamnophis radix*
   • red-sided garter (E) *Thamnophis sirtalis*
toad, Great Plains (E) *Bufo cognatus*
   Woodhouse's *Bufo woodhousii*
turtle, painted *Chrysemys picta*
   snapping (E) *Chelydra serpentina*
   yellow mud (E) *Kinosternon flavescens*

Birds
blackbird, red-winged *Agelaius phoeniceus*
• **bobwhite, northern** (E) *Colinus virginianus*
chickadee, black-capped *Parus atricapillus*
coot, American *Fulica americana*
• cuckoo, yellow-billed *Coccyzus erythropthalmus*
egret, snowy *Egretta thula*
flicker, northern *Colaptes auratus*
flycatcher, ash-throated *Myiarchus cinerascens*
goose, Canada *Branta canadensis*
grebe, western *Aechmophorus occidentalis*
grosbeak, black-headed *Pheucticus melanocephalus*
hawk, red-tailed *Buteo jamaicensis*

heron, black-crowned night *Nycticorax nycticorax*
   • **great blue** *Ardea herodias*
• **jay, blue** (E) *Cyanocitta cristata*
kingbird, eastern *Tyrannus tyrannus*
   western *Tyrannus verticalis*
kingfisher, belted *Ceryle alcyon*
magpie, black-billed *Pica pica*
mallard *Anas platyrhynchos*
mockingbird, northern *Mimus polyglottos*
oriole, • **northern** *Icterus galbula*
   • orchard *Icterus spurius*
owl, common barn *Tyto alba*
   great horned *Bubo virginianus*
pintail, northern *Anas acuta*
rail, Virginia *Rallus limicola*
robin, American *Turdus migratorius*
screech-owl, eastern (E) *Otus asio*
   western *Otus kennicottii*
sparrow, lark *Chondestes grammacus*
   song *Melospiza melodia*
swallow, barn *Hirundo rustica*
   cliff *Hirundo pyrrhonota*
   northern rough-winged *Stelgidopteryx serripennis*
tern, black *Chlidonias niger*
   Forster's *Sterna forsteri*
thrasher, brown (E) *Toxostoma rufum*
warbler, yellow *Dendroica petechia*
woodpecker, downy *Picoides pubescens*
   Lewis *Melanerpes lewis*
   • red-headed (E) *Melanerpes erythrocephalus*
wood-pewee, western *Contopus sordidulus*
wren, Bewick's *Thryomanes bewickii*
   house *Troglodytes aedon*
   marsh *Cistothorus palustris*

Mammals

bat, big brown *Eptesicus fuscus*
  little brown myotis *Myotis lucifugus*
    western small-footed myotis *Myotis ciliolabrum*
beaver *Castor canadensis*
- **cottontail, eastern** (E) *Sylvilagus floridanus*
coyote *Canis latrans*
deer, mule *Odocoileus hemionus*
  - white-tailed *Odocoileus virginianus*
fox, red *Vulpes vulpes*
mink *Mustela vison*
mouse, deer *Peromyscus maniculatus*
  house* *Mus musculus*
  western harvest *Reithrodontomys megalotis*
    white-footed (E) *Peromyscus leucopus*

muskrat *Ondatra zibethicus*
- opossum, Virginia (E) *Didelphis virginiana*
raccoon *Procyon lotor*
- rat, hispid cotton (E) *Sigmodon hispidus*
shrew, masked *Sorex cinereus*
skunk, **striped** *Mephitis mephitis*
  western spotted *Spilogale gracilis*
- **squirrel, fox** (E) *Sciurus niger*
vole, meadow (E) *Microtus pennsylvanicus*
  prairie (E) *Microtus ochrogaster*
weasel, long-tailed *Mustela frenata*
woodrat, eastern (E) *Neotoma floridana*

- Breeds almost exclusively in lowland riparian woodlands.
* Introduced species
Species in bold-faced type are more abundant.

·5·

Mountain Riparian Ecosystems

Identifying Traits

Mountain riparian ecosystems form long, sinuous, discontinuous bands of varying width adjacent to streams, ponds and lakes. Deciduous trees and moisture-loving shrubs dominate the ecosystems, forming small meadows, tree groves, shrub thickets, or mixtures of the last two. They color valleys red and yellow when sap flows in spring, and they fill canyons with flowers in early summer and with yellow falling leaves in autumn. In winter the ecosystems are drab browns and tans compared to surrounding green coniferous forests. The only other deciduous ecosystems in the mountains, quaking aspen and montane shrublands, are on mountain slopes.

Streambank habitats as well as wetlands associated with ponds and lakes support a diverse array of plant communities that in turn provide food and cover for many animal species. Thus riparian ecosystems have an abundance of wildlife whose activity contrasts with the quieter surrounding forests and meadows.

J.C. Emerick.

Location

Mountain riparian ecosystems are found throughout the forested mountains (5600 to 11,000 feet) on moist sites. They are usually at the base of slopes on terraces adjacent to streams, ponds and lakes. Mountain meadows are commonly intermixed. Occasionally riparian ecosystems extend up onto those hillsides that afford adequate moisture. Such sites include pockets or terraces with a high water table, seeps, irrigation ditches, rocky areas that trap and hold moisture, and ravines and gulches, particularly those with a northern exposure. Riparian ecosystems are not as extensive as most other types of mountain ecosystems.

Since streams run through the mountains at all altitudes, riparian ecosystems form continuous strands that cross the subalpine and montane forests. At their upper edges the ecosystems pass through krummholz and tundra marshes. They merge with lowland riparian ecosystems at their lower limits and thus are important migration routes for some animals.

Periodic flooding and bank erosion have killed these conifers, illustrating the dynamic, everchanging nature of riparian ecosystems. Elsewhere, newly formed sandbars will be colonized by willows and other vegetation. *W. Perry Conway.*

Site Characteristics

The climate of mountain riparian ecosystems changes with altitude, as does mountain climate in general. Only a few generalizations are consistently true. Riparian ecosystems are colder than those of adjacent hillsides because of cold air drainage and stagnation. As a result the frost-free season is as much as twenty-five to fifty days shorter than that of nearby ridge tops; riparian trees leaf out later and turn fall colors earlier than upslope trees. Atmospheric humidity is supplemented by cloud layers that roll up the lower canyons in spring and fall. When adjacent slopes are steep and shade the valley floor, patches of snow last late into the spring.

Soil texture varies from fine silts on level floodplains to coarse gravels and cobbles interspersed with boulders in steeper canyon bottoms. Some areas are subject to periodic flooding, a process that erodes some soils and buries others with sand, gravel, and other materials from upstream. Sites also vary with regard to soil drainage and depth to the water table. Soils associated with marshes and fens (see Chapter 3) are usually dark and high in organic matter.

Plant Characteristics

Mountain riparian ecosystems are dominated by alder and species of cottonwood, willow, and birch. Several other plants are common, including two of our most majestic conifers, the Colorado blue spruce and the white fir. The ecosystems are neither homogeneous nor simple but are actually a mosaic of stands that differ in structure and species composition. Structurally, they may be tree groves, shrub thickets, or a mixture of the two, sometimes interspersed with patches of wet meadows and fens. Tree groves and shrub thickets are found throughout the lower elevations; shrub thickets, called carrs, dominate subalpine regions.

As climate changes with increasing elevation, so does the species composition of riparian ecosystems. The flora is especially rich in canyons of the foothills and plateaus where lowland riparian species mix with mountain species. Only plants with the broadest climatic ranges are found in all riparian ecosystems.

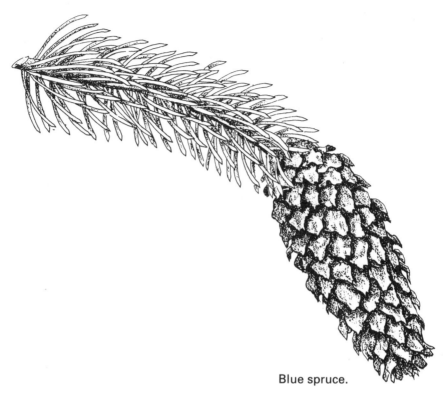

Blue spruce.

The cottonwood and peach-leaved willow that dominate lowland riparian ecosystems extend into the canyons at the base of the mountains. These species are replaced by the narrowleaf cottonwood and shrubby willows as the climate abruptly becomes cooler in the canyon bottoms. Both the plains and valley cottonwood interbreed with narrowleaf cottonwood in lower canyons, producing lanceleaf cottonwood. These trees can be distinguished by their leaf shapes. Plains and valley cottonwood leaves are broadly triangular and similar in appearance, narrowleaf cottonwood leaves are long and thin, and lanceleaf cottonwood leaves are intermediate in width. Narrowleaf cottonwood extends up into the subalpine. Occasionally balsam poplar may be found, although this is a more northern species that extends far into Alaska and northern Canada. Central Colorado is at the extreme southern edge of its range, so the species exists only in scattered locations along mountain watercourses. Its long leaves (up to seven inches) are the largest of our native poplars. The inch-long terminal buds produce a camphor-like fragrance when squeezed, possibly accounting for an alternative name, "balm-of-Gilead."

The numerous moisture-loving shrub and tree species associated with lower mountain canyons include box elder, mountain maple, wild plum, chokecherry, beaked hazelnut, hackberry, and species of hawthorn. Some of these are found on a variety of sites. They may form large patches on north-facing canyon sides and in protected washes on southern exposures. Wild plum and chokecherry may extend onto drier sites. Hawthorn extends out onto mesas on rocky soils that provide more moisture than nearby deeper, finer grassland soils. From central Colorado southward, New Mexico locust is frequent in canyons and valleys of foothills. It may form large, dense thickets up to twenty feet high.

Alder and river birch join riparian ecosystems from the base of the foothills to the subalpine. These tree shrubs, which grow to forty feet tall, are distinguished by the deep red bark of the river birch and woody, persistent cones of the alder. Mountain maple and red-osier dogwood also have a broad altitudinal range and are common on streamsides and upland moist sites.

Riparian ecosystems of montane and subalpine regions have fewer species than at lower elevations, but diversity is still high compared to most adjacent ecosystems. Narrowleaf cottonwood

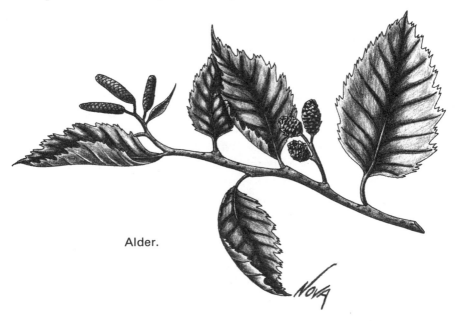

Alder.

is the dominant tree species, and between 7000 and 10,000 feet, it mixes in places with Colorado blue spruce and white fir. Contrary to popular thought, blue spruce is not always bluish; older trees are often dark green. At its upper limits, it hybridizes with the Engelmann spruce. White fir is common in southern Colorado, northern New Mexico and Arizona, sometimes mixing with blue spruce. Both conifers dominate the streamside vegetation in many areas, and often extend far up adjacent hillsides. Above 10,000 feet riparian ecosystems are characterized by bog birch and numerous species of shrubby willows.

Riparian herbaceous understory is lush and diverse when it is not disturbed. Forbs, grasses, sedges, rushes, climbing vines, mosses, lichens, and liverworts are present. Weedy invaders are common. It is not unusual for a valley floor to contain three times the number of species of adjacent upland forests.

On broad floodplains, vegetation is segregated into zones roughly parallel to the creek. Streamsides are bordered with discontinuous belts of willow, alder, and river birch thickets. Tree groves may be interspersed. Large meadows lie between riparian stands and upland forests, and meadows and forests are separated by a band of quaking aspen at the base of the hillside. Fine-grained soils, often saturated with water much of the year, frequently prevent invasion of these meadows by trees.

As streams flow across floodplains, new channels are formed and old meanders are abandoned, leaving oxbow ponds. These ponds gradually fill with vegetation and a rich organic soil develops. Open ponds become marshes with submerged aquatic vegetation, such as pondweeds, bur-reed, and mares-tail, and taller semiaquatic plants around the margin, including bulrush and broad-leaved cat-tail (at lower elevations), Canadian reedgrass, and several species of sedge. With time soil depth increases, and the marshes become willow carrs and wet meadows dominated by sedges, rushes, or reedgrass. Floodplains commonly contain many of these communities, all representing various stages of succession.

Characteristic subalpine riparian ecosystems are fens and shrub carrs in U-shaped valleys that have been carved and dammed by glaciers. These ecosystems often occupy sites that were once ponds or lakes but have gradually filled with sediment and organic material. They are dominated by dense, short willow

A subalpine willow carr along a mountain stream. *W. Perry Conway.*

species, bog birch, sedges and spike rushes. Typically, fens occur in the wetter areas and shrubs in sites with moderate soil moisture. Because soils of shrub carrs are better drained and aerated, usually representing a later successional stage, carrs support a higher diversity of herbaceous species than do fens.

Many high-elevation ponds and lakes are relatively cold, deep, and poor in mineral nutrients and accumulated organic matter. In these situations, the diversity of aquatic plants is low. Other subalpine ponds that have shallow margins and wave action that is not too severe often support a variety of submerged plants and rooted plants with floating leaves, such as pondweed, bur-reed, and water lilies. Such ponds and lakes are likely to change over time as they are invaded by semiaquatic vegetation at their edges, which gives way to concentric bands of wet meadow communities (see Chapter 3).

A good example of these processes can be seen at Red Rocks Lake in the Brainard Lake Recreation Area northwest of Denver. Here floating moss and sedge mats are slowly growing out over the pond. Willow and bog birch are invading the sedge mats and in turn are being invaded by coniferous trees.

Animal Characteristics

Riparian ecosystems are busy places for animals. Abundant food and cover in the dense tree foliage and lush understory, numerous nesting and denning sites, and the presence of free water produce a large and diverse animal community. In addition to resident species, the ecosystems are used part of the time by nonresidents that come to drink, by semiaquatic animals that live in the water, and by carnivores and insectivores that are attracted to the abundance of prey. Common small mammals in lush streamside ecosystems include the water shrew, muskrat, montane vole, and western jumping mouse. Mink and other weasel species prey on smaller mammals. Raccoons are often abundant in lower canyons, where they eat birds, small mammals, and insects, as well as a great variety of plant material. Chipmunks, squirrels, and rabbits, common in other surrounding ecosystems, are seen frequently at streamsides.

The beaver, a familiar mammal in riparian ecosystems, is the largest rodent in North America. Its habit of building dams often results in the flooding of substantial bottomlands. Beaver ponds conserve water, decrease erosion, and provide sites for increased animal diversity. The ponds also collect silt and saturate nearby soils, resulting in elimination of conifers as well as promoting favorable conditions for aspen, willow, alder, and birch. Beaver prefer aspen and willow for food and for building their dams and lodges, and extensive removal of these plants opens and perpetuates aspen or willow groves once the beavers have moved to other sites.

Established beaver families may number over a dozen animals, and over time will begin to eliminate all preferred food and building materials in the vicinity of their ponds. Unable to maintain their dams and at increased risk of predation, the beaver abandon their homes. Their ponds slowly drain or are colonized by semiaquatic vegetation, beginning a successional cycle similar to that described for oxbow ponds. Willow and aspen return, and eventually so do the beaver.

Two mammals have been recently reintroduced to Colorado. Small populations of moose have been released in northern Colorado, and sightings have become commonplace in some areas. In Colorado willows form a large component of their diet, so moose benefit indirectly from beaver activity. River otters have been reintroduced in scattered locations. Otters were once present in every major drainage in the state, but they probably never were common. They are excellent swimmers and seldom are found far from water. These carnivores eat a large number of aquatic organisms as well as birds and small mammals.

The diversity of nesting bird species is significantly higher than in other mountain ecosystems. Yellow warblers, American gold-finches, willow and cordilleran flycatchers, western wood-pewees, black-capped chickadees, fox sparrows, belted kingfish-ers, and warbling vireos are some of the nesting birds. Lincoln's and white-crowned sparrows nest in shrubs in subalpine riparian ecosystems, where they usually choose protected south-facing sites that allow for maintenance of a nearly constant nest temper-ature. The small yellow-and-black Wilson's and MacGillivray's warblers nest in subalpine willows. Hawks and owls use riparian trees for hunting perches. Waterfowl are present during migra-tion, and mallards and common snipes occasionally nest high into the mountains. Green-winged teal typically nest along higher beaver ponds. The dipper, a common inhabitant of moun-tain streams, feeds under water and bobs continuously when perched on rocks in streams. If waterfalls are present, it raises its young behind the falls on moisture-holding, mossy nests.

Riparian ecosystems are the home of several mountain dwelling reptiles and amphibians. These include the tiger sala-mander, the boreal toad, and the wood frog. The boreal toad is strictly a mountain species in Colorado, being most common between 8500 to 11,000 feet but occasionally inhabiting tundra ponds. A few isolated populations of the wood frog frequent the mountains of northern Colorado. Most wood frogs live north of the Arctic Circle. Wood frog populations in scattered Rocky Mountain locations apparently remain from a period of wide-spread distribution when the climate was cooler several thousand years ago. The striped chorus frog, northern leopard frog, west-ern terrestrial garter snake, and the smooth green snake are also found along streamsides in the mountains.

Dragonflies are common in riparian ecosystems, and abundant insects and insect galls are evident on shrubs. Most noticeable

Western screech owl. *James C. Halfpenny.*

are the tent caterpillars—moth larvae that build large, gossamer tents that they leave for foraging trips in search of tender leaves and buds.

Human Use

Riparian ecosystems have been greatly altered by human use. Ranchers have consistently removed beavers and converted willow thickets to hay meadows. Such removal of streamside shrubs hastens bank erosion and siltation of rivers and streams. Cattle have heavily utilized these areas because of their lush forage and the availability of drinking water. Grazing changes herb composition, increasing the dominance of weedy species. Trampling destroys the remaining herb cover and kills young trees and shrubs. Heavy recreational use has similar effects.

Transportation routes, commonly located adjacent to streams, have destroyed continuous riparian stands and produced disturbed areas (road cuts and shoulders) that serve as invasion routes for weedy species, and sources of sedimentation and other water pollution. Species such as white dutch clover were moving into the mountains *en masse* via disturbed creek beds at the turn of the century. By that time the character of riparian ecosystems had been disturbed by fire and by the lumbering of Colorado blue spruce and Douglas fir.

Peat bogs have been mined for decades. One is near the old townsite of Caribou west of Boulder. Recently riparian ecosystems have become centers for housing developments. All of these disruptions are regrettable, considering the small size of the ecosystems, their rich animal and plant life, and their func-

Beaver. Through its dam-building activities, this industrious mammal plays a greater part than any other wild animal in the modification of riparian ecosystems.

tion of maintaining water quality by preventing streambank erosion and by filtering water before it enters streams.

In the mineral belt, acidic, heavy metal–laden drainage from thousands of inactive mines has poisoned hundreds of miles of streams and rivers. Many aquatic reaches are stained yellow or orange with mineral deposits and are devoid of insects and fish. In some cases these waters flow through wetlands, which help remove some of the pollutants, although decreasing the health and diversity of the wetlands. Elsewhere, the contaminated waters simply flow downstream, a hazard to the well-being of humans and wildlife, until the metals are sufficiently diluted by other streams, or until they precipitate onto rocks and sediments in the streambed. While some scientific research has been directed at reducing this mine drainage problem, it will be decades before real solutions are implemented in many of the worst areas.

The American dipper, a small gray bird with a short tail, is often seen flying along mountain streams just a few feet above the water. It feeds on aquatic insects that live under stones in the streambed and frequently submerges itself completely as it searches for its meal. *Stephen Jones.*

Plants and Animals of Mountain Riparian Ecosystems

Mountain riparian ecosystems traverse a broad elevational range. Their character changes distinctly from foothill canyons where they are tree-dominated and share many species with lowland riparian ecosystems, to high elevations where they are dominated by shrubs and often found in association with ponds and bogs. Listed birds are mainly summer residents.

PLANTS

Trees

aspen, quaking *Populus tremuloides*

cottonwood, lanceleaf *Populus X acuminata* (at foothills-plains boundary)

narrowleaf *Populus angustifolia*

fir, white *Abies concolor*

poplar, balsam *Populus balsamifera*

spruce, Colorado blue *Picea pungens*

Shrubs

alder *Alnus incana*

birch, bog *Betula glandulosa*

birch, river *Betula fontinalis*

chokecherry *Padus virginiana*

cinquefoil, shrubby *Pentaphylloides floribunda*

dogwood, red-osier *Swida sericea*

gooseberry, common *Ribes inerme*

hawthorn *Crataegus* spp.

hazelnut, beaked *Corylus cornuta*

honeysuckle, bush *Distegia involucrata*

locust, New Mexico *Robinia neomexicana*

maple, mountain *Acer glabrum*

plum, wild *Prunus americana*

willows *Salix* spp.

Herbaceous Plants

angelica, giant *Angelica ampla*

bitter-cress *Cardamine cordifolia*

bog orchid, northern *Limnorchis hyperborea*

bulrush *Schoenoplectus lacustris*

bur-reed *Sparganium angustifolium*

cat-tail, broad-leaved *Typha latifolia*

checkermallow, white *Sidalcea candida*

chiming bells *Mertensia ciliata*

clover, white dutch* *Trifolium repens*

cow parsnip *Heracleum sphondylium*

gentian, star *Swertia perennis*

horsetail, field *Equisetum arvense*

mannagrass *Glyceria* spp.

mares-tail *Hippuris vulgaris*

monkey flower, common yellow *Mimulus guttatus*

pond lily, yellow *Nuphar luteum*

pondweeds *Potamogeton* spp.

reedgrass, Canadian *Calamagrostis canadensis*

rush, subalpine *Juncus mertensianus*

sedges *Carex* spp.

senecio, arrowleaf *Senecio triangularis*

shooting star *Dodecatheon pulchellum*

spike-rush *Eleocharis* spp.

virgin's bower, western *Clematis ligusticifolia*

ANIMALS

Reptiles and Amphibians

frog, striped chorus   *Pseudacris triseriata*
>   **northern leopard**   *Rana pipiens*
>   • wood   *Rana sylvatica*

salamander, **tiger**   *Ambystoma tigrinum*
snake, • smooth green   *Opheodrys vernalis*
>   wandering garter   *Thamnophis elegans*

• toad, boreal *Bufo boreas*

Birds

chickadee, black-capped   *Parus atricapillus*
mountain   *Parus gambeli*
• **dipper, American**   *Cinclus mexicanus*
flycatcher, **cordilleran**   *Empidonax difficilis*
>   • willow *Empidonax traillii*

goldfinch, American   *Carduelis tristis*
hawk, Cooper's   *Accipiter cooperii*
killdeer   *Charadrius vociferus*
kingfisher, belted   *Ceryle alcyon*
magpie, black-billed   *Pica pica*
mallard   *Anas platyrhynchos*
owl, great horned   *Bubo virginianus*
robin, American   *Turdus migratorius*
sandpiper, spotted   *Actitis macularia*
screech-owl, western   *Otus kennicottii*
snipe, common   *Gallinago gallinago*
sparrow, • fox   *Passerella iliaca*
>   **Lincoln's**   *Melospiza lincolnii*

song   *Melospiza melodia*
white-crowned   *Zonotrichia leucophrys*
swallow, tree   *Tachycineta bicolor*
violet-green   *Tachycineta thalassina*
teal, green-winged   *Anas crecca*
thrush, Swainson's   *Catharus ustulatus*
vireo, warbling   *Vireo gilvus*
warbler, **MacGillivray's**   *Oporornis tolmiei*
>   • **Wilson's** *Wilsonia pusilla*
>   **yellow**   *Dendroica petechia*

wood-pewee, western   *Contopus sordidulus*
woodpecker, downy   *Picoides pubescens*
>   hairy *Picoides villosus*

wren, house   *Troglodytes aedon*

Mammals

bear, black   *Ursus americanus*
beaver   *Castor canadensis*
bobcat   *Felis rufus*
chipmunk, least   *Tamias minimus*
cottontail, Nuttall's   *Sylvilagus nuttallii*
coyote   *Canis latrans*
deer, mule   *Odocoileus hemionus*
lion, mountain   *Felis concolor*
mink   *Mustela vison*
moose*   *Alces alces*
mouse, deer   *Peromyscus maniculatus*
>   **western jumping**   *Zapus princeps*

muskrat   *Ondatra zibethicus*
otter, river*   *Lutra canadensis*

Mammals (continued)

raccoon *Procyon lotor*
shrew, masked *Sorex cinereus*
   montane *Sorex monticolus*
   water *Sorex palustris*
skunk, striped *Mephitis mephitis*
vole, long-tailed *Microtus longicaudus*
   meadow *Microtus pennsylvanicus*
   montane *Microtus montanus*
weasel, long-tailed *Mustela frenata*

● Breeds almost exclusively in mountain riparian ecosystems.
* Introduced in parts of Colorado
Species in bold-faced type are more abundant.

·6·
Shrublands

Shrub communities cover large areas of Colorado and other western states. A rolling, silvery blue mantle of sagebrush dominates lower elevations of the Western Slope. Ragged stands of greasewood occupy semidesert bottomlands, and dense thickets of oak cloak foothill and montane hillsides. Shrubs often form part of the forest understory but also occur in distinct communities of various sizes at all elevations. Shrub communities described in this chapter include semidesert shrublands found in dry lowlands, sagebrush shrublands that occupy a wide range of elevation from the Colorado Plateau to high mountain valleys, and montane shrublands other than sagebrush, characteristic of foothills and mountain regions. Other types of shrub communities are important components of riparian, tundra, and other ecosystems; these are discussed elsewhere.

In spite of their ubiquity, shrubs tend to defy definition. They are usually woody plants with numerous stems and are under ten feet in height, but many grow to be much taller and look like small trees, while others are low with a single stem at their base. So what is a shrub? Perhaps a more useful definition is that if you have to walk around it, it is a shrub, but if you can walk under it, it is a tree.

A dense thicket of Gambel oak and serviceberry cloaks the hillside in the foreground. *J.C. Emerick.*

SEMIDESERT SHRUBLANDS

Identifying Traits

Low, greenish-gray expanses of shrubs in arid lowlands mark
the appearance of semidesert shrublands. The height and density
of the shrubs vary, but the plants are usually short and uncrowded, sparsely interspersed with a few grasses and forbs, because dry climate and poor soils impose severe limitations on
plant growth. To some people these shrublands are lonely, deso-
late regions of dusty weeds, almost devoid of life. To others it is
a world of many interesting plants and animals uniquely adapted
to withstand the rigorous environment.

Greasewood, four-winged saltbush, and shadscale are the most
common dominants of these shrublands in Colorado and northern New Mexico. In many places on the Colorado Plateau in
Utah and northern Arizona, blackbrush forms a distinctive community. Sagebrush also occurs here, but it is not restricted to
lowlands and is described in the "Sagebrush Shrublands" section
of this chapter.

Greasewood appears in alkaline depressions as scraggly,
bright green stands that turn yellow or pale orange in fall. Its
succulent leaves may be up to one-and-a-half inches long. The
male flowers, which lack petals and occur in small catkinlike
spikes, are very distinctive when present. With adequate moisture, greasewood may grow to a height of eight feet.

Gray-green stands of four-winged saltbush usually grow on
higher ground, often around the margins of greasewood populations. Saltbush is usually smaller than greasewood (six feet tall or
less), is very irregular in shape, and has numerous brittle
branches growing from the base. Its flowers are inconspicuous,
but the distinctive fruits have four papery wings.

Shadscale is a compact, spiny shrub that typically grows in
dense clumps from one to three feet high. Its fruits have two
wings instead of four and commonly turn a rose color at maturity, giving shadscale stands a pink blush in late summer and fall.

Blackbrush forms uniform blue-gray stands on shallow sandy
soils. Each shrub has a rounded, well-groomed appearance, although not as compact as shadscale's.

Location

Semidesert shrublands are prevalent throughout the Colorado Plateau region. They are most common at the lowest elevations, but may extend upward to eight thousand feet. Travelers see shadscale and greasewood communities along Interstate 70, from eastern Utah into Colorado, with greasewood reaching as far east as the town of Eagle. Four-winged saltbush is common along arid valley slopes of western Colorado and Utah. Blackbrush occurs along the Colorado and Dolores rivers in Colorado and becomes widespread in the vicinity of Arches and Canyonlands National Parks in eastern Utah.

East of the Continental Divide semidesert shrublands extend from the southern part of Colorado into New Mexico. Greasewood forms extensive stands in the San Luis Valley and extends eastward in the drainages of the Arkansas River and its tributaries, growing on sites from 4500 to 7500 feet in elevation. Four-winged saltbush has a similar distribution, with an elevational range of four to eight thousand feet. It is common but scattered near Walsenburg, Colorado, where it often borders piñon pine–juniper woodlands, occupying a transition zone between woodlands and grasslands. Shadscale is found mostly in Grand Valley and other arid basins along the western edge of

Greasewood bottomland community. *J.C. Emerick.*

Colorado and into Utah, but a few isolated shadscale communities occur near Pueblo and Cañon City.

Site Characteristics

The climate of semidesert shrublands is typified by hot summers and cold winters, with temperatures in January and February often well below freezing. Average precipitation is low, usually less than ten inches, although higher elevations and areas in the southeastern part of the state receive slightly greater amounts. Most of the precipitation falls during the winter months. Still, occasional thunderstorms moisten the soil during summer and regenerate the parched plant life. These conditions have led to the term "cool desert" which is applied to the Great Basin region between Colorado and California as well as to the semiarid lowlands of western Colorado.

Soils of semidesert shrublands are variable, but typically alkaline. Soils developing on shales such as the widespread Mancos Formation are typically high in clay and silt. Water from brief thunderstorms does not easily penetrate these soils, so on slopes water tends to quickly run off the surface, to be retained in poorly drained depressions. High evaporation rates during the hot, dry summers lead to a concentration of salts, which may actually form a white crust on the surface of these low places.

Sandy soils accumulate on weathering sandstone formations and in areas where sands are deposited by wind. In contrast to clay soils, sandy soils are very well drained, and quickly absorb falling rain. However, if not intercepted by plant roots, the moisture will continue to move downward, out of reach of shallow-rooted plants.

Plant Characteristics

Greasewood can be found in nearly pure stands on alkaline soils with a consistently high water table. In drier or less alkaline soils, it mixes with shadscale, four-winged saltbush, rabbitbrush, winterfat, and big sagebrush. Greasewood is often associated with grasses or other herbaceous species, such as saltgrass, alkali sacaton, blue grama, foxtail barley, kochia, whiteweed, and marsh elder.

Shadscale also grows in nearly pure stands in highly alkaline soils but more commonly is found mixed with greasewood, big sagebrush, four-winged saltbush, snakeweed, and rabbitbrush. It is one of the most common shrubs growing in clay soils, and can almost always be found near outcrops of the Mancos, Morrison, and other shale formations of the Colorado Plateau.

Because of the presence of certain mineral salts contained in some sedimentary rock formations of the Colorado Plateau, some unusual plant associations have been found. An example is a group of plants that are consistently associated with soils containing high amounts of the element selenium. Particularly notable are several species of milkvetch, which accumulate selenium to toxic levels and have poisoned livestock. During the 1950s, it was discovered that the distribution of selenium matched the distribution of uranium on the Plateau, and geologists were able to identify locations of uranium deposits by finding places where these selenium-loving species grew.

Four-winged saltbush is one of the most adaptable and widespread western shrubs, occurring in a variety of arid environments. It grows on less-alkaline, better-drained soils than shadscale or greasewood—soils of mesas, slopes, sand dunes, and gravelly washes, for example. In some areas, it is the dominant shrub growing with galletagrass, Indian ricegrass, and blue grama.

Extensive blackbrush stands are found in areas where sand has accumulated over bedrock to a depth of one to six feet. The roots of blackbrush grow downward to the top of the bedrock, where they intercept stranded pockets of water. In deeper sands, and in poorly-stabilized dunes, blackbrush gives way to Mormon tea, which can spread by roots. Blackbrush often grows in association with Indian ricegrass, another very successful species in sandy soils.

Little is known about successional patterns in semidesert shrublands. Because of their high salt tolerance, greasewood and shadscale stands are probably the climax vegetation of very alkaline soils. Greasewood will invade nearby rabbitbrush and saltbush stands if the water table of these stands rises. Four-winged saltbush may invade intensively grazed grasslands.

Animal Characteristics

Semidesert environments are rigorous for animals as well as plants, and many animal species have distinct adaptations for survival in these regions. Most of the smaller mammals do not need to drink water; they can obtain all they need from the plants that they eat. The foliage of some semidesert plants accumulates salts that are toxic to many animals, but physiological adaptations of certain desert animals permit them to eat these plants with impunity. For example greasewood often accumulates soluble oxalates that render the plant poisonous or unpalatable to most animal species; yet for the black-tailed jackrabbit, it is an important food.

High summer temperatures cause many animals to retreat into burrows or under rocks. The large ears of the jackrabbit are effective heat radiators, enabling the animal to stay a few degrees cooler as it seeks shady refuge under shrubs. Many semidesert animals are nocturnal in their habits, while others are active during the morning and evening. Only the reptiles seem to be conspicuous during the day, and even they seek shade during the hottest hours.

Several mammalian species are associated with Colorado's semidesert shrublands. The ubiquitous coyote frequently roams through the brush in search of desert cottontails and black-tailed jackrabbits. Occasionally one sees a badger, but more often finds only abandoned excavations where they have dug for white-tailed antelope squirrels, Gunnison's prairie dogs, and Ord's kangaroo rats. Semidesert shrublands provide cover and forage for mule deer and pronghorn.

Gambel's quail is a common resident of these shrublands in extreme western Colorado, and roadrunners are occasionally seen in these ecosystems in the southern part of the state. Northern harriers and Swainson's hawks may be seen as they hunt for small rodents. Among the most noticeable animals are reptiles such as the sagebrush lizard, side-blotched lizard, western whiptail, striped whipsnake, Great Basin gopher snake, and bullsnake.

Human Use

Semidesert shrublands are used for cattle grazing, and some areas have been converted to agricultural production, notably

Sagebrush shrublands in northeastern Colorado. *J.C. Emerick.*

portions of Grand Valley and the San Luis Valley. Removal of the more palatable herbaceous plants occurs rapidly if grazing pressure is excessive. Recovery of the range from overgrazing is slow because of low annual precipitation.

Because they accumulate salts, many semidesert shrub species such as four-winged saltbush and greasewood may become toxic to livestock. Poisoning and death of hungry animals may occur if they have had little or nothing else to eat.

SAGEBRUSH SHRUBLANDS

Identifying Traits

Sagebrush dominates extensive areas in western Colorado and forms one of the most common types of shrubland in the region. Sagebrush ecosystems occur as dense, rolling, grayish-green or grayish-blue stands, varying from two to seven or more feet tall. Older branches may exceed three inches in diameter and have dark, shredded bark. The species most commonly seen is big sagebrush, which occurs in the mountain and plateau regions of the state. Sand sagebrush, a related species, grows in sandy soils of plains grasslands and was mentioned in Chapter 2.

The Latin name of big sagebrush, *Seriphidium (Artemisia) tridentatum,* refers to the shape of the sagebrush leaf, which is elongate, slightly narrower at its base, and has three lobes or teeth ("tridentate") at its tip. When crushed the leaves emit a distinct sagelike odor, but this is not culinary sage which is a member of the mint family. Big sagebrush and other species of *Seriphidium* belong to the sunflower family, but their flowers bear little superficial resemblance to sunflowers. The tiny flowers have no petals and are clustered in numerous whitish vertical spikes. The aroma of the foliage pervades the sagebrush ecosystem, barely discernable in dry weather but full and pungent following a rainstorm.

Location

Sagebrush shrublands are extensive on the Western Slope of Colorado and in the Great Basin and are found throughout Wyoming. They are less prevalent on Colorado's Eastern Slope but do occur in scattered locations. Two subspecies of big sagebrush are common. Great Basin big sagebrush is a larger form

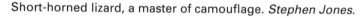

Short-horned lizard, a master of camouflage. *Stephen Jones.*

more typical of lower elevations up to approximately 8000 feet on the western slope. It covers large areas in Rio Blanco and Moffat counties in the northwestern part of Colorado, where it often exceeds ten feet in height in the bottom of intermittent drainages.

Mountain big sagebrush, a smaller shrub, seldom exceeds four feet. It occurs at elevations between seven and ten thousand feet or higher on both the Western and Eastern Slope of the Continental Divide. Mountain big sagebrush forms large stands in North Park, Middle Park, and in the Beaver Meadows area on the eastern side of Rocky Mountain National Park. It can also be seen along the upper reaches of the Arkansas River Valley near Leadville and along U.S. Highway 285 as it crosses Poncha Pass, extending down into the San Luis Valley.

Site Characteristics

The region's sagebrush ecosystems are best developed at low elevations on the western slopes of Colorado and Utah, where Great Basin big sagebrush tolerates desert conditions during the summer. Soils of big sagebrush stands are usually deep, and moderately fine-grained, and can be either acid or alkaline.

At higher elevations mountain big sagebrush withstands the climatic rigors of coniferous forests, such as a mean annual precipitation of twenty inches or more and cool average temperatures of less than 40°F. Here, it usually grows in well-drained soils, often consisting of decomposed granite (grus), or on gravel terraces in valley bottoms.

Plant Characteristics

Great Basin big sagebrush grows in semidesert lowlands over much of its range and is often associated with four-winged saltbush, greasewood, and shadscale. Rabbitbrush also is an important co-dominant at lower elevations up to 9000 feet and may form nearly pure stands in some areas. On slopes, Great Basin sagebrush interfingers with the piñon pine–juniper woodlands directly above them. The woodland species grow on shallower, stony soil overlying bedrock.

Several species commonly associate with mountain big sagebrush, so these ecosystems often have a greater plant diversity than adjacent coniferous forests. Rabbitbrush, bitterbrush, and snowberry are frequent. Slender wheatgrass, Junegrass, and bunchgrasses such as Arizona and Idaho fescue, as well as a few sedges, may intermingle with the shrubs. Wildflowers, such as blanket flower, Mariposa lily, scarlet gilia, and common lupine decorate sagebrush stands during the summer. One of the most colorful wildflowers is Indian paintbrush, whose roots grow semiparasitically with those of sagebrush and other plants. While the leaves of the paintbrush are photosynthetic and produce food for the plant, its roots obtain additional water and nutrients from roots of surrounding plants.

Bare soil is quickly colonized by sagebrush and other shrubs and, once established, sagebrush competes well with trees if soil conditions are appropriate. The margins of sagebrush stands that border coniferous forests are often distinct and appear to be relatively stable. Because of its tolerance of montane climatic conditions, it may form an edaphic climax (a climax that is permitted by locally favorable soil conditions), or a long-lived successional stage. Elsewhere sagebrush ecosystems are invaded by aspen, which in turn are succeeded by shade-tolerant conifers.

Because cattle do not find sagebrush palatable, they eat only the herbaceous understory and create bare, disturbed soil between the sagebrush shrubs. This disturbed soil eventually is invaded by sagebrush. Such stands become very dense. Sagebrush also may invade meadows that are being intensively grazed.

Sagebrush is very intolerant of fire, and when a stand is burned, usually only a small percentage of the sagebrush survives. Thus fire has been used as a range management technique to increase the quantity of grasses for livestock grazing. However, other nonpalatable shrubs, such as rabbitbrush, sprout from their stumps when burned and actually may increase in abundance.

Animal Characteristics

Many mammals rely on sagebrush for food and cover. Sagebrush and bitterbrush are important browse for mule deer and pronghorn. Nuttall's cottontails and white-tailed jackrabbits are never far from the protective cover of the shrubs, and many rodents, such as the northern grasshopper mouse, least chipmunk, golden-mantled ground squirrel, and long-tailed vole, also find shelter in them. Striped skunks and coyotes prowl the sagebrush in search of rodents, berries, insects, or anything else that will satisfy their omnivorous feeding habits.

Several bird species breed in sagebrush habitats, including Brewer's and sage sparrows, sage thrasher, and the sage grouse. High-elevation stands of sagebrush rarely harbor amphibians or reptiles, but Great Basin big sagebrush communities at lower elevations have a complement of reptiles similar to that described for semidesert shrublands.

Sagebrush ecosystems are home for many insects, including a large number of ant species, beetles, and grasshoppers. Many insect galls are found on sagebrush stems and leaves.

Human Use

Sagebrush ecosystems are used for little besides rangeland for cattle. In some parts of the state, sagebrush has been ripped from the soil and the area has been planted with crops or forage grasses. Sagebrush shrublands are important winter range for big game and should be protected when other suitable range is in short supply.

Western rattlesnake. *James C. Halfpenny.*

MONTANE SHRUBLANDS

Identifying Traits

Shrublands occur throughout the lower mountains of the region, often forming transitional belts between plains grasslands and coniferous forests along the eastern foothills or interposed between piñon pine–juniper woodlands and montane coniferous forests. These mountain shrublands are highly variable in composition and appearance but are characterized by dense-to-sparse deciduous shrubs. They often occupy dry, rocky sites, and are sometimes given the term *saxicoline*, meaning "rock inhabitants." The two most common dominant shrubs are Gambel oak and mountain mahogany, which may occur separately or intermixed.

Gambel oak forms dense thickets, often covering steep slopes. Dark green oak foliage may turn to brilliant red and orange in autumn. The leaves of Gambel oak are usually two to four inches long, with deep, rounded lobes. Acorns, the characteristic fruit of oaks, are small, less than an inch in diameter. Gambel oak usually grows six to ten feet tall, although it can grow much taller. In some parts of its range, it grows into a large, handsome tree, with a trunk several feet in diameter.

Mountain mahogany is a shorter shrub, rarely exceeding eight feet in height. It frequently occurs in sparse patches, particularly in very rocky soils, and the shrubs have a somewhat ragged appearance. Its oval leaves are a dull green, up to two inches long and toothed only on the upper margins, not near their base. Mountain mahogany seeds are distinctive. Each has a long,

Mexican woodrat.

curved, hairy "tail" that acts as a parachute, allowing the sharply pointed seed tip to reach the ground first. The "tail" slowly flexes with changes in humidity, drilling the seed into the soil. Thus the seeds are self-planting.

Location

Gambel oak is widespread on the Western Slope from an elevation of 5500 to 10,000 feet. However, oak communities appear to reach their maximum growth between 7000 and 8500 feet, where they form a transitional zone between piñon pine–juniper woodlands and ponderosa pine and Douglas fir forests, such as along US 550 north of Durango and along Colorado 82 east of Basalt.

Along the Eastern Slope, mountain mahogany and Gambel oak mix to form a narrow, discontinuous band between the lower edge of the ponderosa pine forest and the upper margin of the plains grasslands and piñon–juniper woodlands. They extend upward, interrupting ponderosa forest on warm, south-facing slopes and also covering the sides of mesas and hogbacks. Gambel oak is conspicuously absent from Eastern Slope shrub communities north of Morrison, Colorado. Nearly pure mountain mahogany stands can be seen near Lyons, Colorado, and around North and South Table Mountain near Golden, Colorado.

Mountain mahogany ecosystems are typical of semiarid sites, particularly ponderosa pine parklands, piñon–juniper woodlands, and dry mountain meadows. Along Colorado Highway 12, west of Trinidad, and elsewhere, they extend upward, interfingering with montane forests.

Site Characteristics

Mountain mahogany ecosystems are typical of soils that are well-drained, shallow, coarse-textured to rocky, and eroding. Bare rock may cover much of the ground surface. Runoff is high. Rocky outcrops and south-facing, fissured cliffs seldom lack members of the dry shrub complex. Here soils may be present only in rock crevices. Well-developed mountain mahogany ecosystems may be exposed to high winds, intense solar radiation, and moisture and temperature extremes. Rock crevices provide moist, protected sites for animals and plants.

Gambel oak requires a slightly warmer climate than mountain mahogany. Soils are deeper and moister, and the ground, which is well shaded by the dense foliage, is often covered by a thick layer of litter.

Plant Characteristics

Many other shrub species mix with Gambel oak and mountain mahogany, and some of these may form nearly pure stands. Skunkbrush and serviceberry are two of the most common associates. Bitterbrush, wild rose, and members of the currant family are also common. Wavy-leaf oak, smaller than Gambel oak, grows along the bases of mesas in southeastern Colorado. Numerous

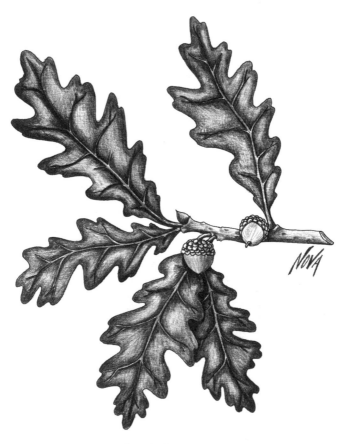

Gambel oak.

grasses and broad-leaved herbs including needle-and-thread, blue grama, western wheatgrass, side-oats grama, mountain muhly, goldenrod, blanket flower and Colorado locoweed are present in oak and mountain mahogany ecosystems.

Stands of Gambel oak at lower elevations in Colorado are probably climax communities where soil conditions are optimal. In Utah, the estimated age of some Gambel oak stands approaches 4000 years. Oak and other shrubs are important invaders following fire or other disturbances. In burned ponderosa pine stands, successional oak may remain for decades, the dense cover providing poor conditions for the reestablishment of ponderosa seedlings. At higher elevations oak provides protected microsites for shade-tolerant conifers and is eventually replaced by them.

North of Denver where oak is absent from the brushlands, mountain mahogany mixes with skunkbrush, bitterbrush, ninebark, buckbrush, rabbitbrush, and hawthorn. In gullies wild plum forms dense thickets. A combination of plains grassland and mountain species comprise the herbaceous understory, but these are sparse except on patches of well-developed soils. Mountain mahogany ecosystems are probably climaxes on very rocky, dry, coarse soils, although little is known about their successional patterns.

Animal Characteristics

Shrubs rapidly recycle nutrients into fruits, seeds, and juicy leaves, providing animals with an abundance of food. When on a rock substratum, shrub ecosystems provide protected nest and den sites. The fauna of oak and mountain mahogany ecosystems is rich and distinctive. Rufous-sided towhees sing from shrubs where they are nesting; in the higher mountains they are replaced by green-tailed towhees. Noisy bands of scrub jays are common in oak, and indigo and lazuli buntings and Virginia's warblers also nest in the dense foliage.

Chipmunk and golden-mantled ground squirrel holes abound, as do rabbit "forms"—protected depressions where rabbits rest. The ubiquitous deer mouse is thought to be more abundant in mountain mahogany shrub ecosystems, where it nests in rock crevices, than in any other regional ecosystem. Merriam's and dwarf shrews, Townsend's big-eared bats, yellow-bellied marmots, brush mice, bobcats, and occasional mountain lions all may be present.

Eastern Slope shrublands on rocky sites below eight thousand feet have more mammal species than any of our other mountainous areas. Here on south-facing sites that provide the necessary warmth, food, and shelter, a number of species extends northward along a narrow band, reaching the limits of their distribution in Boulder and Larimer counties. These include the Mexican woodrat, Colorado chipmunk, rock squirrel, rock mouse, and gray fox. The western small-footed myotis (a bat) and spotted skunk are also found on these sites but do not reach their northern limits here.

Areas that are used intensively by small mammals are marked by growth of the bright orange lichen, *Caloplaca*. It thrives where nitrogen compounds are concentrated, such as sites near dens where mammals urinate.

Oak and mountain mahogany stands provide excellent winter habitat for mule deer. The oak provides good cover, and moun-

Mountain mahogany. *J.C. Emerick.*

tain mahogany and bitterbrush are excellent forage plants. These latter shrubs are often severely damaged when herds are large and grazing intensity is high.

Human Use

Montane shrub ecosystems have been used for cattle grazing, and the oak has been cut for posts and firewood. Because soils beneath oak are rich in humus, some of these communities have been cleared for crop production. Dry mountain mahogany stands are not conducive to any particular human use.

Plants and Animals of Shrubland Ecosystems

Shrub ecosystems are variable in species composition, and plant and animal associations often include species from neighboring forest, meadow, or grassland communities. The following species occur in semidesert shrublands (D), sagebrush shrublands (S), or mountain shrublands (M). Some species are found only on the Eastern Slope (E) or Western Slope (W). Listed birds are mainly summer residents.

PLANTS

Shrubs
big sagebrush, Great Basin (D,S)
Seriphidium tridentatum
mountain (S) *Seriphidium vaseyanum*
bitterbrush (S,M) *Purshia tridentata*
blackbrush (D) *Coleogyne ramosissima*
buckbrush (M) *Ceanothus fendleri*
chokecherry (M) *Padus virginiana*
cliffrose (M) (W) *Purshia stansburiana*
greasewood (D) *Sarcobatus vermiculatus*
hawthorn (M) *Crataegus* spp.
mahogany, mountain (M)
Cercocarpus montanus
Mormon tea (D) *Ephedra* spp.
ninebark (M) *Physocarpus monogynus*

oak, **Gambel** (M) *Quercus gambelii*
gray (wavy-leaf) (M) *Quercus grisea*
plum, wild (M) *Prunus americana*
rabbitbrush (D,S,M)
Chrysothamnus spp.
rose, Wood's (S,M) *Rosa woodsii*
saltbush, four-winged (D) *Atriplex canescens*
serviceberry (S,M) *Amelanchier* spp.
shadscale (D) *Atriplex confertifolia*
skunkbrush (M) *Rhus aromatica*
snakeweed (D) *Gutierrezia* spp.
snowberry (S,M) *Symphoricarpos* spp.
spray, mountain (M) *Holodiscus dumosus*
winterfat (D,S,M) *Krascheninnikovia lanata*

Grasses

barley, foxtail (D,S,M)   *Critesion jubatum*

cheatgrass (S,M)   *Anisantha tectorum*

fescue, Arizona (S,M)   *Festuca arizonica*

Idaho (S,M)   *Festuca idahoensis*

galletagrass (D)   *Hilaria jamesii*

grama, **blue** (D,S,M)   *Chondrosum gracile*

side-oats (M)   *Bouteloua curtipendula*

Junegrass (S,M)   *Koeleria macrantha*

muhly, mountain (M)   *Muhlenbergia montana*

muttongrass (S,M)   *Poa fendleriana*

needle-and-thread (M)   *Stipa comata*

ricegrass, Indian (D,S,M)   *Stipa hymenoides*

sacaton, alkali (D)   *Sporobolus airoides*

salt grass (D)   *Distichlis stricta*

scratchgrass (D)   *Muhlenbergia asperifolia*

wheatgrass, slender (D,S,M)   *Elymus trachycaulus*

western (M)   *Pascopyrum smithii*

Forbs

aster golden (M)   *Heterotheca villosa*

balsamroot, arrowleaf (S,M) (W)   *Balsamorhiza sagittata*

blanket flower (S,M)   *Gaillardia aristata*

eriogonum, bushy (D)   *Eriogonum effusum*

nodding (D,S)   *Eriogonum cernuum*

gilia, scarlet (S,M)   *Ipomopsis aggregata*

goldenrod (S,M)   *Solidago* spp.

kochia (D,S,M)   *Kochia sieversiana*

lily, Mariposa (S,M)   *Calochortus gunnisonii*

locoweed, Colorado (S,M)   *Oxytropis lambertii*

Rocky Mountain (S,M)   *Oxytropis sericea*

lupine, common (S,M)   *Lupinus argenteus*

mallow, copper (D,S,M)   *Sphaeralcea coccinea*

marsh elder (D)   *Iva axillaris*

milkvetch (D)   *Astragalus* spp.

mule-ears (S,M)(W)   *Wyethia amplexicaulis*

paintbrush, Indian (S,M)   *Castilleja* spp.

prince's plume (D)   *Stanleya pinnata*

whiteweed (D)   *Cardaria* spp.

ANIMALS

Reptiles

bullsnake (M) (E)   *Pituophis melanoleucus sayi*

lizard, **eastern fence** (D,S,M)   *Sceloporus undulatus*

northern side-blotched (D,S,M) (W)   *Uta stansburiana*

northern tree (D,S,M) (W)   *Urosaurus ornatus*

sagebrush (D,S) (W)   *Sceloporus graciosus*

short-horned (D,S,M)   *Phrynosoma douglassii*

western whiptail (D,S) (W)   *Cnemidophorus tigris*

rattlesnake, western (D,S,M)   *Crotalus viridis*

snake, Great Basin gopher (D,S,M) (W)   *Pituophis melanoleucus deserticola*

whipsnake, striped (D) (W)   *Masticophis taeniatus*

Birds

bunting, indigo (M) *Passerina cyanea*
- lazuli (M) *Passerina amoena*

flycatcher, dusky (S) *Empidonax wrightii*

grosbeak, black-headed (M) *Pheucticus melanocephalus*

gnatcatcher, blue-gray (M) *Polioptila caerulea*

- **grouse, sage** (S) *Centrocercus urophasianus*

harrier, northern (D) *Circus cyaneus*

hawk, Swainson's (D) *Buteo swainsoni*

- **jay, scrub** (M) *Aphelocoma coerulescens*

quail, Gambel's (D,S) (W) *Callipepla gambelii*
- **scaled** (S) *Callipepla squamata*

roadrunner, greater (S) *Geococcyx californianus*

sparrow, black-throated (D) (W) *Amphispiza bilineata*
    Brewer's (S) *Spizella breweri*
- **sage** (S) (W) *Amphispiza belli*

- **thrasher, sage** (S) (W) *Oreoscoptes montanus*

towhee, canyon (D,S) *Pipilo fuscus*
- **green-tailed** (S,M) *Pipilo chlorurus*
- **rufous-sided** (S,M) *Pipilo erythrophthalmus*

- **warbler, Virginia's** (M) *Vermivora virginiae*

Mammals

badger (D,S,M) *Taxidea taxus*

bat, western small-footed myotis (M) *Myotis ciliolabrum*
    Townsend's big-eared (M) *Plecotus townsendii*

bobcat (D,S,M) *Felis rufus*

chipmunk, Colorado (M) *Tamias quadrivittatus*
    least (D,S,M) *Tamias minimus*

cottontail, desert (D,S,M) *Sylvilagus audubonii*
    Nuttall's (S,M) *Sylvilagus nuttallii*

coyote (D,S,M) *Canis latrans*

deer, mule (D,S,M) *Odocoileus hemionus*

fox, gray (D,M) *Urocyon cinereoargenteus*

ground squirrel, golden-mantled (S,M) *Spermophilus lateralis*

jackrabbit, black-tailed (D,M) *Lepus californicus*
    white-tailed (S,M) *Lepus townsendii*

kangaroo rat, Ord's (D,S) *Dipodomys ordii*

lion, mountain (D,S,M) *Felis concolor*

marmot, yellow-bellied (M) *Marmota flaviventris*

mouse, brush (M) *Peromyscus boylii*
    deer (D,S,M) *Peromyscus maniculatus*
    northern grasshopper (D,S) *Onchomys leucogaster*
    rock (M) (E) *Peromyscus difficilis*

prairie dog, Gunnison's (D,M) *Cynomys gunnisoni*
    white-tailed (D,S) *Cynomys leucurus*

pronghorn (D,S) *Antilocapra americana*

shrew, dwarf (M) *Sorex nanus*
    Merriam's (S,M) *Sorex merriami*

skunk, striped (D,S,M) *Mephitis mephitis*
    western spotted (D,M) *Spilogale gracilis*

squirrel, rock (M) *Spermophilus variegatus*
    white-tailed antelope (D,M) *Ammospermophilus leucurus*

vole, long-tailed (S) *Microtus longicaudus*

woodrat, Mexican (M) *Neotoma mexicana*

- Breeds almost exclusively in the designated shrubland. Species in bold-faced type are more abundant.

·7·

Piñon Pine–Juniper Woodlands

Identifying Traits

Dry, sprawling woodlands of mixed piñon pine and juniper grow throughout the Southwest along mountain flanks, along escarpments, and on low mesas and plateaus. These small, shrubby conifers form a transition between arid shrublands and grasslands of lower elevations and mountain forests above. Because of the short stature of piñon pine and juniper, many people refer to the woodlands as "pygmy forests" which, at their lower margins, appear as widely spaced, scattered trees. With increasing elevation, the hillsides and mesa tops become wooly and dark green as the woodlands become dense. Still higher, near their upper limits, the piñons and junipers mingle with tall ponderosa pine and Douglas fir, or with Gambel oak. Piñon-juniper woodlands are typically hot and dry during the summer (although not as dry as the shrublands or grasslands below) with much of the ground under the trees bare and rocky or with a sparse covering of shrubs and grasses.

Piñon–juniper woodlands near Rifle, Colorado. *J.C. Emerick.*

Piñon pine.

The dominant species in Colorado and New Mexico is Colorado piñon, a pine with one- to two-inch-long needles grouped two (and occasionally three) to a bundle. Cones rarely exceed two inches in length, but these small cones bear large, edible nuts that are gathered in huge quantities by both people and wildlife in the fall. Piñon is the Spanish word for "nut," or "nut-tree." Piñon pines can achieve a height of almost fifty feet, but only on the most favorable sites; usually they are less than thirty feet high, with height diminishing as the site becomes drier. When they exist in near-desert conditions, piñon pines grow slowly and use water sparingly, forming low, rounded crowns with misshapen trunks.

Piñon pines are commonly associated with one-seed juniper and Utah juniper. Utah juniper is restricted to the Western Slope, but one-seed juniper grows in southern Colorado on both sides of the Continental Divide. Piñon pine less commonly mixes with Rocky Mountain juniper (western red cedar) near the upper elevational limit of piñon pine distribution. Juniper can grow at lower elevations than piñon pine and thus may form pure stands at the lower margins of the woodlands. Junipers can be recognized by their minute, scalelike leaves that overlap one another like shingles. They have small blue or reddish-blue berries that technically are cones, and thus junipers, usually classified as members of the cypress family, are closely related to the pines.

Location

Extensive stands of piñon-juniper woodlands are found throughout western and southern Colorado, Utah, northern Arizona, and New Mexico at elevations from four to nine thousand feet, with their best development at about five to seven thousand feet in elevation. In western Colorado, these woodlands may be seen in Mesa Verde National Park, Colorado National Monument and Dinosaur National Monument. On the Eastern Slope of the Rockies, piñon–juniper woodlands grow from Colorado Springs southward along the foothills. The woodlands occur up the Arkansas River valley to about the same latitude as Colorado Springs and are found along the lower forest boundary on the

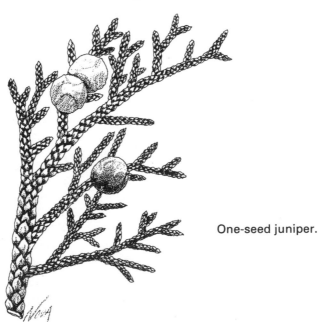

One-seed juniper.

slopes surrounding San Luis Valley. Good stands can be seen along Colorado Highway 115 southwest of Colorado Springs and south of Walsenburg along Interstate 25.

Piñon-juniper woodlands extend eastward from Walsenburg in scattered locations on the plains. As the forests reach the canyons of the Purgatoire and smaller streams to the east, piñon pine is replaced by woodlands of one-seed juniper. These can be seen along Colorado Highway 109 about sixteen miles north of Kim.

An isolated stand of piñon–juniper woodland grows at Owl Canyon, north of Fort Collins. Owl Canyon contains the most northern piñon pine grove along the Eastern Slope, well over a hundred miles from the nearest piñon stand to the south (although groves do occur farther north on the Western Slope). The oldest trees in Owl Canyon are over four hundred years old. Some call this a relict stand from an earlier climate; others think that it is the result of seeds dropped by Indians or birds.

Site Characteristics

Piñon–juniper ecosystems occupy warm, dry sites with mean annual temperatures between 45° and 55°F and annual precipitation between ten and twenty inches. The frost-free season is over eighty days per year and usually much longer. When at higher elevations, stands are always on warmer west- or south-facing slopes.

Piñon–juniper woodlands cover a variety of soils derived from sandstone, limestone, basalt, granite, or other materials. Textures vary from stony, coarse soils to clay, with the optimum being coarse sand and gravels. Soils are usually high in calcium and are alkaline, although the trees grow well in acidic soils. In general, soils of piñon-juniper woodlands are shallow and low in fertility.

Plant Characteristics

Temperature and precipitation determine the relative numbers of piñon pine and juniper in each woodland. Piñon pine is more tolerant of the cold temperatures of higher elevation woodlands, while juniper is more drought-tolerant than piñon pine. Thus juniper dominates low elevation piñon-juniper woodlands but gives way to piñon as elevation increases. In southern Colorado above 7600 feet, Rocky Mountain juniper replaces one-seed juniper. Woodlands of piñon pine and Rocky Mountain juniper can be seen in the Great Sand Dunes National Monument.

Many species of shrubs are found under the conifers, although the precise combination of shrubs depends on site characteristics and the woodland's history of disturbance. Sagebrush frequently intergrades with piñon-juniper in complex patterns. Four-winged saltbush, greasewood, and shadscale occur in low elevation stands where soils are alkaline; at higher elevations scrub oak becomes common. Mountain mahogany is well-suited to the dry climate and thin, rocky soils of piñon–juniper stands and along with bitterbrush is common, provided grazing by deer and elk is not too intensive. Serviceberry, snowberry, rabbitbrush, wild rose, skunkbrush, Apache plume, Mormon tea, currant, and winterfat contribute to a broad array of variations in piñon–juniper woodland.

Herbaceous groundcover is usually sparse, particularly where cattle grazing has been extensive. Grasses include blue grama, Indian ricegrass, galletagrass, Junegrass, muttongrass, and needle-and-thread. Broadleaved herbaceous species are rare but when present are frequently members of the sunflower family and include gumweed, golden aster, and fleabane.

Piñon–juniper woodlands in Colorado National Monument. *J.C. Emerick.*

On optimal sites within their range, woodlands of piñon and juniper become climax ecosystems. Succession to this self-perpetuating state requires three hundred years or longer after a major disturbance such as fire. These ecosystems burn well, especially when understory vegetation is abundant. Burned sites are invaded by annuals, such as Russian thistle, tansy mustard, sunflower, and cheatgrass, which are replaced during the next twenty years by blue grama, Indian ricegrass, and other perennial grasses. Invasion by shrubs follows, and they become a thicket in forty to a hundred years. Juniper trees also become established during this time, followed by piñon pines. Eventually the trees overshadow and suppress the shrubs, and an open woodland—with an understory of sparse shrubs, some grasses, and a few wildflowers—is restored.

Grasslands surrounding piñon–juniper woodlands may be invaded by junipers through pressures of grazing. Overgrazing removes taller grass species, and the ensuing reduced competition and fire hazard allow establishment of junipers. Juniper berries are eaten by birds, coyotes, deer, and domestic livestock, which then disseminate the juniper seeds in their droppings. Once established, trees usually take over as dominants. Coarse-textured soils in particular favor the establishment of trees.

Overgrazing of existing woodlands may have long-lasting effects. Where intensive grazing by domestic or wild animals is allowed, palatable grasses and shrubs may be decimated. Bare soil is increased, and the woodland is invaded by annual species. A dense tree canopy may prevent any appreciable recovery of the understory. If the woodlands are open, and light and moisture are abundant, perennial grasses and shrubs return in about ten to twenty years if protected from grazing.

In many areas of Colorado, mostly on federally owned land, extensive tracts of piñon–juniper woodlands have been removed by bulldozing or by chaining, a practice in which a large chain pulled between two heavy tractors or bulldozers rips up a wide swath of timber. This method, used as a management tool to increase range grasses for cattle and wildlife, has resulted in reversion of woodlands to an early grass-shrub successional stage in some places. Elsewhere this practice has not achieved substantially greater forage. In most cases the cost effectiveness of the operation is dubious, and the wildlife value of the trees has been ignored.

Animal Characteristics

Many wildlife species thrive in piñon–juniper ecosystems, and a few are year-round residents. Mule deer, the dominant large herbivores, depend on piñon–juniper woodlands for cover, shelter, and forage during severe winters. Elk use the habitat to a lesser degree for winter and spring range. Both species find juniper moderately palatable, although deer prefer shrub species such as mountain mahogany, and their use of a particular woodland area is usually determined by the availability of palatable shrubs. Pronghorn inhabit piñon–juniper woodlands to some extent, usually occupying the more open fringe areas where woodlands grade into grasslands or shrublands. Predators such as mountain lion, bobcat, and ringtail roam piñon–juniper woodlands if nearby rocky areas and cliffs provide den sites. Coyotes, badgers, and long-tailed weasels inhabit areas where sufficient small mammals are available as prey.

Shrubs provide cover for desert cottontails and black-tailed jackrabbits. Jackrabbits often concentrate in the woodlands during periods of heavy snow.

Many small rodents occupy piñon–juniper woodlands, particularly where brushy areas provide cover and food. Woodrats are common, and four of Colorado's six species inhabit piñon–juniper forests. The desert woodrat is found only in the extreme western portion of the state, but elsewhere white-throated, Mexican, and bushy-tailed woodrats are found, and in some areas the three occur together. When this happens, the denning sites of the three species are segregated, thus reducing competition. The white-throated woodrat dens at the bases of shrubs and cacti and commonly uses the spiny cholla joints for nesting materials. The Mexican and bushy-tailed woodrats prefer rocky areas, while the Mexican woodrat occupies horizontal rock shelters at intermediate elevations and the bushy-tailed woodrat dens in vertical fissures and caves at higher elevations. The bushy-tailed woodrat is well known as the "pack rat" or "trade rat" who carries off spoons and other human artifacts to its nest, much to the annoyance of the original owner.

Piñon–juniper woodlands are also the home of the piñon mouse, which is most common in this ecosystem. These arboreal mice usually den in hollow juniper branches. Juniper berries make up much of their diet during the winter, but in summer

Piñon jay.

piñon mice and their cousins, deer mice, eat other types of berries and large numbers of seeds and insects. Other rodent residents include the rock squirrel and Colorado chipmunk.

A variety of birds lives and nests in piñon–juniper woodlands, some of them attracted by the many fruit-bearing shrubs, the nutritious juniper berries, and pine nuts. The gregarious piñon jay is a permanent resident and often travels about in large, noisy flocks. Plain titmice and common bushtits nest almost exclusively in piñon–juniper stands. Other nesting species include the blue-gray gnatcatcher, ash-throated flycatcher, Bewick's wren, black-throated gray warbler, black-billed magpie, common raven, mountain chickadee, and chipping sparrow, many of which nest in shrubs or rocks rather than in trees. Typical ground nesters include the lark sparrow and mourning dove, which may also nest in trees. Many raptors such as prairie falcons, kestrels, red-tailed hawks, golden eagles, and great horned and screech owls nest or hunt in the woodlands.

Warm temperatures and abundant rocks, crevices, and other hiding places make piñon–juniper woodlands an ideal habitat for many reptiles, especially lizards. The collared lizard, eastern fence lizard, tree lizard, side-blotched lizard, plateau striped whiptail, striped whipsnake, Great Basin gopher snake, and western rattlesnake are among the most common species.

During the fall many animals avidly consume ripe pine nuts. Abert's squirrels occasionally descend from ponderosa pine forests. Piñon mice and woodrats as well as rock squirrels, chipmunks, and even black bears enjoy the feast. Piñon jays depend on the nuts and flock wherever the crop is good, and Clark's nutcrackers migrate from higher coniferous forests to harvest nuts in large quantities. Scientists believe that these birds play a critical role in establishment of new piñon pines. Jays and nutcrackers hide large numbers of seeds in the ground, far more than they recover, and many of the seeds germinate to produce new trees.

Human Use

Piñon–juniper ecosystems have a long history of human use. Southwestern Indians depended on piñon nut harvests for centuries, and often a successful harvest was a matter of life and death. Tribes would travel long distances to find groves that were producing nuts, for piñons yield large quantities of seed only once every three to seven years. Indians used piñon and juniper as firewood and for constructing many items. Piñon pitch was used for glue, waterproofing, cooking, and for many medicinal purposes.

Early settlers also made use of piñons and junipers to build houses and stockades, for firewood, and for furniture. They too annually harvested piñon nuts. Cattle have been grazed in piñon–juniper woodlands since well before the turn of the century. While these woodland areas can offer excellent long-term grazing, livestock must be managed properly to prevent damage from overgrazing. Many woodlands overgrazed half a century ago still have not recovered.

Many piñon–juniper forests can be managed to provide grass, trees, and shrubs, and thus supply a number of benefits for humans and wildlife alike. Past management techniques have not been directed at improving the quality of all three of these woodland plant components. Redirection toward this goal would allow a more stable, long-term, productive use of these woodlands.

Plants and Animals of Piñon Pine–Juniper Woodlands

Species composition depends on local site characteristics and history of disturbance, and may vary considerably from one place to another. (E) denotes species found only on the Eastern Slope and (W) denotes species found only on the Western Slope. Listed birds are mainly summer residents.

PLANTS

Trees

juniper, one-seed *Sabina monosperma*
   Rocky Mountain *Sabina scopulorum*
   Utah (W) *Sabina osteosperma*
pine, Colorado piñon *Pinus edulis*

Shrubs

Apache plume *Fallugia paradoxa*
bitterbrush *Purshia tridentata*
cactus, candelabra *Cylindropuntia imbricata*
mahogany, mountain *Cercocarpus montanus*
Mormon tea *Ephedra* spp.
oak, Gambel *Quercus gambelii*
rabbitbrush *Chrysothamnus* spp.
sagebrush, big *Seriphidium tridentatum*
saltbush, four-winged *Atriplex canescens*
serviceberry *Amelanchier alnifolia*
shadscale *Atriplex confertifolia*
skunkbrush *Rhus aromatica*
snowberry *Symphoricarpos rotundifolius*

Herbaceous Plants

aster, golden *Heterotheca villosa*
cheatgrass *Anisantha tectorum*
dropseed, sand *Sporobolus cryptandrus*
feathergrass, New Mexican *Stipa neomexicana*
four o'clock *Mirabilis multiflora*
galletagrass *Hilaria jamesii*
grama, blue *Chondrosum gracile*
   side-oats *Bouteloua curtipendula*
gumweed *Grindelia squarrosa*
Junegrass *Koeleria macrantha*
mallow, copper *Sphaeralcea coccinea*
mustard, tansy *Descurainia pinnata*
muttongrass *Poa fendleriana*
needle-and-thread *Stipa comata*
prickly pear *Opuntia* spp.
ricegrass, Indian *Stipa hymenoides*
Russian thistle *Salsola australis*
squirreltail *Elymus elymoides*
sunflower, prairie *Helianthus petiolaris*
three-awn, red *Aristida purpurea*
zinnia, wild *Zinnia grandiflora*

ANIMALS

Reptiles and Amphibians

bullsnake (E) *Pituophis melanoleucus sayi*
lizard, **collared** *Crotaphytus collaris*
   eastern fence *Sceloporus undulatus*
   northern side-blotched (W) *Uta stansburiana*
   northern tree (W) *Urosaurus ornatus*
    plateau striped whiptail (W) *Cnemidophorus velox*

   sagebrush (W) *Sceloporus graciosus*
   short-horned *Phrynosoma douglassii*
   western whiptail (W) *Cnemidophorus tigris*
rattlesnake, western *Crotalus viridis*
snake, Great Basin gopher (W) *Pituophis melanoleucus deserticola*
whipsnake, striped (W) *Masticophis taeniatus*

Birds

bluebird, mountain   *Sialia currucoides*
bushtit   *Psaltriparus minimus*
chickadee, mountain   *Parus gambeli*
dove, mourning   *Zenaida macroura*
eagle, golden   *Aquila chrysaetos*
falcon, prairie   *Falco mexicanus*
flycatcher, ash-throated   *Myiarchus cinerascens*
  ● gray   *Empidonax wrightii*
gnatcatcher, blue-gray   *Polioptila caerulea*
hawk, red-tailed   *Buteo jamaicensis*
● **jay, piñon**   *Gymnorhinus cyanocephalus*
    scrub   *Aphelocoma coerulescens*
    Steller's   *Cyanocitta stelleri*
kestrel, American   *Falco sparverius*
magpie,   black-billed   *Pica pica*
nighthawk, common   *Chordeiles minor*
owl, great horned   *Bubo virginianus*
    northern saw-whet   *Aegolius acadicus*
poorwill, common   *Phalaenoptilus nuttallii*
sparrow, chipping   *Spizella passerina*
    lark   *Chondestes grammacus*
● **titmouse, plain**   *Parus inornatus*
towhee, canyon   *Pipilo fuscus*
turkey, wild   *Meleagris gallopavo*
vireo, gray   *Vireo vicinior*
    solitary   *Vireo solitarius*
● warbler, black-throated gray   *Dendroica nigrescens*
woodpecker, downy   *Picoides pubescens*
wren, Bewick's   *Thryomanes bewickii*

Mammals

badger   *Taxidea taxus*
bat, long-legged myotis   *Myotis volans*
    pallid   *Antrozous pallidus*
bobcat   *Felis rufus*
chipmunk, **Colorado** (E)   *Tamias quadrivittatus*
    Hopi (W)   *Tamias rufus*
    least   *Tamias minimus*
cottontail, desert   *Sylvilagus audubonii*
    Nuttall's   *Sylvilagus nuttallii*
coyote   *Canis latrans*
deer, mule   *Odocoileus hemionus*
elk   *Cervus elaphus*
fox, **gray**   *Urocyon cinereoargenteus*
    kit (W)   *Vulpes macrotis*
ground squirrel, golden-mantled   *Spermophilus lateralis*
jackrabbit, **black-tailed**   *Lepus californicus*
    white-tailed   *Lepus townsendii*
lion, mountain   *Felis concolor*
mouse, **canyon** (W)   *Peromyscus crinitus*
    deer   *Peromyscus maniculatus*
    ● **piñon**   *Peromyscus truei*
    rock (E)   *Peromyscus difficilis*
porcupine   *Erethizon dorsatum*
ringtail   *Bassariscus astutus*
shrew, Merriam's   *Sorex merriami*
skunk, striped   *Mephitis mephitis*
    western spotted   *Spilogale gracilis*
squirrel, rock   *Spermophilus variegatus*
weasel, long-tailed   *Mustela frenata*
woodrat, **bushy-tailed**   *Neotoma cinerea*
    desert (W)   *Neotoma lepida*
    Mexican   *Neotoma mexicana*
    white-throated   *Neotoma albigula*

● Breeds almost exclusively in piñon-juniper woodlands.
Species in bold-faced type are more abundant.

·8·

Ponderosa Pine Forests

Identifying Traits

No other native conifer in the region has needles as long as those of the ponderosa pine. The four- to seven-inch-long needles grow in bunches of two or three; longer needles are usually produced by less-crowded trees, or by trees growing on moister sites. Older ponderosa pines have thick cinnamon-red bark that forms large vertical flakes and has a vanilla or butterscotch scent. The husky cones, three to five inches long, bear short spines on each scale.

Forests of ponderosa pine occupy sunny, dry mountain slopes of low and intermediate elevations. Ponderosa grow to be 150 feet tall or more with trunks three to four feet in diameter. This is the largest conifer species in the Southern Rocky Mountains. Mature stands of these giants are more open than other mountain forests, often forming savanna-like parklands. The massive, broadly rounded crowns of intermediate-aged trees and the flat-topped crowns of very old ponderosa stand out at a distance. Where trees are not too crowded, the understory consists of numerous grasses, shrubs and wildflowers. As forest density increases the understory becomes sparse.

W. Perry Conway.

Location

Ponderosa pine ecosystems are found throughout lower elevations from 5600 to 9000 feet in the Southern Rocky Mountains. Extensive ponderosa stands are most numerous along the Eastern Slope foothills and in southern Colorado, as well as in northern New Mexico. Ponderosa pine forests are replaced by piñon pine–juniper woodlands at low elevations south of Colorado Springs and on the Western Slope. Good examples of large mature stands can be seen along Interstate 70 in the foothills west of Denver and along U.S. 160 between Pagosa Springs and Durango. Large stands of ponderosa are rare in northwestern Colorado, although scattered individuals mix with other forest types.

Site Characteristics

Ponderosa pine ecosystems are relatively dry, warm forests. Piñon pine–juniper woodlands are the only forests that are drier and warmer. Annual precipitation is low (twenty-five inches or less). On the Eastern Slope, most precipitation falls in spring in the form of snow, although summer thunderstorms also provide significant moisture. Snow depth usually does not exceed one foot, and snow often melts within a few days following a storm. Summers are long and hot with a frost-free season of over four months. The soil is usually coarse, shallow, and rocky with a low moisture content.

Plant Characteristics

Characteristics of mature ponderosa forests depend on elevation, exposure, and soil traits. In the foothills climax ecosystems are open parklands with abundant grasses and a few wax currant bushes. On drier, south-facing slopes, ponderosa are more widely separated than trees on slopes with other exposures. In addition, the sparser understory is composed of species that need less moisture such as blue grama and Rocky Mountain juniper. At elevations above 8000 feet, climax ponderosa ecosystems exist only where soils are unusually dry. Such sites include those with well-drained, fine-textured soils at the base of south-

Ponderosa pine.

facing slopes, those with unusually coarse soils, and those on very warm slopes. Here climax stands are denser than in the foothills; they also contain Douglas fir.

Ecosystems may be of any size, from small clumps in meadows to forests covering entire hillsides. Patches of meadow and dry shrub ecosystems interfinger with ponderosa forests, especially on southern exposures in the foothills. Successional tree species (quaking aspen, lodgepole pine) are interspersed in montane forests. At the base of the foothills, ponderosa extend onto mesas and crown the rocky tops of hogbacks, where they often mix with Rocky Mountain juniper.

Ponderosa pine ecosystems throughout much of the region are denser now than they were 50 to 150 years ago. The change in density is largely a result of human actions: logging, the suppression of fire, and cessation of intensive livestock grazing. These measures, in addition to a wet climatic cycle in the first third of the century, resulted in the successful establishment of an abundance of ponderosa seedlings that matured to form today's dense forests. Under completely natural conditions, the young stands of

Colorado chipmunk. *Stephen Jones.*

ponderosa would have been thinned by ground fire. They would have matured to form open parklands, such as those inside the eastern boundary of Rocky Mountain National Park. Wide spacing is beneficial to ponderosa trees since they require abundant sunshine and must compete among each other, as well as with surrounding herbs, for limited moisture.

The ponderosa pine withstands drought well. Trees collect any available water through a deep taproot (to depths of six feet in porous soils; thirty-five to forty feet in fissured rocks) with long lateral roots (up to 100 feet long in open stands). High temperatures and direct sunlight are required for vigorous tree growth; the low temperatures of high altitudes inhibit growth processes. Seeds germinate well in bare, sunny, hot soils, although some shade is beneficial for maintaining soil moisture.

The amount of herbaceous understory ranges from almost none under dense trees to abundant in parklands. Lack of sun and thick litter in dense stands discourage herb growth. The amount of understory also increases as moisture increases. Parklands have a groundcover of bunchgrass with herb composition similar to that of natural dry meadow ecosystems. Blue grama and yellowish green clumps of sun sedge are both abundant. Common wild geranium, whiskbroom parsley, sulphur flower, miner's candle, pasque flower, and a number of composites are just a few of the common associates. Herbs rarely cover the ground completely, but cover is lush when compared to that of all other coniferous stands.

Shrub and tree associates are numerous. Ponderosa pine and Douglas fir often form mixed stands, with the relative abundance of pine greater on drier sites. Rocky Mountain juniper commonly intermixes with ponderosa pine, especially at lower elevations, and may dominate or form pure stands on sites that are exceptionally dry or rocky. The juniper can be recognized by its well-manicured, often silvery green appearance. Wax currant shrubs seem to be ever present with ponderosa, and kinnikinnik, bitterbrush, and common juniper are also frequent. Species of dry shrub ecosystems such as mountain mahogany mix with ponderosa on rocky soils and outcrops. South of Denver associations of ponderosa and Gambel oak are common at lower elevations, and in southern Colorado may be found even at higher elevations up to 10,000 feet on south-facing slopes. Scattered quaking aspen, lodgepole, and limber pine grow among montane ponderosa.

Lightning frequently starts ground fires which are a natural component of ponderosa ecosystems. While still young, ponderosa begin to develop a thick, corky bark that insulates older trees and protects them from all but severe fires. Ground fires kill seedlings and keep stands open, decreasing the probability of hot crown fires in later years that could kill mature trees. Fires also release nutrients tied up in litter, remove thick litter that suppresses herb growth, and prepare a good ponderosa seed bed. During the last several decades, people have suppressed fires, allowing forests to become more dense and susceptible to severe crown fires. When these occur all trees are killed, converting the forest to shrubland or meadow.

Ponderosa in dense stands unthinned by fire, such as those found throughout the region today, do not receive the nutrients, sun, or water necessary for vigorous growth. The weakened trees are more susceptible to diseases such as infestation by the mountain pine beetle. Beetle epidemics have occurred throughout recorded history and have been responsible for the loss of thousands of acres of ponderosa in the region. The beetles are always present in low numbers, increasing when there is an abundance of unhealthy trees. Weakened trees cannot resist invasion of the woodboring beetles by forcing them out with pitch. When mountain pine beetles are abundant, woodpeckers, nematode parasites, and other natural controls which usually keep beetle outbreaks in check are ineffective.

Mountain pine beetles lay eggs between the bark and nutrient-rich wood of the trees in late summer. The eggs hatch into white larvae that feed on the trees through the winter, developing into beetles and flying to attack new trees the following summer. The rice-sized, black bodies of the beetles carry a fungus that grows inside the trees, staining the wood blue and plugging the cells that transport the tree's nutrients. Trees die and turn brown the summer following infection.

A parasitic plant, dwarf mistletoe is another widespread killer of ponderosa pine. Yellow-orange twigs of these leafless flowering plants grow from pine branches. Its roots grow under the bark and collect nutrients from the pine. Mistletoe disrupts normal growth and branching patterns, and trees develop localized swellings and witches' brooms—highly branched twig clusters. Weakened trees are very susceptible to other types of infections. Trees die slowly, sometimes taking twenty years.

Ponderosa are injured less commonly by a wide variety of additional diseases and insects, including rusts, heart and root rots, other species of bark beetles, and cone insects. Damage from heavy, wet snow, wind, and lightning can be extensive.

Intensive, long-term grazing can form a meadow out of the forest. This occurs because cattle trample and damage seedlings and saplings, preventing the replacement of older dying ponderosa by young trees. Cessation of intensive grazing can result in the opposite extreme. Overgrazed herbs offer little competition to the large number of ponderosa seedlings that invade when cattle are removed. The seedlings survive and create a dense, unhealthy forest susceptible to disease. The forest may slowly return to a parkland or meadow ecosystem as older trees die and as herbs become reestablished, competing with ponderosa seedlings for moisture and nutrients.

Animal Characteristics

Few ponderosa pine or low elevation Douglas fir ecosystems are pure stands of either tree species. Likewise, much of the fauna of the two ecosystems is not unique to either type of ecosystem but is instead correlated with montane forests in general. The density and number of species of small mammals and breeding birds are intermediate between those of dense conifer ecosystems (spruce–fir and lodgepole pine) and those of deciduous mountain ecosystems (riparian, aspen, and shrubland areas). However, animal density varies among ponderosa pine and Douglas fir ecosystems, increasing as the systems become more open and as understory diversity and lushness increase. Population numbers of several species (pygmy nuthatches, red crossbills, and Abert's squirrels) also seem to show strong year-to-year fluctuations that possibly relate to food supply. Intermixing of other ecosystem types (aspen, shrubby areas, small meadows) increases the number of animal species of conifer ecosystems by increasing the variety of cover and food.

Birds are abundant throughout the year. Steller's jays, hairy woodpeckers, white-breasted and pygmy nuthatches, and common ravens are present year-round. Wild turkeys are locally common in the southern part of the state. Mountain chickadees, dark-eyed juncos, American robins, and pine siskins are usually present but may go to lower altitudes on the plains for the winter or when weather is stormy. Many of these birds feed on bark insects or conifer seeds, food sources that remain above snow. At least some bird species avoid competition for identical resources by foraging on different parts of the trees. For example, the pygmy nuthatch forages primarily among pine needles while the white-breasted nuthatch forages on pine trunks and large branches.

The summer avifauna is supplemented by a variety of birds such as the yellow-rumped warbler, western bluebird, tree and violet-green swallows, Williamson's sapsucker, Townsend's solitaire, solitary vireo, and broad-tailed hummingbird. Great horned owls, goshawks, and red-tailed hawks are common predators.

Large dead trees are important nest sites for cavity nesters (flickers, nuthatches, and downy woodpeckers). Other cavity nesters that do not build their own nest holes (such as swallows and mountain bluebirds) depend on existing cavities in these trees. Loose bark on conifers forms crevices used as nest sites by tiny brown creepers.

Some birds roost in ponderosa pine forests at night and migrate daily far out onto the plains. Flocks of American crows, black-billed magpies, and Steller's jays leave the mountain canyons at dawn and return to them at dusk, consistently following the same route day after day.

Several reptiles are found in ponderosa or Douglas fir forests. Typically only the eastern fence lizard and the milk snake are seen in northern Colorado. Several other species, including the many-lined skink, short-horned lizard, bullsnake, and western rattlesnake, occur in these forests in the southern part of the state.

The disturbed, patchy nature of today's forests results in a number of rich mammal habitats. Forests with small meadows abound in chipmunks, golden-mantled ground squirrels, Nuttall's cottontails, mule deer, and elk. Mule deer are concentrated in low elevation, south-facing, shrubby ponderosa stands in the winter. Shrub-covered rocky outcrops support a number of mammal species such as the bushy-tailed woodrat, rock squirrel, yellow-bellied marmot, rock mouse, and deer mouse. When species that roam through several ecosystem types, such as coyote and bobcat, are added to the list, the ponderosa pine–Douglas fir ecosystems have a relatively high diversity and abundance of mammals.

Mule deer.
J.C. Emerick.

The Abert's squirrel is characteristic of ponderosa pine forests. This tassel-eared squirrel commonly occurs in two color forms: gray with white underparts, and uniformly dark brown or black. *R.C. Farentinos.*

A few mammal species have strong affinities for continuous forests. Black bears are present but not common. Several bat species, including the hoary bat, Townsend's big-eared bat, and long-legged myotis, live in and forage over woodlands. The porcupine is most abundant in open ponderosa pine woodlands at moderate elevations. These solitary, quilled rodents are active throughout the year, eating herbs during the summer and preferring the inner bark of ponderosa pine in other seasons. The porcupine's eating habits may kill parts of trees or entire trees since cells that transport the tree's food and water are consumed.

Abert's squirrel, a large tree squirrel with tassels on its ears, is more strictly associated with one plant species than are most mammals of the region. The squirrels use ponderosa pine almost exclusively for food, nesting, and cover. Unlike most tree squirrels, Abert's squirrels do not cache food for the winter. Feeding habits change with the seasons, cones being the favorite summer food and the inner bark of twigs the favorite winter food. Favored feeding trees, recognized by piles of needle clusters, and clipped, peeled twigs at their base, are selected presumably because of high nutritive value or good taste. Tests have shown that squirrels choose trees that have smaller amounts of aromatic chemicals in their sap. Squirrel populations fluctuate and are greatest when food and cover are optimal: when forests contain an abundance of healthy, large trees; when the cone crop is large; and when twigs have a sufficient food reserve of high nutritional quality.

Abert's squirrels decrease the cone crop of ponderosa by as much as 20 percent, but their feeding habits also release seeds from cones. The squirrels' twig cutting can reduce tree growth and provide entrance points for infections. At least forty-four mammal species feed on conifer seeds. Mule deer and elk browse conifers, other mammals eat dwarf mistletoe from the branches, and birds disseminate mistletoe seeds. Tree clumps frequently grow from unrecovered cone caches of small rodents. Northern pocket gophers prune the roots of seedlings, and mice, rabbits, chipmunks, and ground squirrels eat their buds and girdle their stems.

Human Use

Few ponderosa pine ecosystems in the region remain unaltered by human activity. Heavy use of ecosystem resources began with the Gold Rush in 1859. People rushed into the forests, cutting most of the commercial ponderosa stands for fuel, mining timbers, and lumber. Logging and mining roads were built. People settled in mountain towns and homesteads, clearing the forests to increase pasturage and room for cultivation of small grains and potatoes. Settlement peaked before 1900, and the cultivated lands were soon abandoned. The cattle industry in the mountains expanded rapidly in the late 1800s, the open ponderosa forest being one of the most important grazing types in the region. The number of cattle grazed in national forests increased through World War I, and overgrazing was severe in the 1880s and during the War. It decreased after the 1930s.

Today ponderosa forests are used heavily for recreation, hunting, woodcutting, and as sites for mountain residences. Livestock grazing and timber production are still important, as is forest quality for forage production and habitat for big game animals. In some areas these forests are a major source of usable water. Because of these many uses, people are becoming more concerned with the condition of the forests. Management of these ecosystems is becoming more intense, and forestry practices on public lands are being reoriented to accommodate multiple-use demands. Selective tree cutting, controlled burning, and grazing restrictions, coupled with an awareness of ecosystem processes, are a few of the management practices being used today to improve forest quality and offset damage done to these ecosystems during past decades.

Plants and Animals of Ponderosa Pine Forests

Species composition depends on local site characteristics and history of disturbance and may vary considerably from one place to another. Ponderosa pine is frequently found growing in mixed forests with aspen, Douglas fir, piñon pine, and other tree species not listed here. Open, grassy ponderosa parklands support a greater variety of understory plant species as well as more diverse animal populations than dense ponderosa forests. Some species are restricted to the Eastern Slope (E) or Western Slope (W). Listed birds are mainly summer residents.

PLANTS

Trees
pine, ponderosa *Pinus ponderosa*
juniper, Rocky Mountain *Sabina scopulorum*

Shrubs
bitterbrush *Purshia tridentata*
buckbrush *Ceanothus fendleri*

currant, wax *Ribes cereum*
juniper, common *Juniperus communis*
kinnikinnik *Arctostaphylos uva-ursi*
mahogany, mountain *Cercocarpus montanus*
oak, gambel *Quercus gambelii*

Herbaceous plants

bladderpod, mountain   *Lesquerella montana*
blanket-flower   *Gaillardia aristata*
cactus, mountain ball   *Pediocactus simpsonii*
daisy, Easter   *Townsendia hookeri*
geranium, common wild   *Geranium caespitosum*
grama, blue   *Chondrosum gracile*
  side-oats   *Bouteloua curtipendula*
gumweed   *Grindelia subalpina*
Junegrass   *Koeleria macrantha*
larkspur, Nelson   *Delphinium nuttallianum*
lily, sand   *Leucocrinum montanum*
miner's candle   *Oreocarya virgata*
mistletoe, dwarf   *Arceuthobium vaginatum*

muhly, mountain   *Muhlenbergia montana*
needle-and-thread   *Stipa comata*
Oregon grape   *Mahonia repens*
parsley, whiskbroom   *Harbouria trachypleura*
pasque flower   *Pulsatilla patens*
penstemon, greenleaf   *Penstemon virens*
  one-sided   *Penstemon secundiflorus*
sedge, sun   *Carex heliophila*
spiderwort   *Tradescantia occidentalis*
spike fescue   *Leucopoa kingii*
sulphur flower   *Eriogonum umbellatum*
wallflower, western   *Erysimum capitatum*

ANIMALS

Reptiles and Amphibians

bullsnake (E)   *Pituophis melanoleucus sayi*
lizard, **eastern fence**   *Sceloporus undulatus*
  many-lined skink   *Eumeces multivirgatus*
  northern sagebush (W)   *Sceloporus graciosus*
  northern tree (W)   *Urosaurus ornatus*
  short-horned   *Phrynosoma douglassii*
rattlesnake, western   *Crotalus viridis*
snake, milk   *Lampropeltis triangulum*
toad, Woodhouse's   *Bufo woodhousii*

Birds

bluebird, mountain   *Sialia currucoides*
  • **western**   *Sialia mexicana*

chickadee, mountain   *Parus gambeli*
creeper, brown   *Certhia americana*
crossbill, red   *Loxia curvirostra*
crow, American   *Corvus brachyrhynchos*
dove, mourning   *Zenaida macroura*
eagle, golden   *Aquila chrysaetos*
finch, Cassin's   *Carpodacus cassinii*
flicker, northern   *Colaptes auratus*
flycatcher, olive-sided   *Contopus borealis*
  cordilleran   *Empidonax difficilis*
goshawk, northern   *Accipiter gentilis*
grosbeak, evening   *Coccothraustes vespertinus*
hawk, Cooper's   *Accipiter cooperii*
  red-tailed   *Buteo jamaicensis*
hummingbird, broad-tailed   *Selasphorus platycercus*
jay, Steller's   *Cyanocitta stelleri*

Birds (continued)

junco, dark-eyed *Junco hyemalis*
magpie, black-billed *Pica pica*
nighthawk, common *Chordeiles minor*
nuthatch, ● pygmy *Sitta pygmaea*
  white-breasted *Sitta carolinensis*
owl, flammulated *Otus flammeolus*
  great horned *Bubo virginianus*
  northern saw-whet *Aegolius acadicus*
poorwill, common *Phalaenoptilus nuttallii*
raven, common *Corvus corax*
robin, American *Turdus migratorius*
sapsucker, Williamson's *Sphyrapicus thyroideus*
siskin, pine *Carduelis pinus*
solitaire, Townsend's *Myadestes townsendi*
sparrow, chipping *Spizella passerina*
swallow, violet-green *Tachycineta thalassina*
tanager, western *Piranga ludoviciana*
turkey, wild *Meleagris gallopavo*
vireo, solitary *Vireo solitarius*
● warbler, Grace's (W) *Dendroica graciae*
  yellow-rumped *Dendroica coronata*
woodpecker, downy *Picoides pubescens*
  hairy *Picoides villosus*
wood-pewee, western *Contopus sordidulus*
wren, house *Troglodytes aedon*

Mammals

bat, hoary *Lasiurus cinereus*
  long-legged myotis *Myotis volans*
  Townsend's big-eared *Plecotus townsendii*
bear, black *Ursus americanus*
bobcat *Felis rufus*
chipmunk, Colorado *Tamias quadrivittatus*
  least *Tamias minimus*
cottontail, Nuttall's *Sylvilagus nuttallii*
coyote *Canis latrans*
deer, mule *Odocoileus hemionus*
elk *Cervus elaphus*
fox, gray *Urocyon cinereoargenteus*
ground squirrel, golden-mantled *Spermophilus lateralis*
  Wyoming *Spermophilus elegans*
jackrabbit, white-tailed *Lepus townsendii*
lion, mountain *Felis concolor*
marmot, yellow-bellied *Marmota flaviventris*
mouse, deer *Peromyscus maniculatus*
  rock (E) *Peromyscus difficilis*
porcupine *Erethizon dorsatum*
sheep, bighorn *Ovis canadensis*
shrew, montane *Sorex monticolus*
skunk, striped *Mephitis mephitis*
squirrel, ● **Abert's** *Sciurus aberti*
  rock *Spermophilus variegatus*
vole, long-tailed *Microtus longicaudus*
weasel, long-tailed *Mustela frenata*
woodrat, bushy-tailed *Neotoma cinerea*
  Mexican *Neotoma mexicana*

● Breeds almost exclusively in ponderosa forests.
Species in bold-faced type are more abundant.

·9·
Douglas Fir Forests

Identifying Traits

From a distance, Douglas fir forests are dense, dark green conifer stands. Young Douglas fir are Christmas tree-shaped, with crowns narrower than those of ponderosa and limber pine but broader than those of spruce and fir. Mature Douglas fir trees have semi-rounded crowns. In general Douglas fir forests are more crowded than mature ponderosa pine forests but not as dense as spruce-fir forests. At closer range Douglas fir forests are cool and moist when compared to other montane coniferous forests.

The Douglas fir of the Rocky Mountains is a medium-sized tree, seldom reaching 100 feet in height. Elsewhere, such as in coastal regions of the Pacific Northwest, Douglas fir reaches enormous proportions, but in the Rockies its growth is limited by colder temperatures, shorter growing seasons, and more arid conditions. The trees can be recognized by their flat, short (one inch), round tipped needles that occur singly on the twig. Their cones hang down from the branches and are distributed throughout the tree. Lobed bracts resembling the shape of a snake's tongue protrude from between cone scales. Douglas firs are not true firs as are

The dense Douglas fir forest on the opposite side of the valley contrasts sharply with the open, south-facing ponderosa stand from which this photograph was taken. *National Park Service.*

white and subalpine firs, which bear candle-like erect cones limited in distribution to the uppermost portion of their crowns.

Location

Douglas fir forests are found throughout the Southern Rockies from 5600 to 9000 feet. These ecosystems are prevalent over much of the landscape at higher elevations in this range, but at lower elevations they are restricted to north-facing slopes, where they stand in sharp contrast to the more open pine forests on opposite south-facing hillsides. The correlation of tree species composition with exposure is pronounced on small rocky outcrops, where ponderosa pine and Douglas fir grow within a few feet of each other but occupy different sides of the outcrop. Well-developed Douglas fir ecosystems can be seen along most highways that cross the mountain ranges of the region.

Site Characteristics

Although the climate of Douglas fir ecosystems is generally that of the low mountains, the forests are distinctly cooler and moister than neighboring ecosystems. Because of their typical northern exposure, these ecosystems are shadier than others. Little or no direct sunlight penetrates the dense foliage. Snow lasts longer than in ponderosa or meadow ecosystems, soil and air temperatures are cooler, relative humidity is higher, and the frost-free season is shorter. Soils are moist and often fine-textured. Douglas fir also grow from scanty soils that have collected in rock crevices.

Plant Characteristics

Although mature ecosystems on favorable sites are nearly pure Douglas fir, most of today's stands are patchy and mixed with ponderosa pine or with successional tree species such as quaking aspen. The understory of Douglas fir ecosystems contrasts sharply with the lusher ground cover of interspersed meadow and ponderosa pine ecosystems. Unless Douglas fir ecosystems are open and sunlight penetrates to the forest floor, herbaceous understory is sparse and litter is thick. Much of the understory is

Douglas fir. This is the only Rocky Mountain conifer whose cones have conspicuous three-pronged bracts extending from between the cone scales.

shrubs. Common juniper, kinnikinnik, ninebark, thimbleberry, and waxflower are common. Species of dry shrub ecosystems may mix into disturbed stands. Herb species in open Douglas fir stands are those of open ponderosa stands, excluding most of the grasses. Mosses and lichens are abundant in moist, well-shaded locations.

Foothills ecosystems in humid, narrow ravines have an unusual and diverse flora. Rare species, including eastern deciduous forest elements such as paper birch, and a rich moss and lichen flora are found on northern exposures. Moisture loving shrub stands mentioned in the discussion of mountain riparian ecosystems also commonly interfinger with foothills Douglas fir ecosystems.

Although less susceptible to disease and insect attack than ponderosa pine, Douglas fir is subject to a number of insect pests including the spruce budworm and Douglas fir bark beetle. The western budworm and Douglas fir tussock moth may defoliate the trees but do not necessarily kill them. During the late 1980s, a widespread spruce budworm epidemic in the Front Range killed large numbers of Douglas fir. In the areas of heaviest infestations there was vigorous growth of the herbaceous understory as the trees died, benefiting deer and elk populations.

Usually, a few trees in each infested stand survived, and these individuals will serve as seed sources for regrowth of the forest.

Windthrow, fire, and lightning may kill trees. The thick, corky bark of mature Douglas fir protects trees from ground fires, but the dense forests are much more susceptible to hot crown fires than are open ponderosa forests.

Most Douglas fir ecosystems of the Southern Rockies appear to be successional, the pristine ecosystems having been destroyed through lumbering activities. Sites now dominated by Douglas fir will eventually become climax Douglas fir forests, but dominance and density of individual species will change. It is likely that the forests will become more open than they are today, since Douglas fir forests typically become thinner as they mature. On moist sites ponderosa pine would be less abundant than at present, since the pine are unable to reproduce successfully in dense, shady Douglas fir forests.

Foothills forests on northern exposures would be climaxes of Douglas fir or Douglas fir and ponderosa pine. Montane ridgetops with well-developed soils would be covered with Douglas fir and ponderosa pine; climax ecosystems on ridge tops with coarse soils would have fewer trees, more of which would be ponderosa pine. Montane slopes would be covered with climaxes of dense Douglas fir on north-facing slopes and open Douglas fir and ponderosa pine on south-facing slopes.

Animal Characteristics

The animals of Douglas fir forests are also found in other coniferous forest types. Lower, drier Douglas fir forests have a fauna similar to that of ponderosa pine forests which are discussed in Chapter 8. Common distribution of reptile and many bird species is particularly conspicuous. At higher elevations in the montane life zone, animal characteristics of Douglas fir stands are closer to those of lodgepole pine and spruce-fir ecosystems. Mammals such as pine squirrels, martens, and southern red-backed voles, and birds such as Clark's nutcrackers and ruby-crowned kinglets are more common throughout these higher, moister coniferous forests. Reptiles are essentially absent. Faunal characteristics common to these higher coniferous forests are discussed in Chapters 11, 12 and 13.

Pine squirrel, or chickaree. This subspecies of the red squirrel of the northeastern United States is common throughout dense conifer forests of the Rocky Mountain region.

Human Use

In the 1800s Douglas fir ecosystems probably contained the finest lumber in the area. They were heavily cut, the lumber being used for rough bridge timbering and similar purposes. Mining activities, settlements, fire, and lumbering have modified pristine Douglas fir ecosystems throughout the region. Douglas fir forests are still of minor importance to the wood products industry. Recreational use is expanding rapidly. As with other mountain forests, Douglas fir ecosystems are important sources of water.

Plants and Animals of Douglas Fir Forests

Species composition depends on local site conditions and history of disturbance and may vary considerably from one place to another. Douglas fir is often mixed with other tree species, such as ponderosa pine, lodgepole pine, aspen, Engelmann spruce and subalpine fir. At lower elevations species composition of Douglas fir forests is similar to that of ponderosa pine forests. At higher elevations, Douglas fir forests share many plant and animal species with lodgepole and spruce-fir forests. Listed birds are mainly summer residents.

PLANTS

Trees
Douglas fir   *Pseudotsuga menziesii*
juniper, Rocky Mountain   *Sabina scopulorum*

Shrubs
baneberry   *Actaea rubra*
chokecherry   *Padus virginiana*
juniper, common   *Juniperus communis*
kinnikinnik   *Arctostaphylos uva-ursi*
maple, mountain   *Acer glabrum*
mountain ash   *Sorbus scopulina*
mountain lover   *Paxistima myrsinites*
ninebark   *Physocarpus monogynus*
raspberry, wild   *Rubus idaeus*
rose, wild   *Rosa* spp.
thimbleberry   *Rubacer parviflorus*
waxflower   *Jamesia americana*

Herbaceous Plants
arnica, heart-leaved   *Arnica cordifolia*
aster, smooth   *Symphyotrichum laeve*
baby-blue-eyes   *Collinsia parviflora*
bog orchid, green   *Coeloglossum viride*
fairy slipper   *Calypso bulbosa*
hawkweed, slender   *Chlorocrepis tristis*
pipsissewa   *Chimaphila umbellata*
sedge, elk   *Carex geyeri*
Solomon's seal, false   *Maianthemum* spp.
twisted stalk   *Streptopus fassettii*

ANIMALS

Birds
chickadee, mountain   *Parus gambeli*
creeper, brown   *Certhia americana*
crossbill, red   *Loxia curvirostra*
finch, Cassin's   *Carpodacus cassinii*
flicker, northern   *Colaptes auratus*
goshawk, northern   *Accipiter gentilis*
grosbeak, evening   *Coccothraustes vespertinus*
grouse, blue   *Dendragapus obscurus*
hawk, Cooper's   *Accipiter cooperii*
hummingbird, broad-tailed   *Selasphorus platycercus*
jay, Steller's   *Cyanocitta stelleri*
junco, dark-eyed   *Junco hyemalis*
kinglet, golden-crowned   *Regulus satrapa*
    ruby-crowned   *Regulus calendula*
nutcracker, Clark's   *Nucifraga columbiana*
nuthatch, white-breasted   *Sitta carolinensis*

Birds (continued)

owl, great horned   *Bubo virginianus*
raven, common   *Corvus corax*
siskin, pine   *Carduelis pinus*
solitaire, Townsend's   *Myadestes townsendi*
thrush, hermit   *Catharus guttatus*
warbler, yellow-rumped   *Dendroica coronata*
woodpecker, downy   *Picoides pubescens*
        hairy   *Picoides villosus*
wren, house   *Troglodytes aedon*

Mammals

bear, black   *Ursus americanus*
bobcat   *Felis rufus*
chipmunk, Colorado   *Tamias quadrivittatus*
        least   *Tamias minimus*
        Uinta   *Tamias umbrinus*
cottontail, Nuttall's   *Sylvilagus nuttallii*
coyote   *Canis latrans*
deer, mule   *Odocoileus hemionus*
elk   *Cervus elaphus*
ermine   *Mustela erminea*
ground squirrel, golden-mantled   *Spermophilus lateralis*

hare, snowshoe   *Lepus americanus*
jackrabbit, white-tailed   *Lepus townsendii*
lion, mountain   *Felis concolor*
lynx   *Felis lynx*
marmot, yellow-bellied   *Marmota flaviventris*
marten   *Martes americana*
mouse, deer   *Peromyscus maniculatus*
        western jumping   *Zapus princeps*
porcupine   *Erethizon dorsatum*
shrew, masked   *Sorex cinereus*
        montane   *Sorex monticolus*
skunk, striped   *Mephitis mephitis*
squirrel, pine   *Tamiasciurus hudsonicus*
vole, heather   *Phenacomys intermedius*
        long-tailed   *Microtus longicaudus*
        montane   *Microtus montanus*
        southern red-backed   *Clethrionomys gapperi*
weasel, long-tailed   *Mustela frenata*
wolverine   *Gulo gulo*
woodrat, bushy-tailed   *Neotoma cinerea*

Species in bold-faced type are more abundant.

·10·
Aspen Groves

Identifying Traits

Aspen form the only upland deciduous forests in the region. Other native deciduous tree species are found only adjacent to water. In winter the bare light-colored aspen branches contrast sharply with dark-green conifers. Pale-green aspen leaves tremble in the summer breeze, giving the tree the name "quaking" or "trembling aspen." This occurs because the flattened stem of the leaf is perpendicular to the plane of the leaf surface. The change to brilliant shades of yellow and orange heralds the beginning of autumn and brings thousands of sightseers into the mountains to view the spectacular colors.

Aspen ecosystems are characterized by their rich herbaceous understory and abundant and diverse animal life. They are noisy and busy while adjacent conifer ecosystems are relatively silent. Aspen ecosystems resemble mountain riparian ecosystems in lushness of plant and animal life.

Inside an aspen grove. *J.C. Emerick.*

Location

Quaking aspen is the most widely distributed native North American tree species. It is widespread in the eastern United States, Canada and Alaska. In the West, it occurs mainly in the mountains and high plateaus. Aspen groves are common throughout the Southern Rocky Mountain region from 8000 to 10,000 feet. Scattered aspen trees can be found from 5600 feet to treeline in moist, protected sites. At lower elevations aspen typically form small groves that are nestled into valleys or ravines with a north-facing exposure. Here the aspen are surrounded by Douglas fir, ponderosa pine, or piñon pine–juniper forests. At intermediate elevations in the montane forests or the lower subalpine forests, aspen may occur on slopes of any exposure and often cover extensive areas. A narrow band of aspen may border valley bottom meadows below hillside conifer stands. As they approach their upper subalpine limit of distribution, aspen grow on south-facing hillsides in sites protected from the wind. In northwestern Colorado and southeastern Wyoming, aspen often grow in ravines or depressions where sufficient moisture lasts through the summer months. In these locations, the aspen groves are frequently surrounded by sagebrush shrublands.

Aspen forests can be seen throughout the Southern Rocky Mountain region and higher elevations of the Colorado Plateau, particularly in areas once heavily disturbed by mining, logging, or grazing. Old mining districts often have the most spectacular displays of fall aspen colors in the region. Extensive forests grow in the vicinity of Aspen and Crested Butte, and aspen are also abundant in the rugged San Juan Mountains of southwestern Colorado. US 550 offers numerous opportunities to view aspen forests as it winds southward from Ouray to Durango over Red Mountain Pass, a drive considered by many people to be one of the most scenic routes in Colorado.

Site Characteristics

Aspen trees are capable of growing in a variety of soils. They may be dry or wet, loamy, clayey, or rocky, but they are usually deeper and less rocky than soils of coniferous ecosystems. Aspen forests with large trees and lush understory occur on sites that

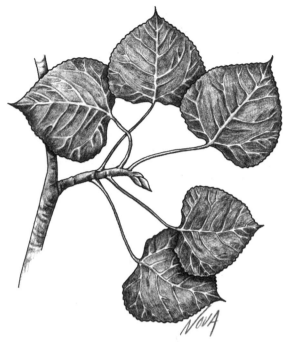

Quaking aspen.

are moist through the growing season, often with a high water table and soils that are loamy and porous.

The presence of an aspen forest improves the quality of the soil. Leaves decompose rapidly because they are low in tannins and resins, substances that retard decomposition of conifer needles. Bacterial decomposition is rapid, and leaf nutrients are returned to the soil rather than held in a thick litter. As an aspen stand matures, the organic carbon content and moisture-retaining capacity of soil increase, and pH becomes more alkaline. Soil invertebrates increase. These events are not pronounced in coniferous ecosystems. However, air temperature, relative humidity, and light intensity do not differ consistently from measurements in coniferous ecosystems in similar locations.

Plant Characteristics

Aspen forests are highly variable, depending on their age and on moisture conditions. Trees may be dense or widely spaced, and they can be large or stunted and shrubby. When soils are rich and moist, aspen trees are large, and the understory is a lush assemblage of forbs and shrubs. The ground surface is shaded completely by one or more leaf layers.

Dry aspen forests have an understory dominated by grasses, frequently Thurber's fescue mixed with slender wheatgrass and blue wild-rye. With increasing moisture, forbs such as Colorado columbine (the Colorado state flower), common lupine, golden banner, strawberry, tall lousewort, cow parsnip, yellow mountain parsley, and grasses such as Junegrass and bluegrasses are common. Common juniper and kinnikinnik, species found in coniferous forests, are occasionally present. The most frequent shrubs in moist Western Slope aspen forests are chokecherry, snowberry, and serviceberry. Bracken fern is abundant only in scattered locations along the Eastern Slope, but it is typical of very moist aspen groves in western Colorado and the eastern United States.

Understory lushness decreases in sites that have less than optimal conditions (little moisture, high wind, or poor soil) or sites that are overused by wild or domestic grazing animals. Even here the understory plant lushness and the number of species typically exceeds that of adjacent conifer stands.

Aspen trees are well adapted to a pioneering role, colonizing disturbed sites. Like other poplars, aspen produce tiny seeds with long silky hairs. The seeds are extremely buoyant and can be dispersed great distances on air currents. Their viability is brief, however, and germination must occur within a few days under optimal moisture and temperature conditions on bare soil. Although a single tree may produce thousands of seeds, only a few germinate, and of those that do only a small percentage of seedlings seem to survive. Once aspen seedlings do become established, further reproduction is effective and is accomplished by means of suckering—production of sprouts (suckers) from a network of shallow, interconnected, lateral roots that can extend outward nearly 50 feet from the parent tree.

Roots are thought to underlie most of the area within the range of aspen, and aspen suckers, present in virtually every mountain ecosystem, seem to light autumn forests as tiny yellow candles. Mature aspen trees produce chemical substances that inhibit suckering. However, when an ecosystem is destroyed, increased exposure to sun and subsequent increase in soil temperature stimulates growth of suckers from the roots. This explains the profusion of suckers along sunny roadcuts. Suckering is also

Colorado columbine.

initiated when all of the larger trees of an aspen grove are re-moved. This happens frequently in avalanche tracks, where aspen suckers often form dense thickets.

Suckers receive food stored in roots and moisture collected by the extensive root system. They grow rapidly the first year, often reaching a height of over two feet and rapidly achieving domi-nance over surrounding vegetation. Because they do not have to compete with herbs for resources, aspen frequently invade meadows. Here the suckers can rely on food produced by inter-connected mature aspen in more favorable sites nearby.

All trees produced from one set of roots form an aspen clone—a group of genetically identical individuals. Thus, all trees from the same clone tend to have similar characteristics. For example, they will all produce leaves at the same time in the spring, and change colors at the same time in the fall. They will have similar bark color and texture as well as a similar leaf shape. Typically, all trees within a clone will produce either male or female flowers, although a small percentage of the trees of any given clone may produce flowers having both male and female parts. Some clones will alternate their sex, producing male flowers one year and female flowers the next. During the fall, color change on some hillsides has the appearance of a patchwork of different colors, ranging from greens through different shades of yellow and orange. Each patch is likely a separate clone, changing color independently from the rest in response to fall temperatures as well as its own genetic makeup.

Aspen trees are susceptible to a large number of injuries and diseases. Major fungal diseases are trunk rots and cankers. The orange coloration of bark found on some aspen also is a fungal disease. Susceptibility to infection is increased by injuries from browsing and bark-eating mule deer and elk and excavation of trunk cavities by woodpeckers. Aspen also are host to many insects, including tent caterpillars, leafrollers, leafminers, aphids, leafhoppers, scale, and other species that may seriously weaken and occasionally completely defoliate trees.

Fragile aspen wood suffers breakage by heavy snows and strong winds. Breakage scars are also entrance points for disease. Bark in open aspen forests is susceptible to being burned by the sun. These and other damaging agents result in most aspen groves containing an abundance of short-lived, sickly, and deformed trees.

Fortunately, the bark of the trunk and branches of aspen is photosynthetic, and like green leaves, has the capability to produce sugar and other important substances from sunlight, water, and minerals. Although bark photosynthesis is only one or two percent of that of the leaves, it could increase the chances for recovery of trees stressed by defoliation caused by insects or severe late-spring frosts.

Aspen rapidly colonize sunny sites from which other forest trees have been removed by fire, landslide, logging, or other disturbance. Usually in such cases either lodgepole pine or aspen invade, but the two species occasionally intermix. Invasion is completed within five to ten years, and maximum density is reached twenty-five to fifty years later. As shade from the growing trees increases, reproduction of aspen declines because reproductive processes require direct sunlight. Seedlings of climax forest species, Douglas fir, Engelmann spruce and subalpine fir, need a shaded forest floor to survive. Thus these species slowly replace the aspen. Soils mature, the fauna changes in response to changes in plant composition, and the ecosystem gradually returns to a climax forest. Conifer invasion is hastened by the dramatic soil improvements made by aspen and is most rapid when the aspen grove is small.

Aspen occasionally form isolated climax ecosystems. Conifers are unable to invade these ecosystems because of lack of a seed source or because of a high water table and dense herb understory. Long-lived quaking aspen ecosystems are common on the Western Slope, with some perhaps several thousand years old. This is far older than the age of individual trees, which seldom exceeds 200 years.

Animal Characteristics

Aspen forests have a varied and abundant animal life, sharing many species with mountain riparian ecosystems. In western North America, this ecosystem provides habitat for over 50 species of wild mammals. The lush understory vegetation provides prime habitat for northern pocket gophers, long-tailed and montane voles, and other rodents. Small carnivores such as the long-tailed weasel and montane shrew are common. Scars on the white bark of larger trees occasionally reveal where black bears climbed to feed on aspen buds and foliage, or to raid bird nests. Mule deer commonly browse the understory, and extensive bark-stripping in some aspen forests bears testimony to heavy elk usage during the winter when other forage is unavailable.

Elk and mule deer are the most important large herbivores to use aspen forests in the Southern Rocky Mountain region. Deer find both cover and browse in the aspen, and frequent this ecosystem primarily in the summer and fall, when tree and associated shrub foliage are at their peak. Aspen groves that are near water and that have a well developed herbaceous and shrub layer are among the best deer habitats.

In the Rocky Mountains, aspen forests are important to many elk populations. Aspen twigs and foliage are avidly sought during all seasons as browse, and during the summer and early fall, elk graze the lush understory. Where aspen occur on elk winter range, the habitat is heavily used. It is during this time that they gnaw aspen bark, leaving their long, thin tooth marks engraved in trees. In the spring, as elk begin to move to higher elevations, pregnant cows leave the herd to give birth to their calves. Mid-elevation aspen forests, especially those with dense shrub understories, are valuable calving grounds, providing critical cover and forage.

After hard winters with late-lying snow, there is evidence of large numbers of microtine rodents having been active under the snow during the winter. They remove bark from stems of shrubs and gnaw large circular or oval patches from lower aspen trunks.

Although pocket gophers themselves are rarely seen, numerous mounds of rich, bare soil under many aspen groves is evidence of their presence. Such places provide good habitat for these rodents because of the abundance of leaves and roots, well-drained and soft soils that allow easy burrowing, and winter snowpacks that are deep enough to prevent the ground from freezing solid. Only mountain meadows that are well drained and rich in plant life provide a better habitat for pocket gophers.

Aspen is critical to beaver in some areas, especially where the riparian zone is too narrow to provide an adequate supply of willow, alder, cottonwood, or other preferred food and building materials. Here, beaver will cut aspen as far as 200 yards away from the stream. Although beaver will cut any size of tree, their preference is for smaller ones with diameters of less than six inches. Beaver can consume lots of aspen. It has been estimated that in some areas a beaver will eat nearly 1500 pounds of aspen per year, requiring about 200 trees. Because of this, beaver colonies that depend on aspen are particularly unstable, since the regrowth of suckers is too slow to sustain the population.

Breeding bird density is high as a result of the large number of plant layers, each a different distance from the ground and providing an assemblage of nesting sites, seeds, insects, and nectar sources used by different groups of nesting birds. Western warbling vireos sing from nests that are almost completely concealed by the dense aspen foliage. The thick understory hides and protects juvenile birds fresh out of the nest. Red-naped sapsuckers nest almost exclusively in aspen forests and, along with northern flickers and hairy woodpeckers, hollow out cavities in the soft aspen trunks that are used in turn by other birds. Such cavity-nesters include tree and violet-green swallows, white-breasted nuthatches, house wrens, mountain bluebirds, and occasional northern pygmy owls. Robins, western tanagers, and cordilleran flycatchers also nest in aspen forests. In Utah and northern states, ruffed grouse populations are strongly associated with aspen and other hardwood forests, where males drum from fallen logs during the breeding season, and where adults feed on aspen buds and catkins, and the chicks on the rich insect fauna of the understory.

Most groups of large soil invertebrates (for example snails, earthworms, spiders, ants) are more abundant in aspen groves than in adjacent coniferous forests. Their abundance is a result of favorable food and moisture conditions. The soil organisms in turn are important soil enrichers. Because of the often-dense herbaceous understory, insect populations in general are diverse and abundant, providing an important food source for birds and insect-eating mammals.

Human Use

Although aspen forests are the result of human or natural disturbance, the small size of trees has discouraged commercial use in all but the larger groves. However, future markets for certain wood products, including paneling, fiber, and excelsior may increase the demand for aspen trees. Because aspen wood is prone to decay, early settlers and miners in Colorado preferred coniferous trees for most construction purposes. Aspen is gathered for firewood, and domestic herbivores graze the understory and trample suckers. Aspen ecosystems are important because they hold soils of disturbed areas in place and by doing so prevent stream siltation. Compared to coniferous forest types, aspen forests have a more beneficial effect on water quality, producing water that potentially is less acidic and has fewer dissolved minerals.

Aspen forests are becoming better recognized for their multiple values regarding wildlife, livestock grazing, forest products, water resources, aesthetics, and recreation. Thus they are being more actively studied and managed by federal agencies than in the past. Such activities undoubtedly will increase our understanding and appreciation of these important ecosystems.

Plants and Animals of Aspen Forests

Understory species composition varies greatly depending on site moisture and stage of succession. The understory of dry forests is dominated by grasses, and as moisture increases, the relative amounts of forbs and shrubs increase. Aspen forests in advanced stages of succession are characterized by numerous Douglas fir, Engelmann spruce, or subalpine fir intermixed with the aspen. Listed birds are mainly summer residents.

PLANTS

Trees
aspen, quaking *Populus tremuloides*

Shrubs
chokecherry *Padus virginiana*
gooseberry, common *Ribes inerme*
honeysuckle, bush *Distegia involucrata*
juniper, common *Juniperus communis*
kinnikinnik *Arctostaphylos uva-ursi*
maple, mountain *Acer glabrum*
rose, Wood's *Rosa woodsii*
serviceberry *Amelanchier alnifolia*
snowberry *Symphoricarpos rotundifolius*

Herbaceous plants
bedstraw, fragrant *Galium triflorum*
bluegrass *Poa* spp.
columbine, Colorado blue *Aquilegia caerulea*
cow parsnip *Heracleum sphondylium*
daisy, showy *Erigeron speciosus*
fern, bracken *Pteridium aquilinum*
fescue, Thurber's *Festuca thurberi*

geranium, white *Geranium richardsonii*
golden banner *Thermopsis divaricarpa*
Junegrass *Koeleria macrantha*
lily, Mariposa *Calochortus gunnisonii*
lousewort, Gray's *Pedicularis procera*
lovage, Porter's *Ligusticum porteri*
lupine, common *Lupinus argenteus*
meadowrue, Fendler *Thalictrum fendleri*
mountain parsley, yellow *Pseudocymopterus montanus*
oniongrass, purple *Bromelica spectabilis*
sneezeweed, orange *Dugaldia hoopesii*
strawberry *Fragaria virginiana* ssp. *ovalis*
vetch, American *Vicia americana*
wheatgrass, slender *Elymus trachycaulus*
wild-rye, blue *Elymus glaucus*
yarrow *Achillea lanulosa*

ANIMALS

Birds

bluebird, mountain *Sialia currucoides*

chickadee, black-capped *Parus atricapillus*

    mountain *Parus gambeli*

flicker, northern *Colaptes auratus*

flycatcher, cordilleran *Empidonax difficilis*

hawk, Cooper's *Accipiter cooperii*

hummingbird, broad-tailed *Selasphorus platycercus*

junco, dark-eyed *Junco hyemalis*

nuthatch, red-breasted *Sitta canadensis*

    white-breasted *Sitta carolinensis*

pygmy-owl, northern *Glaucidium gnoma*

robin, American *Turdus migratorius*

sapsucker, Williamson's *Sphyrapicus thyroideus*

    ● red-naped *Sphyrapicus nuchalis*

swallow, tree *Tachycineta bicolor*

violet-green *Tachycineta thalassina*

vireo, warbling *Vireo gilvus*

warbler, orange-crowned *Vermivora celata*

wood-pewee, western *Contopus sordidulus*

woodpecker, hairy *Picoides villosus*

    downy *Picoides pubescens*

wren, house *Troglodytes aedon*

Mammals

bat, long-legged myotis *Myotis volans*

    silver-haired *Lasionycteris noctivagans*

bear, black *Ursus americanus*

chipmunk, least *Tamias minimus*

cottontail, Nuttall's *Sylvilagus nuttallii*

coyote *Canis latrans*

deer, mule *Odocoileus hemionus*

elk *Cervus elaphus*

ermine *Mustela erminea*

ground squirrel, golden-mantled *Spermophilus lateralis*

hare, snowshoe *Lepus americanus*

lynx *Felis lynx*

marmot, yellow-bellied *Marmota flaviventris*

mouse, deer *Peromyscus maniculatus*

    western jumping *Zapus princeps*

pocket gopher, northern *Thomomys talpoides*

porcupine *Erethizon dorsatum*

shrew, masked *Sorex cinereus*

    montane *Sorex monticolus*

skunk, striped *Mephitis mephitis*

vole, long-tailed *Microtus longicaudus*

    meadow *Microtus pennsylvanicus*

    montane *Microtus montanus*

weasel, long-tailed *Mustela frenata*

● Breeds almost exclusively in aspen forests.

Species in bold-faced type are more common.

·11·
Lodgepole Pine Forests

Identifying Traits

Lodgepole pine forests can be distinguished at a distance by the yellow-green foliage and by upper-tree crowns that are a few feet wide and gently rounded. Trees are dense and even sized; forests often have the consistency of a tree plantation. The straight, pole-like appearance of their trunks gives lodgepole pines their name.

Lodgepole pine needles grow in bunches of two. They are one to three inches long, shorter than the paired needles of ponderosa pine. The tan lodgepole cones are shorter than two inches, and old, gray, closed cones cling to lodgepole branches for as long as forty years.

In contrast to aspen groves, lodgepole pine forests are quiet and typically contain little animal life. They have very little understory, and are less diverse than other ecosystems.

Location

Lodgepole pine are common between 8500 and 10,500 feet in the montane and lower subalpine forests. Below 9000 feet they prevail on north-facing slopes. They are common on all slope

The interior of a lodgepole pine stand. Trees typically are even-sized and, in contrast to aspen forests, the understory vegetation is sparse. *J.C. Emerick.*

exposures at higher elevations. Lodgepole forests are uncommon but present beyond these limits, from 7500 feet to treeline. They may be of any size, from small patches of less than an acre scattered through ponderosa pine, Douglas fir, or spruce–fir ecosystems, to large forests covering entire ridges. Lodgepole pines are common in northern and central Colorado, but occur only in scattered locations in the southern part of the region.

Site Characteristics

Lodgepole pine stands are found in a variety of sites. Soil texture and moisture are not consistent from stand to stand. Climate is generally that of upper mountain forests: cool and moist with a short frost-free season.

Plant Characteristics

Lodgepole pine forests usually are very dense, with trees all approximately the same size. A mosaic of uneven-sized tree patches or a multi-storied ecosystem result when poor climate or seed supply thwarts the typical massive invasion of a disturbed area.

Since little light reaches the forest floor and most of the ecosystem's resources are used by trees, understory is absent or sparse. It increases as trees die from suppression—lack of adequate light and nutrition—and the stand opens up. Common understory species include kinnikinnik, wild rose, buffaloberry, and common juniper; blueberry and wintergreen are found at upper elevations. During summer, the forest floor is brightened by the cheerful yellow blooms of heart-leaved arnica.

Lodgepole pine is considered by foresters to be a "fire-type" conifer; forest fires open the forest, remove the understory vegetation, produce a bare mineral soil, and facilitate the release of lodgepole seeds. Lodgepole have serotinous cones—cones that remain on the tree for many years. The cones must be exposed to high temperatures (113° to 122°F) to melt the resin between cone scales and allow the cones to open up. Strong winds also can open them. Barring strong winds and high temperatures, cones can remain closed on trees for 40 years and still contain viable seed. Germination is best on bare mineral soil, although it can occur on disturbed litter and decaying wood.

Following a fire, often within a few weeks, the ground becomes dotted with tiny lodgepole seedlings. These flourish when exposed to intense sunlight, and in a few years grow into a thick stand of saplings. As the stand continues to develop, faster growing individuals soon top their neighbors, robbing them of precious sunlight and nutrients. The smaller, weaker trees soon die, thinning the stand. As shade from the growing trees increases, reproduction declines, because lodgepole seedlings are intolerant of shade. Over time, the shade-tolerant seedlings of Douglas fir, Engelmann spruce, and subalpine fir appear on the forest floor. These climax species eventually replace the lodgepole.

Lodgepole pine ecosystems are normally successional to Douglas fir in montane forests or Engelmann spruce and subalpine fir in higher forests. Occasionally aspen ecosystems are invaded by lodgepole pine, which are in turn replaced by Douglas fir or spruce–fir forests. Signs of the history and transitory nature of lodgepole pine forests are often abundant. Remnants of distroyed ecosystems remain as charred or saw-cut stumps, bits of charcoal in the soil, and widely scattered survivors that tower above climax trees. These old survivors are important seed sources.

Lodgepole ecosystems can be perpetuated if they are continually disturbed. For example, dense lodgepole provide quantities of fuel for wildfires; these stands may be burned time after time, perpetuating good sites for lodgepole reproduction and destroying all seed trees of other species. Perpetual logging of lodgepole stands plays the same role as periodic fire.

Some lodgepole pine ecosystems may be climax ecosystems. Warm, dry, upland sites with deep, well-drained soils between 8200 and 9300 feet possibly are too hot and dry for successful invasion of Douglas fir or other tree species. While climax lodgepole stands are common farther west in the Sierra Nevada mountains, they are unusual in the Rockies.

Lodgepole pine is susceptible to a number of damaging agents, including the same species of mountain pine beetle that widely attacks ponderosa pine. Dwarf mistletoe typically infests one-third to two-thirds of all lodgepole stands. Infestations reduce growth and seed production of trees. Pine squirrels, elk, birds, and insects eat the protein-rich dwarf mistletoe. A number of lesser insect pests and diseases, windthrow, and gnawing mammals also take their toll, each injury making a tree and stand more susceptible to future injury. For example, stands opened by disease are more prone to windthrow, and trees injured by mammals are more susceptible to fungus and mistletoe attack.

Lodgepole pine.

Animal Characteristics

The chattering and scolding sounds of pine squirrels (often called chickarees) are common in lodgepole pine forests. These small, highly-territorial tree squirrels collect lodgepole cones in large caches, called middens, which are raided by southern red-backed voles, mouselike rodents. The vole is consistently present in lodgepole ecosystems, also eating fungi and small invertebrate animals. Deer mice, Uinta chipmunks, and heather voles also may be present. The weasellike pine marten slinks through the forest, feeding on pine squirrels and other small mammals. These animals form a simple food web. The sparse plant associations do not provide food and cover for many mammalian species.

Small openings in lodgepole pine forests are important to wildlife. Understory flourishes in response to increased light, and wildlife in turn increases. Mule deer and elk use the openings for foraging, blue grouse use them for booming grounds, and small mammals nest and forage here.

Pine marten.

Bird sounds of lodgepole forests are similar to those of other dense conifer forests. Mountain chickadees, dark-eyed juncos, and white-breasted nuthatches move through the forest in family groups after the breeding season, interrupting the quiet surroundings with soft chatterings. During the breeding season, the yellow-rumped warbler's colorless song is joined by that of the ruby-crowned kinglet throughout the day, occasionally inter-rupted by the harsh calls of gray jays or of Clark's nutcrackers. Density of breeding birds is low.

Human Use

Lodgepole pine have been used since prehistoric times, when Indians constructed their dwellings (lodges) with straight poles of this pine. More recently the wood has been used for mining timbers, rough construction, fuel, fences, and railroad ties. Today the wood is used for light frame construction, finishing lumber, posts, poles, and pulp.

Although lodgepole pine ecosystems contain few plant or ani-mal species, they serve the important function of preventing rapid water runoff and of holding soils of disturbed areas in place until more diverse climax ecosystems again are present.

Plants and Animals of Lodgepole Pine Forests

Lodgepole pine forests that are in an advanced state of succession will contain Douglas fir, Engelmann spruce, or subalpine fir mixed with the pines. Forests in earlier successional stages are characterized by relatively few species of plants and animals.

PLANTS

Tree
pine, lodgepole *Pinus contorta*

Shrubs
blueberry *Vaccinium myrtillus*
broom huckleberry *Vaccinium scoparium*
buffaloberry *Shepherdia canadensis*
elder, red-berried *Sambucus microbotrys*
juniper, common *Juniperus communis*
kinnikinnik *Arctostaphylos uva-ursi*

rose, Wood's *Rosa woodsii*
sticky-laurel *Ceanothus velutina*

Herbaceous Plants
arnica, heart-leaved *Arnica cordifolia*
locoweed, drop-pod *Oxytropis deflexa*
mistletoe, dwarf *Arceuthobium americanum*
paintbrush, Wyoming *Castilleja linarifolia*
pinedrops *Pterospora andromedea*
wintergreen, one-sided *Orthilia secunda*

ANIMALS

Birds

chickadee, mountain *Parus gambeli*
creeper, brown *Certhia americana*
crossbill, red *Loxia curvirostra*
finch, Cassin's *Carpodacus cassinii*
grosbeak, evening *Coccothraustes vespertinus*
grouse, blue *Dendragapus obscurus*
hummingbird, broad-tailed *Selasphorus platycercus*
jay, gray *Perisoreus canadensis*
    Steller's *Cyanocitta stelleri*
junco, dark-eyed *Junco hyemalis*
kinglet, ruby-crowned *Regulus calendula*
nutcracker, Clark's *Nucifraga columbiana*
nuthatch, white-breasted *Sitta carolinensis*
raven, common *Corvus corax*
sapsucker, Williamson's *Sphyrapicus thyroideus*
siskin, pine *Carduelis pinus*
thrush, hermit *Catharus guttatus*
warbler, yellow-rumped *Dendroica coronata*
wood-pewee, western *Contopus sordidulus*
woodpecker, hairy *Picoides villosus*
wren, house *Troglodytes aedon*

Mammals

bat, hoary *Lasiurus cinereus*
bear, black *Ursus americanus*
bobcat *Felis rufus*
chipmunk, least *Tamias minimus*
    Uinta *Tamias umbrinus*
cottontail, Nuttall's *Sylvilagus nuttallii*
coyote *Canis latrans*
deer, mule *Odocoileus hemionus*
ermine *Mustela erminea*
ground squirrel, golden-mantled *Spermophilus lateralis*
hare, snowshoe *Lepus americanus*
jackrabbit, white-tailed *Lepus townsendii*
lion, mountain *Felis concolor*
lynx *Felis lynx*
marmot, yellow-bellied *Marmota flaviventris*
marten *Martes americana*
mouse, deer *Peromyscus maniculatus*
    western jumping *Zapus princeps*
porcupine *Erethizon dorsatum*
shrew, masked *Sorex cinereus*
    montane *Sorex monticolus*
skunk, striped *Mephitis mephitis*
squirrel, pine *Tamiasciurus hudsonicus*
vole, heather *Phenacomys intermedius*
    long-tailed *Microtus longicaudus*
    montane *Microtus montanus*
    southern red-backed *Clethrionomys gapperi*
weasel, long-tailed *Mustela frenata*
wolverine *Gulo gulo*
woodrat, bushy-tailed *Neotoma cinerea*

Species in bold-faced type are more common.

·12·
Limber Pine and Bristlecone Pine Woodlands

Identifying Traits

Limber pine and bristlecone pine form woodlands on exposed mountain sites (ridge tops, rocky knobs) where the widely spaced, broad-crowned trees are silhouetted against the sky. Trees usually are short, reaching heights of only thirty to fifty feet. At upper elevations on very windy sites, trees may be as wide as they are tall. Their wood is bent and twisted, and they often lack a central trunk.

The needles of both pines typically grow in bunches of five. Other pine species of the region have only two or three needles per bunch. Limber pine cones are husky and large (three to ten inches long). Branches are of varying lengths, giving limber pine a ragged appearance. Their broad, flat tops strongly contrast with the spirelike crowns of neighboring spruce and fir. These pines often appear to produce numerous trunks at ground level. On exposed, windy sites, the bark of the upper branches is reddish

White wind-scoured trunks of bristlecone pine. *W. Perry Conway.*

Limber pine.

and smooth, almost skinlike. Branches of limber pine are flexible and bend easily in the wind; this characteristic gives these trees their name.

Bristlecones look much like limber pine, although their foliage is stiffer and slightly darker, and in exposed sites their crowns look more ragged. The needles of the bristlecone are distinctive, being shorter (one to one-and-one-half inches long) than limber pine's two- to three-inch needles, and covered with tiny specks of resin. The cones of bristlecone pine also are covered with beads of resin, and each cone scale has a sharp bristle at its tip.

Location

Limber pine ecosystems are present from 7500 feet to timber-line although a few of these pines are scattered at lower elevations on rocky outcrops in northeastern Colorado (Pawnee Buttes) and western Nebraska. Their occurrence at these latter sites is usually restricted to locations where soil moisture is favorable and they are protected from the wind. Whether or not these are relict populations dating back to a cooler, moister climate is a matter for debate. Limber pine, like piñon pine, produce large, edible nuts that could have been carried to the plains by birds or by Indians who hunted in the mountains.

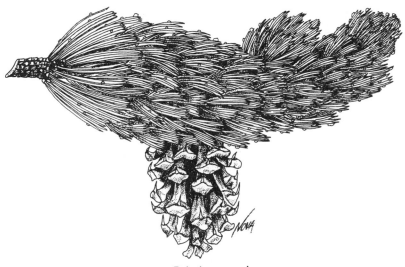

Bristlecone pine.

Bristlecone pine are restricted to elevations above 7000 feet. They are rare north of Berthoud Pass in Colorado and locally abundant south of there. Bristlecone often mix with limber pine in stands ranging from less than an acre to several hundred acres in size. Mixed stands of the two pines can be seen on many south-facing slopes in mid to upper elevations, such as along Interstate 70 above Silver Plume and along Colorado Highway 82 between Twin Lakes and Independence Pass. An especially picturesque stand can be seen at the Mount Goliath Natural Area along the road to Mount Evans in the Front Range. Pure stands of bristlecone grow in South Park and in many other central and southern parts of the Southern Rocky Mountains.

Site Characteristics

Stands of limber and bristlecone pine are typical of windy, exposed sites with coarse, rocky soils. Rock covers three-fourths or more of the ground surface. The climate is dry and sunny, runoff is high, and the ecosystems are the only subalpine areas blown free of winter's snow. Aside from these unusually severe conditions, climate is generally that of montane and subalpine forests. The frost-free season is short, solar radiation is high, and soil and air temperatures are low.

Plant Characteristics

On permanently windy, dry, exposed sites, limber and bristlecone pine ecosystems are climaxes with large trees. No other tree species can invade these harsh sites. Climax limber and bristlecone stands are characteristically open with a sparse understory. Herbs and small shrubs usually cover less than ten percent of the ground, with common species including Junegrass, stonecrop, Colorado locoweed, and whitlow-wort. Lichens cover exposed rock surfaces.

Where fire or logging activities have removed other types of climax coniferous forests, limber and bristlecone pines may form

Clark's nutcracker. *W. Perry Conway.*

successional stands. As the pines mature and reduce wind exposure, they are gradually replaced by the original climax species. The composition of successional stands is variable, depending on their age and on site characteristics. Here the two pines are often found with other tree species such as Engelmann spruce, subalpine fir, lodgepole pine, ponderosa pine, Douglas fir, and aspen. Understory shrubs can include serviceberry, buffaloberry, raspberry, common juniper, and shrubby cinquefoil. Subalpine stands may be moist with a closed canopy, harboring understory shrubs typical of spruce–fir stands such as blueberry and wild rose.

Limber and bristlecone pines are well adapted to a rigorous climate. Little of the ecosystem's limited resources needs to be used by the trees since they are slow-growing, long-lived, and resistant to decay and fire. The bristlecone is the longest-lived tree species in the Southern Rocky Mountains, with some old survivors being a thousand years old or older. Elsewhere, specimens that have been reported to be over 4600 years old are perhaps the oldest living organisms.

Animal Characteristics

Limber pine and bristlecone pine ecosystems do not house a diverse fauna. Deer mice and chipmunks, both seed eaters, are common as a result of the large limber pine seeds and abundant nest sites in rock crevices. Occasionally pine squirrel middens litter the forest floor, and porcupines eat limber pine bark. Otherwise, most birds and mammals are probably visitors from adjacent forests. The gray jay and Clark's nutcracker actively feed on limber pine seeds.

Nutcrackers cache seeds as they do in piñon pine woodlands. Thus germination of limber pine seeds is enhanced by the birds, and in places where numerous seeds are deposited several seedlings often appear. As they mature they look like a single tree with many trunks; however, recent research on such trees has shown that each trunk is genetically distinct. In contrast, bristlecone pines rarely have this growth form. Their seeds are small with papery wings and are usually disseminated by the wind.

Human Use

Most climax limber and bristlecone pine ecosystems in the regions are old. They have escaped large-scale modification by fire because tree crowns are widely separated. The trees have not been lumbered, because their trunks are usually twisted, but in some areas many trees have been mutilated by saws or axes, their picturesque gnarled branches having been removed for landscaping or other decorative purposes. The ecosystems are valuable because they reduce runoff and modify harsh environments on sites that would otherwise be unforested.

Plants and Animals of Limber Pine and Bristlecone Pine Woodlands

Where woodlands of limber pine and bristlecone pine exist in a climax state on exposed rocky outcrops, diversity of associated plant and animal species typically is low. Elsewhere on more protected sites with better soils where the pines may exist in a successional state, diversity is higher because of the presence of many species characteristic of surrounding forests or meadows. For example, favorable sites at timberline may harbor many plants and animals more characteristic of alpine tundra that are not listed here. Because of the small size of many of these stands, the flora and fauna are not as distinctive as for other kinds of ecosystems. Listed birds are mainly summer residents.

PLANTS

Trees
pine, bristlecone *Pinus aristata*
 limber *Pinus flexilis*

Shrubs
broom huckleberry *Vaccinium scoparium*
buffaloberry *Shepherdia canadensis*
cinquefoil, shrubby *Pentaphylloides floribunda*

juniper, common *Juniperus communis*
kinnikinnik *Arctostaphylos uva-ursi*
raspberry, wild *Rubus idaeus*
rose, Wood's *Rosa woodsii*
serviceberry *Amelanchier alnifolia*
sticky-laurel *Ceanothus velutinus*

Herbaceous Plants

alum-root, common *Heuchera parvifolia*
candytuft, mountain *Noccaea montana*
Junegrass *Koeleria macrantha*
locoweed, Rocky Mountain *Oxytropis sericea*
muhly, mountain *Muhlenbergia montana*
muttongrass *Poa fendleriana*
penstemon, alpine *Penstemon glabere*
Whipple's *Penstemon whippleanus*
rockcress, Drummond *Boechera drummondii*
stonecrop *Sedum lanceolatum*
thistle, Hooker *Cirsium scopulorum*
whitlow-wort *Draba* spp.

ANIMALS

Birds

chickadee, mountain *Parus gambeli*
crossbill, red *Loxia curvirostra*
finch, Cassin's *Carpoducus cassinii*
grosbeak, evening *Coccothraustes vespertinus*
jay, **gray** *Perisoreus canadensis*
Steller's *Cyanocitta stelleri*
junco, dark-eyed *Junco hyemalis*
kinglet, golden-crowned *Regulus satrapa*
nutcracker, Clark's *Nucifraga columbiana*
nuthatch, white-breasted *Sitta carolinensis*
raven, common *Corvus corax*
siskin, pine *Carduelis pinus*
thrush, hermit *Catharus guttatus*
warbler, yellow-rumped *Dendroica coronata*
woodpecker, hairy *Picoides villosus*

Mammals

bear, black *Ursus americanus*
bobcat *Felis rufus*
chipmunk, least *Tamias minimus*
cottontail, Nuttall's *Sylvilagus nuttallii*
coyote *Canis latrans*
deer, mule *Odocoileus hemionus*
ermine *Mustela erminea*
ground squirrel, golden-mantled *Spermophilus lateralis*
hare, snowshoe *Lepus americanus*
jackrabbit, white-tailed *Lepus townsendii*
lion, mountain *Felis concolor*
marmot, yellow-bellied *Marmota flaviventris*
marten *Martes americana*
mouse, deer *Peromyscus maniculatus*
porcupine *Erethizon dorsatum*
shrew, masked *Sorex cinereus*
montane *Sorex monticolus*
squirrel, pine *Tamiasciurus hudsonicus*
vole, southern red-backed *Clethrionomys gapperi*
weasel, long-tailed *Mustela frenata*
woodrat, bushy-tailed *Neotoma cinerea*

Species in bold-faced type are more common.

·13·
Engelmann Spruce–Subalpine Fir Forests

Identifying Traits

Engelmann spruce–subalpine fir forests can be recognized from a distance by the very narrow crowns and dark green color of the dense trees. Other ecosystems intermixed with these high altitude forests are dominated by trees of a distinctly different color (lodgepole pine have a yellow-green foliage, and aspen have light green foliage and whitish trunks) or shape (limber and bristlecone pine have broad crowns). A spruce–fir ecosystem has a cool, dark, humid feeling absent from other mountain forests.

Spruce and fir trees can be recognized by their short needles (approximately one inch long) that are attached to twigs singly, not in bunches as are pine needles. Female cones cluster near the tops of both species, a protection against self-pollination and inbreeding. The only other common tree without needles in bunches is Douglas fir, recognized by the cones scattered throughout the entire crown.

Subalpine fir can be distinguished from Engelmann spruce by the upright cones of the fir (spruce cones hang down), by the soft, flat needles of the fir that are rounded at the tip (spruce

National Park Service.

Engelmann spruce.

needles are rigid, square, and have pointed tips), and by the shape of the upper crown. Fir crowns are exceptionally narrow and spirelike, often less than ten inches wide. Spruce crowns may be very narrow, but they often have longer branches of different lengths that give the crown a ragged appearance. Engelmann spruce bark is usually reddish when mature, with outer layers flaking off in small, thin sheets. Subalpine fir bark is smooth except when trees are very old, and fir bark, which appears whitish or silvery, is flecked with regularly spaced horizontal markings. From Pikes Peak south, subalpine fir occurs with a variant called corkbark fir, which is similar in all respects to subalpine fir except that its bark is much thicker and has a cushiony, corklike feel when pressed with the finger.

Location

Spruce–fir ecosystems form the highest, most continuous and pristine forests in the region. Present from 9000 feet to treeline, they are most abundant between 10,000 and 11,000 feet. Dense, homogeneous forests roll for miles across valleys and slopes of all exposures, interrupted only by small meadows, fens, ponds, clumps of limber or bristlecone pine, and lichen-covered rock faces. Spruce and fir forests have a ragged upper border of

Subalpine fir.

krummholz ecosystems that contain the same plant species. Lodgepole pine and quaking aspen stands, many of which have an understory of spruce and fir seedlings, often border lower spruce–fir forests. Spruce–fir forests can be seen along the higher highway passes in Colorado, such as Berthoud, Monarch, and Wolf Creek Passes, and at the eastern and western approaches to Eisenhower Tunnel along Interstate 70.

Site Characteristics

Spruce–fir forests have a cool, moist, windy climate. Most precipitation is in the form of snow that covers the ground to several feet deeper than in any other mountain zone. The United States record for a twenty-four hour snowfall occurred in spruce–fir forests at Silver Lake, west of Boulder. On April 24-25, 1921, seventy-six inches of snow fell. Spruce–fir forests increase their effective precipitation by catching snow blown down from the tundra. Snowpack remains well into the summer, melting later than on much of the tundra. The frost-free season lasts only two months. The dense trees modify the harsh climate by decreasing wind speed and radiation intensity and by holding moisture.

Soils are highly variable. They may be formed from glacial deposits or from igneous or metamorphic bedrock. Texture varies from coarse to fine and in general soils are young. Old, deep, well-developed soils are found in areas that were not glaciated. They are moist through the summer and may be subject to frost heaving.

Plant Characteristics

Some of the largest and oldest trees in the region are found in these forests, some of which have remained untouched by either recent fire or human use. Trees may exceed three feet in diameter, 120 feet in height, and 400 years of age. An excellent example of an old, undisturbed spruce–fir forest is located around Long Lake in the Brainard Lake Recreation Area west of Colorado Highway 72 near Ward.

Fir seedlings establish themselves more successfully in the shade typical of spruce–fir stands, but spruce have a higher survival rate, are less susceptible to disease, and live longer. For these reasons, mature spruce are slightly more abundant than are mature fir. Spruce also extend down into the montane climax region in cool pockets, but fir do not.

The forest floor is littered with rotting logs. Understory growth is patchy and consists primarily of dense, low-growing blueberry and broom huckleberry bushes. Moisture-loving shrubs and herbs such as heart-leaved arnica, lousewort, elk sedge, wintergreen and wild rose are interspersed among the huckleberry. Occasional blooms of twin-flower, woodnymph, and fairy slipper delight the wildflower enthusiast. These forests often have a relatively dense understory compared to other coniferous forests, but the number of plant species is generally low.

Tree seedlings are abundant. They grow slowly, spruce commonly taking forty years to reach a four-foot height. Spruce and fir also reproduce through layering—the sprouting of roots and vertical shoots from tree branches that have been partially covered by litter. To layer, low branches need to be covered by snow well into the spring but cannot be covered long enough to foster growth of a snow mold (fungus) that kills the branches. The perpendicular shoots grow into trees with their own root systems. Layering becomes more common at higher elevations.

Spruce and fir trees are susceptible to a number of damaging agents. The Engelmann spruce beetle is the most serious insect pest. Epidemics have occurred throughout recorded history whenever an abundance of mature trees, slash, or trees killed by windthrow have provided a large beetle food source. Predation on beetles by insect parasites and predators, including woodpeckers, is important in keeping beetle populations under control.

The western spruce budworm attacks both spruce and fir. This is a small, foliage-feeding caterpillar that eats young needles, buds, and pollen. If budworm populations remain high and the infection lasts several years, older needles on the branches will not be replaced. Defoliation gradually ensues, and the trees may die. Wood-rotting fungi are common, more so in fir than in spruce. Windthrow kills trees growing on shallow soils, trees

The effects of fire on subalpine forests are long-lasting. Fire occurred here before the turn of the century, and the area is slowly being recolonized by Engelmann spruce. *J.C. Emerick.*

with defective roots, trees already injured by disease, and trees in overly dense stands that have been recently opened and exposed to strong winds. Lightning damage is frequent.

Spruce–fir ecosystems are climax ecosystems. No other tree species can reproduce in shade at these altitudes, and thus spruce and fir replace themselves and continue to dominate. Protected from fire by moist summers and from lumbering by remote and rugged terrain, sections of these high forests have maintained their basic character for thousands of years.

Once disturbed, forest recovery is slow because of slow growth and the short, cool growing season. Recovery rate depends on the severity of disturbance and on the type of community that invades after disturbance, which in turn depends on altitude. When an area is lightly burned, vegetation and soils are not severely altered. In their range lodgepole pine or aspen invade rapidly, these being replaced by spruce and fir within as little as fifty years. Most subalpine forests below 10,000 feet are now composed of these successional ecosystems. Above 10,000 feet, spruce and fir rapidly invade directly, providing that increased wind speeds do not favor invasion of limber and bristlecone pine. Since spruce seedlings are more tolerant of full sunlight than are fir, disturbed sites have a large proportion of spruce seedlings.

When sites below 10,000 feet are severely burned, lodgepole pine, aspen, or dry meadow ecosystems invade. At higher elevations, a sedge-bluegrass meadow invades. If plants of either type of meadow are dense, successful establishment of spruce and fir seedlings will require as much as three centuries. Tree invasion is more rapid on northern exposures and on light, gravelly soils derived from granite.

Recovery is slowest on disturbed areas adjacent to treeline. When these sites are no longer protected from the harsh alpine climate by mature trees, wind and solar radiation increase dramatically, snow accumulation and soil moisture decrease, and tree seedlings cannot survive. Tundra plants invade and treeline is depressed for centuries.

Animal Characteristics

The cool, moist environment of subalpine spruce–fir forests supports fewer animal species than do most lower elevation

Snowshoe hare. The hares, such as snowshoes and jackrabbits, bear young that are furred, alert, and able to move about soon after birth. Rabbits, such as cottontails, bear young that are naked, blind, and helpless.

forests. Deep, long-lasting winter snow cover restricts the movements of animals, and the short growing season limits the variety of berries, seeds, and other food from the understory vegetation.

Mammals regularly present are the pine marten, an arboreal weasel that feeds on pine squirrels and other small animals; the mouselike southern red-backed vole; and the widely distributed deer mouse. Other species include the snowshoe hare, a nocturnal solitary animal that changes color from brown to white with the seasons; the Canada lynx, a member of the cat family that preys on hares and mice; and the carnivorous wolverine. The lynx and wolverine have decreased during the last century. Their numbers in the region are now extremely low, and evidence of their existence is scant. They are considered endangered in Colorado.

Any disturbance that opens the forests and results in an increase of understory also increases mammalian abundance and diversity. Openings encourage flowering and fruiting of strawberries and blueberries, resulting in an increase in fruit-eating deer mice, least chipmunks, and southern red-backed voles. Slash provides abundant homes for small mammals. Forests with openings are more heavily used by mule deer and elk, and thickets in forests or openings with downed logs provide booming grounds for male blue grouse. Pine squirrels affect tree reproduction by eating a significant number of tree seeds, but they also enhance tree establishment by abandoning seed caches that eventually result in clumps of even-sized trees. Young fir trees are browsed by big game.

Most bird species eat bark insects and seeds. The gray jay, Clark's nutcracker, brown creeper, pine siskin, Townsend's solitaire, golden-crowned kinglet, and mountain chickadees are common. Goshawks fly swiftly through the forest in search of birds and small mammals, and rarer boreal owls occasionally nest here. Ruby-crowned kinglets sing persistently from tops of tall trees all day during the breeding season. Their songs are interrupted by chatterings of woodpeckers, softer "inks" of red-breasted nuthatches, and whistling notes of pine grosbeaks. Early mornings and evenings are graced by the ethereal, flutelike song of the hermit thrush.

When spruce–fir ecosystems are attacked by the Engelmann spruce beetle, downy, hairy, and three-toed woodpeckers move into the area. Woodpeckers can remove nearly all beetles from infested trees and are an effective natural control. Bark and wood-boring beetles also invade the forest following a fire. Woodpeckers increase correspondingly; one of the best places to see three-toed woodpeckers is in burned subalpine forests during the first few years after fire.

Human Use

Until the 1950s subalpine forests were seldom logged, although mining camps did use the trees for lumber in the late 1800s. Rugged terrain and remoteness have kept these ecosystems in pristine condition relative to other mountain forests. Their greatest human-related alterations probably have been caused by fire. Many of the extensive fires of the late 1800s and early 1900s were set purposefully by miners to clear the forests. Some of these fires moved upslope to treeline, cutting wide swaths through the spruce and fir.

Spruce–fir forests are extremely important as snow collection areas. Water is stored in their soils and in subalpine reservoirs. The greatest effective precipitation in the region occurs in these forests. Most of the major metropolitan areas along the Eastern Slope receive a substantial portion of their water from these ecosystems. The forests are also heavily used for hiking, skiing, and other forms of recreation.

Plants and Animals of Engelmann Spruce-Subalpine Fir Forests

PLANTS

Trees
fir, corkbark *Abies arizonica*
 subalpine *Abies bifolia*
spruce, Engelmann *Picea engelmannii*

Shrubs
blueberry *Vaccinium myrtillus*
broom huckleberry *Vaccinium scoparium*
cinquefoil, shrubby *Pentaphylloides floribunda*
cranberry, high-bush *Viburnum edule*
currant, Colorado *Ribes coloradense*
elder, red-berried *Sambucus microbotrys*
mountain lover *Paxistima myrsinites*
rose, Wood's *Rosa woodsii*

Herbaceous Plants
arnica, broad-leaved *Arnica latifolia*
 heart-leaved *Arnica cordifolia*
columbine, Colorado blue *Aquilegia caerulea*
 red *Aquilegia elegantula*
fairy slipper *Calypso bulbosa*
gentian, blue *Pneumonanthe affinis*
Jacob's ladder *Polemonium pulcherrimum*
lousewort, curled *Pedicularis racemosa*
muttongrass *Poa fendleriana*
needlegrass, Letterman *Stipa lettermanii*
pipsissewa *Chimaphila umbellata*
sedge, elk *Carex geyeri*
senecio, Wooton *Senecio wootonii*
sneezeweed, orange *Dugaldia hoopesii*
twin-flower *Linnaea borealis*
wintergreen, lesser *Pyrola minor*
woodnymph *Moneses uniflora*

ANIMALS

Birds
chickadee, mountain *Parus gambeli*
creeper, brown *Certhia americana*
crossbill, red *Loxia curvirostra*
finch, Cassin's *Carpodacus cassinii*
flycatcher, olive-sided *Contopus borealis*
Goshawk, northern *Accipiter gentilis*
grosbeak, evening *Coccothraustes vespertinus*
 ● **pine** *Pinicola enucleator*
grouse, blue *Dendragapus obscurus*
jay, **gray** *Perisoreus canadensis*
 Steller's *Cyanocitta stelleri*
junco, dark-eyed *Junco hyemalis*

kinglet, golden-crowned *Regulus satrapa*
 ruby-crowned *Regulus calendula*
nutcracker, Clark's *Nucifraga columbiana*
nuthatch, red-breasted *Sitta canadensis*
 white-breasted *Sitta carolinensis*
owl, boreal *Aegolius funerius*
raven, common *Corvus corax*
sapsucker, Williamson's *Sphyrapicus thyroideus*
siskin, pine *Carduelis pinus*
solitaire, Townsend's *Myadestes townsendi*

Birds (continued)

thrush, **hermit**   *Catharus guttatus*
    Swainson's   *Catharus ustulatus*
warbler, yellow-rumped
    Dendroica coronata
woodpecker, hairy   *Picoides villosus*
    • three-toed   *Picoides
    tridactylus*

Mammals

bat, hoary   *Lasiurus cinereus*
    long-legged myotis   *Myotis
    volans*
bear, black   *Ursus americanus*
bobcat   *Felis rufus*
chipmunk, least   *Tamias minimus*
    Uinta   *Tamias umbrinus*
cottontail, Nuttall's   *Sylvilagus
    nuttallii*
coyote   *Canis latrans*
deer, mule   *Odocoileus hemionus*
elk   *Cervus elaphus*
ermine   *Mustela erminea*
ground squirrel, golden-mantled
    Spermophilis lateralis
hare, snowshoe   *Lepus americanus*
jackrabbit, white-tailed   *Lepus
    townsendii*

lion, mountain   *Felis concolor*
lynx   *Felis lynx*
marmot, yellow-bellied   *Marmota
    flaviventris*
marten   *Martes americana*
mouse, deer   *Peromyscus
    maniculatus*
    western jumping   *Zapus princeps*
porcupine   *Erethizon dorsatum*
shrew, masked   *Sorex cinereus*
    montane   *Sorex monticolus*
    water   *Sorex palustris*
squirrel, pine   *Tamiasciurus
    hudsonicus*
vole, heather   *Phenacomys
    intermedius*
    long-tailed   *Microtus
    longicaudus*
    montane   *Microtus montanus*
    southern red-backed
    Clethrionomys gapperi
weasel, long-tailed   *Mustela frenata*
wolverine   *Gulo gulo*
woodrat, bushy-tailed   *Neotoma
    cinerea*

• Breeds almost exclusively in spruce-fir forests.
Species in bold-faced type are more common.

·14·
The Forest–Tundra Transition

Identifying Traits

Stunted, windswept trees mark the upper limit of forest growth. Here freezing temperatures and erosive blasts of ice crystals whipped by howling winter winds fragment the forest edge into isolated tree islands, often shaping individual trees into grotesque forms. This zone of transition between the treeless alpine tundra and the dense subalpine coniferous forest is known as *krummholz*, a German word meaning "crooked wood."

As elevation and wind intensity increase, trees of the upper subalpine forest begin to diminish in height. The tops of their crowns become one-sided as the windward branches are killed, producing "flag trees." On more exposed sites, flag trees are replaced by shrublike "cushion trees"—low-branching tree mats which often have a highly streamlined or pruned appearance. On higher slopes tree islands become more deformed and asymmetrical, smaller and less frequent, until trees are the size of small shrubs. Interspersed meadows of tundra herbs and shrubs increase in size with increasing altitude.

Flag trees. *National Park Service.*

Location

Krummholz ecosystems are found at the upper fringes of mountain forests, where they form a distinctive area of mixed subalpine and alpine species called the subalpine-alpine tundra ecotone. The ecosystems form a discontinuous band on all exposures between 11,000 and 12,000 feet. They are bordered on the bottom by timberline—continuous subalpine forests of upright trees—and on the top by treeline—the upper limit of tree species of any shape or size.

The size of krummholz bands varies. East-facing slopes have depressed timberlines and broad krummholz belts. Steep northern exposures and avalanche paths have narrow krummholz belts. Krummholz is found in valley bottoms and cirque heads of low elevations and is more extensive and higher on convex surfaces than on concave surfaces.

Site Characteristics

The climate of krummholz is within the limits necessary for tree survival but severe enough to limit tree growth to favorable microsites where wind and temperature extremes are moderated. Krummholz ecosystems throughout the Rockies are located approximately where the average temperature of the warmest month of the year is 50°F. The exact placement of krummholz depends on local wind, snow, soil, and animal conditions. Disturbance by avalanche or fire temporarily depresses the treeline.

Wind speeds may exceed 100 miles per hour, and snow may accumulate to depths of twelve feet or more. The frost-free season is less than two months. Annual average summer temperatures are low (44° to 48°F), and mean annual soil temperatures are near freezing. Soil factors may be locally important, but in general soil does not limit plant growth.

Plant Characteristics

The dominant trees in krummholz ecosystems are Engelmann spruce and subalpine fir; limber pine are abundant on especially windy, rocky sites. Bristlecone pine mixes with limber pine in the central and southern part of the region south of Berthoud Pass. Small numbers of quaking aspen and lodgepole pine may be present. Vegetation between the tree islands consists of herbs,

Upper treeline near Trail Ridge in Rocky Mountain National Park. *J.C. Emerick.*

willows, bog birch, and mosses of subalpine forests that are replaced by tundra herbs and willows as altitude increases. Some patches of ground remain bare. Because of the mixing of species of both climax regions, krummholz has a far richer flora than either of these other climax regions.

Krummholz trees are growing at the limits of their environmental requirements. Growth is slow; krummholz spruce several hundred years old may have a trunk diameter of four inches and be only a few feet tall. The summer krummholz temperatures are just warm enough for tree survival. Trees cannot survive lower temperatures or shorter growing seasons because they cannot make enough food to maintain their existing tissues and replace plant parts killed during the winter. Cold winter temperatures do not in themselves limit tree growth; the growing season must be long enough to allow new tissues to harden before the onset of winter.

Several factors determine the size and shape of trees. Although trees may grow symmetrically in the summer, needles on the windward side of the tree turn yellow or brown the following winter. Ice crystals carried by the wind pit the needles, causing desiccation. Windward twigs lose their needles and are broken off; windward buds fail to open.

Snow accumulates in dense branches on the leeward side of tree islands. The snow forms a blanket that protects trees from severe temperatures and winds. However, if snow is too deep or remains too long into the summer, it may harm trees. The snow's weight can physically injure and break branches, the growing season is significantly shortened, and snow mold kills branches under late-lying snow. Thus optimal tree growth occurs when neither wind or snow conditions are extreme, when the wind moves snow into drifts that are neither too deep nor too shallow.

The interactions of wind and snow result in tree islands of predictable shapes. Where snow accumulation is great, the leeward branches are killed by the snow mold while windward branches are killed by wind. The only tree branches and seedlings to survive are those on the sides of islands, where neither snow nor wind are excessive. As seedlings to the sides of islands mature and reproduce, tree islands slowly grow into thin bands crossing hillsides horizontally. Where wind is more severe, the only branches and seedlings to survive are those protected by snow on the leeward side of islands. These tree islands form long, narrow strips that run vertically upslope.

Growing tree islands overrun meadow ecosystems or change their environment and species composition. For example, increased snow accumulation in the lee of the island destroys meadows of kobresia, since this small sedge does not tolerate snow cover. Other herbs that are more tolerant of snow cover replace kobresia.

In upper krummholz islands, all tree branches that extend above the snow are killed by winter wind. This does not occur in lower, more protected krummholz islands. Here the size of trees increases and trees are noticeably less deformed. Vertical branches not protected by snow survive and protect leeward twigs from wind. The vertical branches and horizontal twigs form flag trees.

In addition to the stresses of wind and snow, krummholz trees must perform all of their physiological process during a very short growing season. Tree growth does not begin until late June to mid-July, depending on the tree species and microenvironment. Willow species start growing first, followed by quaking aspen, limber pine, fir, and spruce. Conifer buds grow only 0.6 to 1.7 inches a year. Little growth occurs after mid-August.

Tree islands originate where seedlings are sheltered from wind by a rock, crevice, or stump. As the seedling grows, it alters the wind speed and snow accumulation patterns, forming microsites where additional tree reproduction can occur. Following initial seedling establishment, most reproduction occurs through layering—sprouting of roots from existing tree branches that are covered with snow and debris. Once roots are established, a vertical stem grows into a new trunk. Thus, the slow growing krummholz trees do not expend a large percentage of their energy producing seeds, a process that requires several summers of favorable weather conditions and energy storage.

Over decades some tree islands slowly migrate over the landscape. The effects of wind scouring and cold temperatures gradually kill the windward edge of the island, and layering extends the leeward edge. Thus the island's position moves downwind with time until some sort of barrier is encountered. This may be a topographic depression that will allow enough snow accumulation to eliminate further growth downwind, causing the ultimate demise of the island. Evidence of such movement has been observed on Niwot Ridge west of Ward. Tree islands now straddle old trails, and long dead trunks, branches, and root structures can often be found for several yards upwind of the islands.

Limber and bristlecone pines do not reproduce by layering,

A small tree island composed of subalpine fir. *National Park Service.*

The yellow-bellied marmot, a resident of parklands and meadows throughout the mountains, is frequently seen by hikers at timberline. Their loud chirps are often heard echoing off rock walls of high mountain basins; thus, these rodents are also known as "whistle-pigs." *Stephen Jones.*

but twisted trunks of individual trees extend across the krummholz where wind blows all snow cover from the branches.

Although treeline is advancing in some parts of the world, it is thought to be in equilibrium with the climate in the Rocky Mountains; that is, unless climatic conditions change, treeline location will remain the same. Time modifies the shape, size and age of individual tree islands, but the integrated character of any large section of krummholz is consistent as long as disturbance is excluded. In this sense, undisturbed krummholz is a climax ecosystem.

If treeline is depressed by avalanche, extensive collection of campfire wood, fire, or similar disturbance, reinvasion of trees is extremely slow. Tree removal exaggerates the severity of climate. Wind and solar radiation increase, snow cover and soil moisture decrease, and shrubs and herbs are the only species that can survive. These meadows are invaded by spruce, fir, or limber pine only where climate is moderate, such as sites in the lee of rocks. Even here tree invasion is hampered by rodents and birds that eat tree seeds and seedlings and by competition from herbs. Areas burned in the 1800s still have not recovered.

Animal Characteristics

Animals of krummholz ecosystems are largely those found on the tundra. Krummholz ecosystems are important animal habitats because they combine the positive aspects of forests and tundra ecosystems. Krummholz herbs provide a seasonally rich food source, and dense mats of tree island needles provide protective cover. White-tailed ptarmigan spend the winter in the shelter of krummholz, and mule deer and elk rest here during hot summer days. White-crowned sparrows nest primarily in krummholz.

Human Use

Krummholz ecosystems have been altered by fire and recreational use. Numerous fires were started purposefully by miners at lower elevations in the late 1800s, and the fires sometimes burned upslope, destroying strips of krummholz. The most obvious recreational pressure is the cutting of ski slopes through krummholz. Less obvious but equally destructive is collection of twisted krummholz wood for campfires or home decoration. Krummholz wood, even if dead, serves the important function of protecting tree parts from the wind. Once dead branches are removed, windward sections of tree islands die. High altitude ecosystems are extremely sensitive to small changes in their environment. They often require centuries to recover from change and thus demand unusually careful human use.

White-crowned sparrow.

·15·
Alpine Tundra

Identifying Traits

Alpine tundra is a windswept, treeless area that includes the highest altitudes of the mountains. It is an area of contrasts. A hiker might need to hide from intense sunshine one hour and the next hour be caught in a summer thunderstorm. Much of the tundra appears to be barren rock, but acres of tundra with deep soils have abundant small plants, insects, birds, and mammals. Some areas contain vegetation comparable in lushness to rich prairies. Plants are arranged in a complex mosaic of widely differing types of communities, which change with varying soils, wind exposures, snow accumulation, and other factors. During the winter areas free of snow may lie a few feet from snowdrifts fifteen feet deep. In some places, one can walk a hundred feet and cross half-a-dozen types of plant communities. Some sections of tundra have been called a high altitude desert, but this "desert" may be interspersed with meltwater ponds and wet meadows.

The key to understanding tundra ecosystems is to reduce one's sense of scale. One needs to get down on hands and knees to see the ecosystems, as well as to see the tremendous variations in communities and environments that can occur in one small area.

A pageantry of wildflowers begins in late spring and often is well underway before the plants of lower subalpine forests begin to bloom.
J.C. Emerick.

Location

The tundra lies above krummholz ecosystems, extending from treeline (11,200-12,000 feet, depending on latitude and slope exposure) to the mountain tops. Plant communities vary tremendously in shape and plant composition, but these qualities are not conspicuously correlated with changes in slope exposure. Communities may vary in size from a few square inches to several acres.

Alpine tundra of the Rockies is a high altitude counterpart to the high latitude, treeless stretches of Arctic tundra. The two areas share many of the same plants. Tundra is also a counterpart to the nearly treeless plains: both areas are dominated by herbs because climate is too severe to support tree life.

Site Characteristics

The climate of the alpine tundra is cold and windy and is similar in many respects to Arctic climate. Annual precipitation is between forty and sixty inches, most falling in the winter as snow. The effective precipitation is far below forty inches, since much of the snow is blown from the tundra into krummholz and subalpine areas. Some snow remains as an addition to permanent snowfields. Wind speeds exceed 100 mph, with extreme gusts from October to February. The mean annual temperature is below freezing, and the frost-free season is approximately one-and-one-half months long. Diurnal temperature variations are slight because of air mixing by constant winds.

The texture and moisture of tundra soils varies widely from site to site. Deep, mature, residual soils cover portions of unglaciated ridges. They are scattered between large rocks brought to the surface over a thousand years ago when soils were churned as they were repeatedly frozen and thawed. These rocks often form large reticulate patterns across the landscape, called stone polygons. Some of these polygons may be several yards across. On steeper slopes similar processes have formed elongate rows of rocks called stone stripes. Today freeze-thaw processes are limited mainly to the upper few inches of soil on sites where there is an abundance of soil moisture in spring and fall. Soil ice is found in all soils in the winter. Soil temperatures

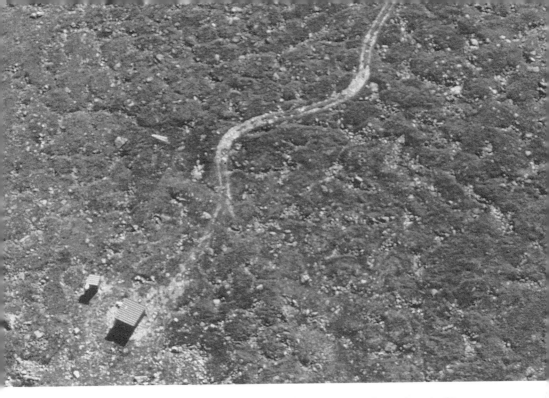

Stone polygons, a patterned ground feature, as seen from the air. These polygons on Niwot Ridge in the Front Range were formed when the climate was more moist than it is now. For scale, the roof of the hut at the bottom of the picture measures 14 by 16 feet. *J.C. Emerick.*

are sufficiently low in some areas to allow the formation of isolated patches of permafrost, soils that are permanently frozen. In valleys that were shaped and scoured by glaciers, most soils are young and very rocky and have originated from glacial debris.

Plant Characteristics

Tundra vegetation consists of a low growth of shrubs, cushion plants, and small forbs with brilliantly colored flowers, and of lush meadows of narrow-leaved sedges and grasses. These plants cover gentle slopes and rock crevices filled with soil. Rock surfaces are partially covered with more primitive plants—lichens and mosses.

Tundra plant communities are subjected to a rigorous climate and very short growing season. Plant adaptations to these factors are numerous. All species are slow-growing perennials except for the rare annual koenigia, a tiny member of the buckwheat family.

Plants save energy by using the same root masses from year to year. Ninety percent of the total structure of some alpine tundra communities consists of subterranean roots, which store reserves of nutrients and energy for periods of poor growing conditions. Although flowers are often large, other plant parts are dwarfed, again saving energy and resulting in forms that have minimal wind resistance. The common low rosettes and mats of leaves, many of which are covered with a waxy layer of cutin or with dense hairs, lose a minimal amount of water and heat to the wind. Tundra plants produce flowers and fruits within a matter of weeks. Although most alpine tundra species are physiologically active only from April through October, many of them have green, viable leaves through the winter. Tundra plants can start to grow and break bud before the soil thaws or snow cover melts.

Plants set viable seed, and seedlings cover some sites profusely. However, as is true whenever climate places severe restraints on plant growth, asexual means of reproduction are utilized frequently. For example, some of the flowers of alpine bistort are replaced by swollen buds called bulblets, which

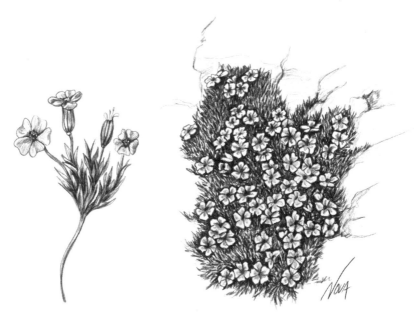

Moss pink, one of the cushion plants of alpine tundra in the Rocky Mountains, also occurs in tundra regions in the Arctic and throughout the Northern Hemisphere.

sprout leaves, fall to the ground, and sprout roots. The roots can take hold immediately and absorb water and nutrients for the rapidly growing plant.

Some tundra species, such as alpine avens and American bistort, are found in many types of tundra communities, but most species are limited by specific environmental requirements. The plants form a patchwork quilt of numerous miniature plant communities, the environment of each patch differing slightly from that of its neighbors. One can easily step on two or three different communities at one time.

The location of most communities is correlated with the length of time snow covers the ground. Snow accumulates in depressions and to the lee of objects; strong winds remove it from other sites. Melting snow contributes to the soil moisture of downslope communities. Other factors such as soil development, drainage, movement of soil by small animals, frost action, and gravity contribute to the determination of community location. These factors contrast sharply with those of lower mountain forests, where slope exposure and resulting variations in temperature, light, and moisture control ecosystem location.

Two communities are found on areas that are snow free through the winter. Dense clumps of the fine-leaved sedge kobresia dominate level or gently rolling areas with fine-textured, humus-rich, stable, deep soils that are moist through the growing season. This community supports more species of wildflowers, grasses, and mosses than any other tundra plant community. Kobresia communities are often located in the center of ancient patterned ground figures. Bands of rock selaginella, alpine avens, and dwarf clover form successional bands on the coarser soils between the kobresia and the large boulders of patterned ground. Kobresia stands may cover acres of gentle alpine ridges with lush vegetation.

The tundra's colorful rock gardens, fellfields, are found on sites tipped into the wind. Here wind removes snow throughout the winter and subjects plants to severe desiccation. The communities are described as alpine deserts. Plant shapes minimize wind resistance. The low round mats, cushion plants, are nestled against the earth, with taproots that protrude into soil between exposed rocks. Flower size is large relative to the rest of the plant. A variety of species is found in fellfields, common species including moss pink, alpine sandwort, alpine phlox, alpine avens, nailwort, dwarf and whiproot clovers, and mountain avens (mountain dryad).

Some areas have snow cover through the winter that melts in spring or early summer. If soils of these areas are moist into the summer, they are dominated by the bunchgrass, tufted hairgrass. Hairgrass forms lush meadows that may be interspersed with flowering plants, such as alpine avens and bistort and occasionally prostrate willows.

Dense willow thickets often occupy depressions on the lee side of broad ridges. During the winter these thickets, which may be several feet in height, are completely covered by snow that disappears by late spring. This blanket of snow protects the overwintering buds of the willows from freezing temperatures and blowing snow. Thus willows have the tallest perennial structure of any species growing above the krummholz.

Shallow depressions that collect snow through the winter and hold it until early summer are dominated by the purple-flowered Parry's clover and dwarf willows. The yellow-flowered snow buttercup dominates deeper depressions that hold snow even longer. This is the buttercup whose blooms push through the edges of receding snowbanks.

On some ridge sides, the action of heavy wet snows and freeze-thaw processes have formed depressions that hold snow nine months or more of each year. Melting snowbanks shorten the growing season of areas they cover and provide abundant water to nearby downslope ecosystems. Receding snowlines reveal zones of plants that need moist soil and can survive their momentary summers. Each zone is dominated by a different species of sedge, grass, or rush, or by the small, yellow-flowered sibbaldia. Drummond's rush and Pyrennian sedge are common, as are lichens and mosses. Zones exposed late in the summer have few species and smaller, more widely spaced plants than zones exposed early in the summer.

Some areas have very moist soils through the summer because of high groundwater levels. In some cases, this accumulation of moisture may be due to underlying permafrost, which restricts drainage. On ridge sides these areas form terraces that are slowly sliding downslope—solifluction terraces. The moist soil on top of the terraces is covered with a lush growth of forbs, grasses, and sedges, dominant species being Rocky Mountain sedge, marsh marigold, elephantella, and rose crown.

Very moist areas on flat sites or gentle slopes without late-lying snow commonly are covered with soil hummocks dominated by willows and sedges. The large hummocks (to three feet wide and eighteen inches tall) are interspersed with pools of water.

All of the plant communities discussed to this point appear to be climax communities because they change so slowly. Numerous other plant communities can be found, several of which are typical of disturbed areas. Tundra ecosystems are subjected to frequent disturbance from soil movement and small animals. Northern pocket gophers produce miles of burrows that push up

Alpine avens.

White-tailed ptarmigan, winter plumage. *James C. Halfpenny.*

the soil and disrupt plant cover. The gophers also eat the plant roots, and voles can overgraze acres of above-ground plant parts.

Many patterned ground features are relicts dating from 1000 to 4000 years ago, when the climate was wetter. However, soil moving processes still operate on a smaller scale. Wet, poorly drained soils are churned by repeated freezing and thawing, and solifluction terraces still roll imperceptibly down the slopes. Once plant cover is removed, thin strands of needle ice form in the soil, pushing it upward, dislodging seeds, uprooting seedlings and delaying revegetation.

After disturbance has ceased, revegetation is slower than in any other mountain ecosystem because of the short growing season and harsh climate. Recovery may require centuries. Successional communities vary with the length of time since disturbance. The most conspicuous are "gopher gardens." Here the moist soils tilled by northern pocket gophers grow dense, tall plants that

White-tailed ptarmigan, summer plumage. *Stephen Jones.*

have large, bright flowers. Common species include alpine avens, sky pilot, bistort, green mertensia, and grasses (bluegrasses, wheatgrass, alpine timothy). The "gopher gardens" are invaded by cushion plants after wind has eroded the mounds of fine textured soil particles, leaving only gravel.

Animal Characteristics

The tundra fauna is composed of a small number of species, but due to the lack of forest cover and the animals' conspicuous habits, many are well-known to the hiker. Three bird species nest primarily on the tundra. The brown-capped rosy finch nests on cliffs. It forages on permanent snowfields, where insects blown in from surrounding tundra and lower elevations become inactive and are easily caught. The American pipit nests in tundra meadows, where it is seen bobbing its tail while standing on a rock. The white-tailed ptarmigan is the only year-round bird resident. This grouse is pure white during the winter, becoming a mottled brown in summer. It survives in the winter by bedding in snowdrifts protected from the wind and by eating the energy-rich buds of willow shrubs. Horned larks nest in tundra meadows as well as in plains grasslands, and tundra willow thickets and krummholz are nesting habitats for white-crowned sparrows. Common ravens are frequently seen riding air currents over cliffs where they nest along rocky ledges. Other birds are seen in the alpine tundra in late summer—especially hawks, which migrate along the mountains.

No mammal species are restricted to the tundra, although several species are abundant here as well as at lower elevations. A large rodent, the yellow-bellied marmot, and the pika, a small relative of the rabbit, both live on rocky areas and alert hikers with their high pips. Yellow-bellied marmots hibernate through the winter, but the pika is active year-round. It harvests forbs and grasses into large hay piles for a winter food source. The pika lives chiefly in alpine and upper subalpine rock fields.

Pika.

Bighorn sheep. *W. Perry Conway.*

Northern pocket gophers and microtine rodents such as montane and long-tailed voles are active in tundra turfs and meadows, where they significantly influence vegetation. The gophers make extensive burrows that are also used by microtines. Burrowing action changes the environment for plants by smothering them with soil, aerating and fertilizing the soil, and increasing the potential for wind and water erosion and needle ice formation. Plant species composition changes dramatically and climax species might not return for centuries.

The number of microtine rodents on the tundra fluctuates dramatically. Some years animals can hardly be found. Other years they are so abundant that acres of tundra appear to be mowed after the small voles have grazed. Such grazing can change plant succession; for example, heavily grazed rocky areas are profusely invaded by alpine avens.

Mule deer and elk feed on the tundra in summer. Bighorn sheep were formerly seasonal tundra residents and were plentiful until the late 1800s. They are still present but in smaller numbers. White-tailed jackrabbits, snowshoe hares, least chipmunks, shrews, long-tailed weasels, ermine, coyotes, bobcats, and red foxes may be found on the tundra. Mountain goats have been introduced in some areas and can be seen occasionally on the tundra in the vicinity of Mount Evans.

Invertebrates are abundant, although the number of types is not large. Leafhoppers, grasshoppers, mites, scarab beetles, wolf and crab spiders, flies, bees, and a few butterfly species are active during the day. Abundant ground beetles, dwarf spiders, and millipedes are active during the cold nights. Insects are often wingless or have reduced wings, a trait usually explained as an adaptation to strong winds. Tundra spiders do not build webs for the same reason. Insect larvae may require two or more years to mature because of the short growing season.

Human Use

In spite of their inaccessibility, tundra ecosystems have been used by humans since prehistoric times. High terraces were used as butchering and camping sites by early hunters over 7000 years ago. Domestic sheep have grazed tundra areas throughout the Rocky Mountains since the turn of the century. This practice still continues in many parts of Colorado. Sheep have cut trails across slopes and trampled areas where they have bedded. Butterfly populations have been reduced as meadows were overgrazed, and areas of heavy use have suffered increased erosion. Undoubtedly other ecosystem changes occurred but were not recorded. Since high altitude causes heart failure in cattle, cattle herds have not been extensively grazed in the tundra. More recently off-road vehicles have ruined sections of tundra, as have hikers who do not use established trails.

Even moderate recreational use can alter tundra ecosystems for centuries. Almost three decades of studies in Rocky Mountain National Park revealed that trampling by large numbers of people resulted in changes in the species present and in a decrease in the number of plant species, plant density, and flower and seed production. Ecosystems vary in their vulnerability to trampling. Areas of high soil moisture are more easily damaged than dry areas. Lush herb stands with large forbs are more easily damaged than grass and sedge turfs. Fellfield ecosystems can be destroyed by a few weeks of heavy use, but they can recover within a few decades if undisturbed. Kobresia meadows, on the other hand, are relatively disturbance resistant, but once the turf is broken, estimated recovery time is a thousand years.

Even minor disturbances in the tundra can have large effects. A piece of litter can kill the plants it covers in three or four summer weeks. Return of vegetation may take twenty years. The removal of a rock can start a cycle of erosion and needle ice activity that results in the disturbed area concentrically expanding. The erosion of a small amount of soil may seem like a minute disturbance, but on the tundra, small amounts of soil require centuries to replace.

Tundra communities are small, complex, and delicate. The plants are growing close to the limits of possible life. Like other high-altitude ecosystems, a small change in exposure to climatic variables can bring large results, and ecosystems with cold, short growing seasons recover slowly. More than ecosystems of lower altitudes, tundra ecosystems need to be treated with great care.

Plants and Animals of the Alpine Tundra

Species composition depends on local site characteristics, notably soil moisture, soil depth and rockiness, amount of snow accumulation, and exposure to wind. Listed birds are mainly summer residents.

PLANTS

Shrubs
willow, arctic *Salix arctica*
barrenground *Salix brachycarpa*
planeleaf *Salix planifolia*
snow *Salix reticulata* ssp. *nivalis*

Grasses and Grasslike Plants
bluegrass, alpine *Poa alpina*
skyline *Poa cusickii* ssp. *epilis*
hairgrass, tufted *Deschampsia cespitosa*
kobresia *Kobresia myosuroides*
rush, Drummond's *Juncus drummondii*
sedge, Pyrennian *Carex crandallii*
Rocky Mountain *Carex scopulorum*
timothy, alpine *Phleum commutatum*
trisetum, spike *Trisetum spicatum*
wheatgrass, spreading *Elymus scribneri*
woodrush, spike *Luzula spicata*

Forbs
avens, alpine *Acomastylis rossii*
mountain *Dryas octopetala*
bistort, alpine *Bistorta vivipara*
American *Bistorta bistortoides*
bitterroot, pygmy *Lewisia pygmaea*
buttercup, snow *Ranunculus adoneus*
clover, dwarf *Trifolium nanum*
Parry's *Trifolium parryi*
whiproot *Trifolium dasyphyllum*

daisy, one-headed *Erigeron simplex*
black-headed *Erigeron melanocephalus*
elephantella *Pedicularis groenlandica*
forget-me-not, alpine *Eritrichum aretioides*
gentian, arctic *Gentianodes algida*
king's crown *Rhodiola integrifolia*
koenigia *Koenigia islandica*
lily, alp *Lloydia serotina*
marsh marigold *Psychrophila leptosepala*
mertensia, green *Mertensia lanceolata*
nailwort *Paronychia pulvinata*
old-man-on-the-mountain
Rydbergia grandiflora
paintbrush, alpine *Castilleja puberula*
phlox, alpine *Phlox pulvinata*
pink, moss *Silene acaulis*
rock selaginella *Selaginella densa*
rose crown *Clementsia rhodantha*
sandwort, alpine *Lidia obtusiloba*
saxifrage, snowball *Micranthes rhomboidea*
sibbaldia *Sibbaldia procumbens*
sky pilot *Polemonium viscosum*
sorrel, alpine *Oxyria digyna*
stonecrop *Sedum lanceolatum*
wallflower, alpine *Erysimum capitatum*

ANIMALS

Amphibians (in moist places)
frog, boreal chorus *Pseudacris triseriata*

toad, boreal *Bufo boreas*

Birds
falcon, prairie *Falco mexicanus*

● **finch, rosy** *Leucosticte arctoa*

lark, horned *Eremophila alpestris*

● **pipit, American** *Anthus rubescens*

● **ptarmigan, white-tailed**
Lagopus leucurus

raven, common *Corvus corax*

sparrow, white-crowned
Zonotrichia leucophrys

wren, rock *Salpinctes obsoletus*

Mammals
badger *Taxidea taxus*

bobcat *Felis rufus*

chipmunk, least *Tamias minimus*

coyote *Canis latrans*

deer, mule *Odocoileus hemionus*

elk *Cervus elaphus*

ermine *Mustela erminea*

fox, red *Vulpes vulpes*

goat, mountain* *Oreamnos americanus*

ground squirrel, golden-mantled
Spermophilus lateralis

hare, snowshoe *Lepus americanus*

jackrabbit, white-tailed *Lepus townsendii*

lion, mountain *Felis concolor*

marmot, yellow-bellied *Marmota flaviventris*

marten *Martes americana*

mouse, deer *Peromyscus maniculatus*

western jumping *Zapus princeps*

pika *Ochotona princeps*

pocket gopher, northern
Thomomys talpoides

sheep, bighorn *Ovis canadensis*

shrew, dwarf *Sorex nanus*

masked *Sorex cinereus*

montane *Sorex monticolus*

vole, long-tailed *Microtus longicaudus*

montane *Microtus montanus*

weasel, long-tailed *Mustela frenata*

woodrat, bushy-tailed *Neotoma cinerea*

● Breeds almost exclusively in the tundra.

* Introduced

Species in bold-faced type are more common.

·16·

Aquatic Ecosystems

Earlier chapters of this book have discussed terrestrial, or land-based, ecosystems, with only brief mention of aquatic habitats in the chapters on riparian lands. This chapter describes life in the watery realm within streams, rivers, ponds, lakes, and reservoirs. Because of significant fundamental differences between aquatic and terrestrial ecosystems, the organization of this chapter differs from that of previous ones.

Adaptations of aquatic organisms differ greatly from those of terrestrial plants and animals. The relative importance of certain environmental factors also is different. In aquatic ecosystems, the distribution of organisms is determined by water temperature, clarity, current, the amount and kind of dissolved materials, and the types of materials that line the stream or lake bottom.

Water tends to provide a more constant environment for its inhabitants than does air because water moderates climatic fluctuations. Most notably, water temperatures lag behind fluctuations in air temperature, with water temperatures rarely reaching the extremes of air temperatures. Thus, aquatic creatures often remain active in their ice-covered watery realms long after migrating birds have left and the first snows of fall have driven the smaller terrestrial animals to the comfort of nests and dens.

Many substances dissolve in water, which transports them from

Tony Oswald

place to place. The amount of dissolved plant nutrients, such as nitrogen, potassium, and phosphorus, is of critical importance to the growth and abundance of algae and other aquatic plants that form the base of most aquatic food chains. In contrast, the type and number of insects, fish, and other animals that will thrive in a particular location often are dictated by levels of oxygen and other dissolved materials. Many streams in mineralized regions are devoid of aquatic animals because of high heavy metal concentrations or extreme acidity. Countless ponds and streams are affected by pesticides, herbicides, and other pollutants. The water chemistry (and therefore the organisms) in virtually all of our aquatic ecosystems has in some way been influenced by human activities.

Water current is among the most important factors that influence aquatic life forms. Current affects the amount of water turbulence, concentrations of dissolved gasses, and characteristics of the bottom sediments. The lifestyles of organisms found in any given location are dictated by the strength of the currents to which they are subjected. Organisms and environments of the moving-water ecosystems of streams and rivers are much different than those of relatively still lake and pond waters. Because of this, the discussion of moving waters has been separated from that of lakes and ponds.

STREAMS AND RIVERS

Environmental Characteristics

Characteristics of streams, and thus the habitats they provide for animals and plants, change with elevation as the streams flow from the mountains to lower elevations. At the highest reaches, water from melting snow has little opportunity to dissolve materials from the rocks and soil. The water is cold and almost as pure as distilled water. Stream beds are steep and strewn with boulders over which the water tumbles in noisy cascades, pausing from time to time in quieter pools. Levels of dissolved oxygen in the water are high because of the agitation and cold temperatures.

At middle elevations, stream channels are not as steep. Currents decrease although the volume of water is greater. Stream beds alternate between boulders and rocks (in sections of rapids) and sand and gravel (in slower waters). In the lower sections of many glacial valleys, stream beds are nearly flat, and bottoms are covered by mud and silt. In such places, streams meander through meadows and willows, or may enter beaver ponds or small lakes. The water is still high in oxygen, but by now it has accumulated a moderate concentration of dissolved minerals. Summer water temperatures may be relatively warm. Below glacial valleys, stream beds may steepen again, returning to stretches of rapids.

Where mid-elevation stream beds have a moderate gradient, relatively deep, quiet pools alternate with riffles: shallower areas with a steeper slope, faster current, and a bed of larger, often cobble-sized rocks. Pools and riffles each provide a unique habitat to stream inhabitants, their differences being reflected in the types of insects and other invertebrates found in each area and in the area's use by fish.

A section of riffles and pools along a mountain stream. *Tony Oswald*

At lower elevations, where streams leave the mountains, stream gradients decline sharply and current velocities slow considerably, particularly on the Eastern Slope. Concentrations of dissolved salts are relatively high, and oxygen content is often much lower than in the mountains, particularly when water temperatures are warm during the summer. Accumulations of suspended particulate materials and other substances reduce the water's clarity. At times streams are extremely turbid, especially during spring run-off or heavy thunderstorms in the mountains. The sediments of low elevation stream beds are more fine-grained than in the mountains, and consist of gravel, sand, or silt.

On the Eastern Slope, as the larger river channels reach the plains, they widen and divide, forming braided channels with many sandbars and islands. During periods of high flow, the channels shift from side to side, removing some islands and forming new ones. However, Western Slope rivers in many places have downcut into the relatively soft sedimentary formations of the Colorado Plateau, forming narrow valleys or canyons that confine channels and reduce braiding.

Some streams provide special habitats for aquatic life. Geothermal springs, for example, supply their inhabitants with warm water all year. In contrast, in intermittent streams, water is found year-round only at spring-fed headwaters or in potholes.

In the Rocky Mountains, much of the annual precipitation falls as snow in the higher elevations. The snow accumulates over the winter months and above 9000 feet, maximum depths typically are reached in April. With warming spring temperatures, melting snow begins to increase flows in mountain streams and rivers. Peak stream flows are reached during the spring and early summer, when they are often ten times greater than the lowest flows in the fall.

High springtime flows are a natural event and are important to the ecology of the aquatic ecosystems as well as to the surrounding riparian zones. Flooding produces and maintains floodplains, and scours and rejuvenates pool and riffle areas. During peak flows, water overflows stream banks to flood adjacent lowlands and wetlands, replenishing soil moisture and encouraging the sprouting and growth of riparian vegetation. Most aquatic life forms typical of mountain stream habitats are adapted to seasonal flooding and are not greatly affected unless the floods are of unusually high intensity. During the summer, thunderstorms may cause local flooding, and run-off occasionally is so great that it produces severe and destructive scouring of the stream channel.

Healthy riparian ecosystems are of prime importance to associated aquatic habitats. Riparian vegetation helps hold stream bank soils in place, which in turn reduces the sediment loads of streams. Riparian lands also contribute organic detritus to the streams, which often serves as the most important source of energy for aquatic food webs.

Aquatic Life

As elevation and the stream environment change, so do communities of aquatic organisms. Few aquatic plants can survive the cold, swiftly moving, nutrient-poor waters of the highest streams. In these places the major energy source is organic detritus, mainly leaves, twigs, and other plant fragments, which serve as food for microbes, aquatic insects, and other small organisms.

Brown trout, common in many of the larger mountain streams, was introduced to the region before the turn of the century. *Tony Oswald*

At middle elevations, where currents lessen and more phosphorus, nitrogen, and other plant nutrients are available in the water, a slippery coating of periphyton covers the stream bed rocks. This living film, also known as *aufwuchs*, is an extremely important food source for insects and other invertebrates, and consists of green algae, diatoms, golden brown algae, red algae, blue-green bacteria, and water moss (commonly *Fontinalis*). Periphyton increases the biological productivity of mid-elevation streams far above that of higher reaches.

Especially productive are the riffles, where periphyton-covered rocks support a diverse insect community. The silty bottoms of intervening pools do not contain appreciable growths of periphyton. However, pools accumulate detritus and may be important sites for organic decomposition and nutrient recycling. Sedges, rushes, and other rooted aquatic vegetation may grow along slowly flowing stream margins in pool areas. Riffles are important feeding areas for trout, while pools provide quieter water for them to rest.

Farther downstream, as streams widen and coalesce to form rivers, turbidity limits in-stream growth of aquatic plants, although marshes in quiet backwaters may be very productive. Marshes are important rearing areas for many fish species, and often harbor diverse aquatic plant communities typically dominated by cattail and bulrush.

Streams and rivers are inhabited by a variety of aquatic organisms. The largest organisms are vertebrate animals—fish and a few amphibians and reptiles. Beaver, muskrat, water shrews, and other mammals are associated with aquatic ecosystems; these animals are discussed in the riparian ecosystem chapters. Far more numerous are the invertebrates: insects, snails, flatworms, leeches, scuds, and other small animals without backbones. These are called macroinvertebrates because they can be seen without magnification. Microinvertebrates such as water fleas, copepods, protozoans, rotifers, and other groups are also present.

Insects in their immature stages form one of the largest groups of aquatic macroinvertebrates; few adult forms of insects are actually aquatic with the exception of water beetles. These immature stages (nymph, larva, and pupa) typically represent most of the insect's life cycle, sometimes lasting for two or more years, while the adult insect may live only an hour to a few weeks. The emer-

gence of adults from the immature aquatic stage is highly syn-
chronized in some species. Dense swarms of mating mayflies may
appear suddenly, but last only a few hours or days.

Insects show a wide range of behavioral or structural adaptations to life in turbulent waters. Many are strongly flattened or
otherwise streamlined to reduce resistance to the current. They
often have claws, hooks, friction pads, or suckers, enabling them
to cling tenaciously to submerged rocks and branches. Other organisms, such as blackfly and caddisfly larvae, depend on sticky
secretions to attach themselves to objects. Still others avoid the
strongest currents, living instead under or between rocks. Some
caddisfly larvae live in portable cases to which they attach large
grains of sand or gravel as ballast to keep from being swept
away. In lowland reaches, where currents are slow and the bottom
is soft and fine-grained, some mayfly larvae construct burrows, although these may be more for protection against predators than
an adaptation to water currents.

Many, if not most, insects face into the current and tend to
move upstream. This helps compensate for their being periodi-
cally swept downstream. Nevertheless, many insects are displaced
by the current, a phenomenon known as drift. It is common for
adults of some aquatic species to fly upstream before laying eggs,
a behavior that also helps to counteract drift.

Feeding habits of aquatic insects are varied. Most feed on fine
organic debris when newly hatched from eggs, but as they grow
larger they develop more specialized habits of feeding and are
thus named scrapers, collectors, shredders, and predators. Scrapers feed on periphyton that is attached to rocks, wood, and other
firm surfaces. Collectors gather organic detritus, some by crawling
along the bottom, others by filtering detritus from the water. Some
caddisfly larvae construct silk nets to collect waterborne detritus.
Shredders feed on relatively large items: herbivore shredders on
leaves and stems of aquatic plants, and detritivore shredders on
large fragments of detritus. Predators feed on insects or other animals, including fish larvae.

The relative importance of each of these feeding types in any
particular stream segment largely depends on the type of food
available. In the highest streams where most of the available food
consists of detritus, collectors and shredders typically predominate. Where nutrients and light favor the establishment of peri-

phyton on rocks, scrapers are an important component. In lower streams and rivers where turbidity and soft bottoms limit periphyton, and where most organic material consists of fine particles, perhaps eighty to ninety percent of the fauna consists of collectors. Predators abound in all areas where other insects occur.

Stoneflies, mayflies, caddisflies, true flies (especially blackflies and midges), and riffle beetles collectively comprise about ninety percent of the total macroinvertebrate fauna of the region's streams and rivers. Stoneflies are the most important cold-water group in high mountain streams. Most are leaf and detritus shredders. In contrast to stoneflies, mayflies reach their maximum diversity in low-elevation warm waters. Most mayflies are scrapers or collectors. Caddisflies are a large and diverse group that includes all feeding types. Most caddisfly larvae build portable cases out of sand grains or organic detritus, although some are free-living and do not make cases. True flies are another diverse group that also includes all feeding types.

Native cutthroat trout were once abundant in the mountain streams of Colorado. Since the introduction of non-native fish species a century ago, including brown, rainbow, and brook trout, native cutthroats have been reduced to isolated populations restricted to the highest and steepest streams. In some locations, such as in Rocky Mountain National Park, intensive fish management programs designed to reduce populations of introduced species have been successful in rejuvenating cutthroat numbers.

Brook trout, introduced to the region in the late 1800s, are highly adaptable and very prolific. They are capable of utilizing a wide range of stream habitats, and are tolerant of poor water quality. "Brookies" are the most abundant high-elevation trout.

A favorite of fishermen because of their fighting ability and flavor, rainbow trout are more specific in their habitat requirements than brook trout. Generally occupying mid-elevation streams, rainbow trout are intolerant of very cold water. They prefer deeper pools behind large boulders, and spawn on gravel bottoms where the water flows freely and is well aerated.

Brown trout occupy larger mountain streams, preferring the deeper and slower runs and pools. They are more tolerant of heavy metal pollution than rainbow trout. In the upper Arkansas drainage, browns can survive to reproductive age, despite relatively high heavy metal contamination from nearby mining districts.

Other fish species, such as white suckers, are common in pools of mountain streams and rivers and in lakes. Fathead minnows, johnny darters, and freshwater sculpins serve as food for birds, mammals, and larger fish.

Fish communities of low-elevation streams and rivers differ greatly from those of mountain streams. Warmer waters eliminate trout species and favor channel catfish and various sucker species. Because of many introductions, it is nearly impossible to know whether some of the fish species are native or introduced. In the Colorado River system on the Western Slope, several native species once plentiful are now endangered, including the Colorado squawfish, bonytail chub, and humpback chub. Major dams have tamed the flow of the Colorado, a change which together with increased agriculture in bottomlands has altered and reduced habitat for these fish species. Competition from non native fish species has also contributed to the decline of native populations.

Few reptile and amphibian species occupy streams and rivers. Those that do are restricted to slow-moving waters of low elevations. These include bullfrogs, northern and plains leopard frogs, snapping turtles, and spiny softshell turtles. All of these species occur in pond and lake environments as well.

PONDS AND LAKES

Environmental Characteristics

In the Rocky Mountain region, most natural lakes have been created through glacial action and thus are found at higher elevations, above 9000 feet. In some places, the ice scooped out depressions in the bedrock, leaving small lakes called tarns. Elsewhere, dams formed by glacial moraines have produced lakes in valley bottoms. A few lakes have formed in depressions on the tops of moraines. Below 9000 feet, most "lakes" are actually reservoirs, constructed mainly for water storage. Reservoirs can resemble lakes in many ways, with the degree of similarity dependent on how the reservoirs are constructed and managed. For example, storage reservoirs with widely fluctuating water levels usually are less diverse than natural lakes.

Ponds, although not always distinctive from lakes, are generally

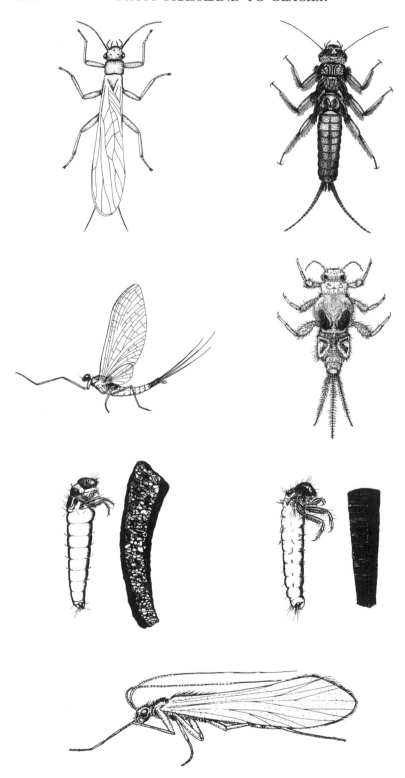

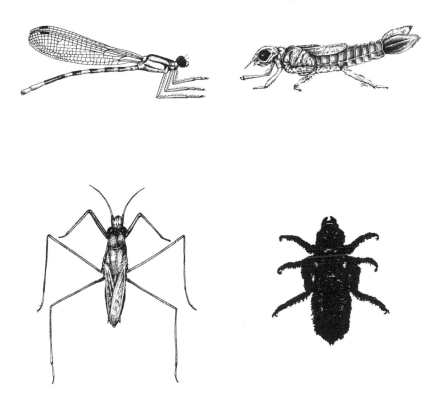

Typical aquatic insects of the Rocky Mountain Region. Opposite page: top, stonefly adult and nymph; middle, mayfly adult and nymph; bottom, two caddisfly larvae with cases, above adult caddisfly. The caddisfly larvae live in the cases, enlarging them as they grow. The case on the left is made from fine sand grains, and the one on the right is made from bits of plant detritus. On this page are insects found in pond environments, and include: top, damselfly adult and nymph; bottom left, water strider; and bottom right, the nymph of a dragonfly. Caddisfly larvae also are common in pond and lake environments. (Drawings of immature insect forms reprinted from *An Illustrated Guide to the Insects of Colorado*, by J.V. Ward and B.C. Kondratieff, with permission of University Press of Colorado. Drawings of insects reprinted from *An Angler's Guide to Aquatic Insects and Their Imitations*, by Rick Hafele and Scott Roederer, illustrations by Richard Bunse).

smaller and shallower, and may have a considerable amount of emergent vegetation growing around their margin. A pond with emergent vegetation extending to its center is sometimes called a marsh. Wind action on the surface of larger lakes may cause enough wave turbulence to reduce aquatic vegetation around the shoreline. Such turbulence is rarely a factor in ponds. Potholes—ponds that often dry up during the summer—exist in many forms and locations: in intermittent stream beds, in small depressions in forest or prairie soils, and as erosion craters in exposed bedrock.

Lakes at the highest elevations above timberline usually have very low dissolved mineral concentrations, are cold, and may be covered by ice and snow for over half the year. Water is usually supplied to these lakes by snowmelt and shallow groundwater movement, and has few nutrients. The surrounding tundra communities typically provide little organic material; thus these lakes usually have low biological productivity because of the paucity of nutrients.

Where fish exist at all, their population size often is limited by lack of dissolved oxygen during the winter as well as by food. Although the larger high-altitude lakes usually do not freeze to

Dragonfly. *Tony Oswald*

the bottom, once the lakes are covered by ice and snow, oxygen content of the remaining water may drop so low that fish die. The oxygen content of these lakes rises again in the spring, once the mountain winds can circulate and aerate the water.

A large percentage of the bottom of high lakes is often bedrock or broken rock, with perhaps only a thin layer of fine material consisting of organic matter and wind-blown debris. The chemistry of these lakes is largely dependent on the characteristics of surrounding rocks. Lakes occurring on sedimentary rock tend to be more alkaline, while those on granites, schists, and gneisses are often somewhat acidic. Scientific data suggest that the acidity of these latter lakes may be increasing in some areas because of acid precipitation, which could reduce organism diversity.

Natural lakes at lower elevations are more amenable to aquatic life. Waters entering the lakes are richer in plant nutrients than waters of higher altitude lakes, and surrounding forests may contribute substantial quantities of nutrients in the form of organic matter. The lakes are warmer than those higher up, and thaw earlier in the spring. Bottom sediments typically consist of fine-grained sediments, often with large percentages of organic matter.

Overturn of lake waters is important for replenishing oxygen to the lower sections of deeper lakes, and for bringing nutrients up to the surface waters where they can be used by aquatic plants. Overturn usually happens in the fall, when surface waters cool and become denser and heavier. With the aid of the wind, these denser oxygen-rich surface waters sink to the lake bottom, pushing the deep nutrient-rich waters up to the lake's surface. A second overturn usually occurs in spring when the ice melts. Water in deep lakes stagnates between the two overturns during the summer, when warmer, less dense surface waters float stably above cooler bottom waters, and during the winter, when ice covers the lakes.

As soon as they form, lakes start collecting sediments and organic debris that eventually fill the lake. Accumulated nutrients favor the growth of plants, which in turn enhances the further build-up of organic sediments. As lakes age, they become more biologically productive because of nutrient accumulation, a process called eutrophication. This process is accelerated when streams carry fertilizers and organic pollutants, such as municipal wastes, into lakes.

The many reservoirs scattered throughout lower elevations provide a still-water habitat where none was available a century or so ago. Reservoirs built for recreational purposes may have relatively stable water levels; here rich aquatic communities similar to those of lakes may develop. Aquatic communities in general, and shoreline plant communities in particular, are poorly developed in reservoirs with wide daily or annual fluctuations in water level. Such fluctuations are a trait of many reservoirs constructed for temporary water storage or for pump-storage at electrical power facilities.

Aquatic Life

The absence of current makes the environment of ponds and lakes much different than that of streams, where turbulent mixing of the water ensures a rapid and relatively even distribution of dissolved components. In standing water, different zones, set apart by differences in temperature, oxygen content, nutrient concentrations, and available light, strongly influence the distribution of aquatic plants and animals.

This is particularly noticeable in large lakes. Aquatic vegetation is restricted to shallow margins, where there is ample light for growth. The vegetation provides food and cover for aquatic fauna, and the water is warmer and relatively well oxygenated. Thus these shallow zones are usually the most biologically diverse and productive areas in lakes. In deeper areas, where low light restricts the growth of rooted vegetation, invertebrate detritus feeders dominate the lake's bottom. Zonation is not as pronounced in small lakes and ponds.

A group of organisms that is essentially absent from streams but important in standing waters is plankton: those microscopic plants and animals that float or weakly swim through the water. Single-celled and small multi-celled algae, protozoans, water fleas, and copepods are some of the minute planktonic forms. These organisms are often so abundant in nutrient-rich conditions that they cloud the water. They are an important food source for insect larvae, fish larvae, tadpoles, and a variety of filter-feeding organisms that strain their food from the water, such as clams, fresh water sponges, and fairy shrimp.

Wood frog. Though common in more northern areas of North America, this amphibian is found only in the northern part of the Southern Rockies in the mountains near North Park and upper tributaries of the Colorado River. *W. Perry Conway*

Ponds and lakes support a more diverse group of aquatic plants than do streams. Many plants, including duckweed, among the smallest of the flowering plants, the carnivorous bladderwort, and the primitive quillworts, are unique to pond environments. Yellow pondlily produces one of the most beautiful blossoms of any plant in the Rockies. A rooted subalpine plant with long-stemmed leaves and flowers that float on the surface, it is often a mystery why one lake will support a healthy population of pondlily, while another lake with seemingly similar conditions has none.

Animal diversity also is higher in ponds and lakes than in streams or rivers. Clams, aquatic earthworms, freshwater sponges, and hydras are part of the rich assortment of invertebrate pond life. While most aquatic insect orders found in streams are represented in ponds and lakes, some groups seem to have a much stronger affinity for still waters. These include backswimmers, water boatmen, water scorpions, diving beetles, and the larvae of craneflies and mosquitos.

Small ephemeral ponds and potholes are frequently home to fairy shrimp. These small arthropods can be found throughout a wide range of elevations, from the tundra to the desert, as long as there are few predators in the water. As they swim on their backs with their legs beating like little oars, fairy shrimp feed on plankton and other bits of floating organic material. Eggs are produced before the pond dries up, and apparently are distributed by birds or mammals, or blown about by the wind. Ponds may hold fairy shrimp during some years and not in others.

Ponds, lakes, and reservoirs, particularly those at lower elevations, offer a variety of fish species. The introduced lake trout, or mackinaw, is the largest trout in North America and prefers cold waters and deep mountain lakes. Unlike its close relative, the vigorous brook trout, "Macks" are slow-growing fish that take six years to reach seventeen inches. Another successful introduction is the kokanee (or red) salmon, which has thrived in several large, fluctuating reservoirs. Native cutthroat are found in many high lakes. Reservoirs and lakes at lower elevations commonly have populations of largemouth and smallmouth bass, bluegill, channel catfish, yellow perch, bullhead, green sunfish, and crappie.

One of the most widespread amphibians is the tiger salamander, which occurs from the plains up to 12,000 feet. Tiger salamanders lay their eggs in ponds, lakes, and reservoirs of almost

any size. The eggs hatch into aquatic larvae which develop feathery external gills. At lower elevations the larvae metamorphose into air-breathing adults two to five months after hatching. In cool mountain ponds, salamanders may remain as larvae for up to two years, becoming sexually mature and breeding before metamorphosing to the adult form.

HUMAN ACTIVITIES

Aquatic ecosystems are impacted by a broad range of human activities that span all of the ecosystem types discussed in this book. Modifications to woodlands, prairies, or other terrestrial environments frequently affect the water quality of nearby streams and lakes. Because of this, the following paragraphs discuss not only human use of the region's water bodies, but also impacts of land-based activities on these aquatic resources.

Greenback cutthroat trout (left) and brook trout (right). Cutthroat trout are the only native trout in the region. The greenback cutthroat is the rarest variety, restricted to the Eastern Slope, and can be distinguished from the brook trout by a light body with dark spots on its back and sides near the tail. Cutthroats also have a crimson slash on each side of the throat beneath the lower jaws. The brook trout is mostly dark with white spots, and red spots surrounded by blue. The lower fins of the brook trout also are edged with white. *Tony Oswald*

Today, few streams and natural lakes, if any, have been left untouched by human activities. The onset of the Gold Rush brought a permanent end to many of the area's pristine waters. Heavy metal pollution from acid mine drainage killed the fish as well as the invertebrates of many streams. One-third to one-half of the total stream mileage in Colorado now has heavy metal loads in excess of the state's water quality standards. Some metal load is natural in a mineral-rich region like the Rocky Mountains, but a significant amount, perhaps half, is due to pollution from thousands of inactive (and thus uncontrolled) metal mines.

Other forms of water pollution are also common. Dust and oil from roads, pesticides, fertilizer, animal wastes, high sediment loads from agricultural areas, industrial wastes, heat from power plant condensers, and treated and untreated discharges from municipal sewage treatment plants all affect aquatic life. As if the above list were not enough, evidence suggests that some of our high mountain streams and lakes are being impacted by acid precipitation.

Because of the aridity of regional lowlands, reservoirs and transbasin water diversion projects were well underway before the turn of the century. Reservoirs have largely tamed the rivers of the region. Before they were put into place, seasonal water levels fluctuated widely, from raging springtime torrents to mere trickles in the fall. Now, water discharges are regulated so that relatively uniform year-round flows can be maintained. While this uniformity permits a greater variety of fish to live in the streams, the natural flooding cycle has been disrupted, eliminating some stream habitats. Native fish are adapted to survive in extreme flows, and in the absence of such fluctuations are often unable to compete with introduced fish. Species requiring flowing waters are eliminated in reservoir impoundments. Warm-water fish and insects are eliminated downstream from reservoirs in which released water is drawn from the bottom and is cold.

Transbasin water diversions often severely reduce the flow of mountain streams, disrupting natural stream dynamics and, as in the case of reservoirs, eliminating or reducing some stream habitats. Agricultural diversion has similar effects.

Many species have been introduced to provide more game fish or forage fish, including several bass species, kokanee salmon, pike, lake trout, smelt, carp, goldfish, and various minnows and suckers. Some introductions have been useful from the standpoint of providing a stable fishery for anglers. However, many of the introductions have resulted in severe competition with native species. Some natives have been eliminated, while populations of others have been reduced.

Human modifications have reduced the number of destructive floods, increased the number of fish species that test the skills of anglers, and provided the water that is vital to our regional economy. These modifications also have decreased the number of free-flowing streams and healthy aquatic ecosystems to the point that they have become as endangered as our rarer native species. Because of their sensitivity to environmental perturbations, aquatic ecosystems serve as barometers of environmental quality. They reveal how well we are managing our forests, our air, and our water, and they provide early warning of conditions potentially affecting human health. Perhaps this is reason enough to persevere in seeking to assure that remaining natural aquatic ecosystems retain their health and integrity.

Plants and Animals of Aquatic Ecosystems

Occurrence of each species depends on local site conditions, such as history of disturbance, water quality, elevation and presence or absence of other competing or predaceous species, and may vary considerably from one place to another. (P) denotes species found in ponds, lakes, or very slow moving water and (S) denotes species found in streams or rivers; (E) denotes species restricted to the Eastern Slope and (W) to the Western Slope.

PLANTS

Arrowhead (P) *Sagittaria* spp.

bladderwort, great (P) *Utricularia vulgaris*

buckbean (P) *Menyanthes trifoliata*

bulrush (P,S) *Scirpus pallidus*

burreed (P,S) *Sparganium* spp.

buttercup, floating (P) *Ranunculus palustris hyperboreus*

cattail, broad-leaved (P) *Typha latifolia*

　　Narrow-leaved (P) *Typha angustifolia*

crowfoot, water (S) *Batrachium* spp. *Ranunculus gmelinii*

ditchgrass (S) *Ruppia cirrhosa*

duckweed (P) *Lemna* spp.

hornwort (S,P) *Ceratophyllum demersum*

mannagrass (P) *Torreyochloa pauciflora*

mare's tail (P,S) *Hippuris vulgaris*

milfoil, water (P) *Myriophyllum sibiricum*

pondlily, yellow (P) *Nuphar luteum*

pondweed (P) *Potamogeton* spp.

pondweed, horned (S) *Zannichellia palustris*

quillwort (P) *Isoetes* spp.

rushes (P,S) *Juncus* spp.

sedges (P,S) *Carex* spp.

smartweed, scarlet (P) *Persicaria coccinea*

　　water (P) *Persicaria amphibia*

spikerush (P) *Eleocharis* spp.

starwort, water (S,P) *Callitriche* spp.

waternymph (P) *Najas guadalupensis*

waterweed (P) *Elodea* spp.

ANIMALS

Major Insect Orders

backswimmers (P) *Hemiptera*

beetle, diving (P) *Coleoptera*

　　riffle (S) *Coleoptera*

　　whirligig (P) *Coleoptera*

damselflies (P,S) *Odonata*

dobsonflies (P,S) *Megaloptera*

dragonflies (P,S) *Odonata*

caddisflies (P,S) *Trichoptera*

craneflies (P) *Diptera*

mayflies (P,S) *Ephemeroptera*

midges (P,S) *Diptera*

mosquitos (P) *Diptera*

stoneflies (S) *Plecoptera*

water-boatmen (P) *Hemiptera*

water scorpions (P) *Hemiptera*

Other Macroinvertebrates

　(Phylum, Class)

clams (P) *Mollusca, Pelecypoda*

crayfish (P,S) *Arthropoda, Crustacea*

earthworms, aquatic (P) *Annelida, Oligochaeta*

fairy shrimp (P) *Arthropoda, Crustacea*

hydra (P) *Cnidaria, Hydrozoa*

leeches (P) *Annelida, Hirudinea*

scuds (P,S) *Arthropoda, Amphipoda*

snails (P,S) *Mollusca, Gastropoda*

sowbugs (P,S) *Arthropoda, Isopoda*

sponge, fresh water (P) *Porifera, Demospongiae*

planarians (flatworms) (P) *Platyhelminthes, Turbellaria*

Lowland Aquatic Systems:

Fish

bass, largemouth (P,S) *Micropterus salmoides*
    smallmouth (P,S) *Micropterus dolomieui*
bluegill (P) *Lepomis macrochirus*
bullhead, black (P,S) *Ictalurus melas*
carp (P,S) *Cyprinus carpio*
catfish, channel (P,S) *Ictalurus punctatus*
chub, bonytail* (S)(W) *Gila elegans*
    creek (S)(E) *Semotilus atromaculatus*
      humpback* (S)(W) *Gila cypha*
      roundtail (S)(W) *Gila robusta*
crappie, black (P)(E) *Pomoxis nigromaculatus*
dace, longnose (S) *Rhinichthys cataractae*
    speckled (S)(W) *Rhinichthys osculus*
killifish, plains (S) *Fundulus zebrinus*
minnow, fathead (P,S) *Pimephales promelas*
perch, yellow (P) *Perca flavescens*
smelt, rainbow (P)(E) *Osmerus mordax*
stickleback, brook (P)(E) *Culaea inconstans*
squawfish, Colorado* (S)(W) *Ptychocheilus lucius*
sucker, bluehead (S)(W) *Catostomus discobolus*

sucker, **longnose** (P,S) *Catostomus catostomus*
    white (P,S) *Catostomus commersoni*
sunfish, **green** (P,S) *Lepomis cyanellus*
    orange-spotted (P)(E) *Lepomis humilis*
    pumpkinseed (P)(E) *Lepomis gibbosus*
whitefish, mountain (S) *Prosopium williamsoni*

Reptiles and Amphibians

bullfrog (P,S) *Rana catesbeiana*
frog, northern leopard (P,S) *Rana pipiens*
    plains leopard (P,S)(E) *Rana blairi*
    striped chorus (P) *Pseudacris triseriata*
salamander, tiger (P) *Ambystoma tigrinum*
snake, northern water (S)(E) *Nerodia sipedon*
turtle, painted (P) *Chrysemys picta*
    snapping (P,S)(E) *Chelydra serpentina*
    spiny softshell (P,S)(E) *Trionyx spiniferus*
    yellow mud (P)(E) *Kinosternon flavescens*

Mountain Aquatic Systems:

Fish

darter, johnny (S) *Etheostoma nigrum*

minnow, fathead (P,S) *Pimephales promelas*

salmon, kokanee (P) *Oncorhynchus nerka*

sculpin, mottled (S)(E) *Cottus bairdi*

sucker, longnose (P,S) *Catostomus catostomus*

   white (P,S) *Catostomus commersoni*

trout, cutthroat (P,S) *Oncorhynchus clarki*

   rainbow (P,S) *Oncorhynchus mykiss*

trout, **brook** (P,S) *Salvelinus fontinalis*

   brown (S) *Salmo trutta*

   lake (P) *Salvelinus namaycush*

Reptiles and Amphibians

frog, striped chorus (P) *Pseudacris triseriata*

   northern leopard (P) *Rana pipiens*

   wood* (P) *Rana sylvatica*

salamander, tiger (P) *Ambystoma tigrinum*

Species in bold-faced type are more abundant.
*Endangered or greatly reduced in number.

Epilogue

The prairies, forests, and other ecosystems of the region are the result of continuous dynamic interaction between living organisms and their environment through past millennia. Geologic events have changed the shape of the land, and shifting climates have converted forests into deserts and back into forests again. Extinction of some species as well as evolution of new ones have occurred, while other species have migrated to the region from surrounding areas. The petrified stumps of giant redwoods can be seen at the Florissant Fossil Beds west of Colorado Springs. During the last ice age, elephant-like mastodons roamed the lowlands, and their bones, teeth, and tusks occasionally appear at the surface of eroding prairie sediments.

Ecological change is as old as life itself, and the chapters of this book provide many examples of the dynamic nature of ecosystems. In a sense the landscape we see today is only a snapshot in the passage of time. Ponds will become meadows, later to be replaced by forests. Colorful aspen groves gradually will be succeeded by dark coniferous stands. Drier climates or new ice ages will shift the positions of treelines.

As we grow to appreciate these changes that occur under natural circumstances, we must also be aware of the human capability to be a dominant and pervasive ecological force. We are fortunate in that many of the region's ecosystems have retained their character despite human activities. Yet for much of the area the opposite is true. Grasslands have become a patchwork of cultivated land and rangeland that is too heavily grazed to support the plant communities that once grew here. Undisturbed riparian habitat is almost nonexistent. Ecosystem changes resulting from logging, accidental forest fires, livestock grazing, agriculture, urbanization, and numerous other human activities are occurring at an alarming rate. Destruction of vegetative cover is accelerating erosion, causing a loss of valuable topsoil. Pesticides, toxic wastes, and other chemicals are polluting water, air, and soil. Many of these forces are producing irreversible changes that will require many decades or centuries for natural ecological succession to run its course.

The use of natural resources for the good of our society should and will continue. In the end society will determine the extent to which our natural resources will be exploited, the degree to which wildlife or wildlife habitat should be protected, and the need to conserve our natural ecosystems. The responsibility is great and demands a knowledge of ecological processes and ecosystem tolerances. We are all called upon to educate ourselves so that we can take stock of our actions before damage to the environment is manifest. Accomplishing this, we can understand, enjoy, and use our natural resources in harmony with the wild creatures that remain.

Self-Guided Tours to Regional Ecosystems

The ecosystems of the region are so distinct that they can be distinguished from a moving car. The following self-guided tours in Colorado are designed to help you identify the ecosystems discussed in this book. Each tour can be accomplished easily in a day. We suggest that you take a picnic lunch along and make the trip a leisurely one, with frequent stops to investigate the plants and animals in each ecosystem. You may wish to bring binoculars and one or more of the field guides suggested in the reference list.

As you make these ecological tours, identify growth forms of the dominant plants—are they trees, shrubs, or herbs? Identify the altitudinal zone, the ecosystem position on a slope, and the degree of soil rockiness. In forests, observe foliage color and shape and density of trees. Take a close look at cone structure and at bark and needle characteristics. A key to the tree species follows the tours and will help you identify the dominant trees in the forested ecosystems. Differences among ecological units will soon become obvious.

Tour routes are marked with arrows on accompanying maps. All mileages refer to the distances traveled from the beginning of the tour; if your car has a resettable trip odometer, it should be set to 0.0 miles when you begin the tour.

As you proceed on the tour, the accumulated mileage shown on your car's odometer may differ slightly from the numbers shown here, so you may have to adjust your distances accordingly at major intersections or other landmarks given in the tours. Stopping points are marked with asterisks. Elevations above sea level noted in parentheses for each stopping point are approximate and refer to the elevation of the road.

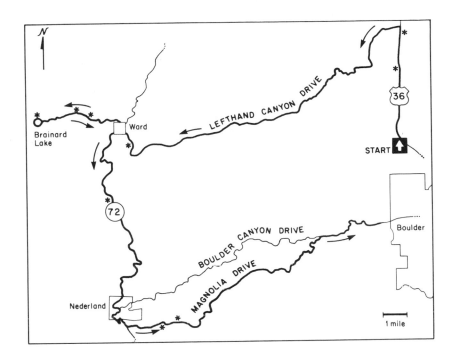

TOUR NO. 1: BOULDER COUNTY LOOP

This tour begins one mile north of Boulder, on US 36, and is approximately 61 miles long.

Start: 0.0 miles, and north to 4.8 mi.	North from the junction of North Broadway and US 36 (North Foothills Highway): As you drive north, notice the low, small, dense *montane shrub ecosystems* on eroding hogbacks to the west. Ponderosa pine crown hogbacks above the shrubs, forming the lower treeline.
*2.7 mi. (5550′)	Just north and east of the Beechcraft plant: *Plains grassland ecosystems* are in unusually good condition here. Look for short, curly leaved blue grama and notice interspersed taller bunchgrasses. As you continue north, you can imagine plains grasslands rolling hundreds of miles eastward, interrupted only by winding bands of streamside cottonwoods and wet pockets of cat-tails and pondweeds.

*4.5 mi. (5580')	0.3 miles south of the junction of US 36 and Lefthand Creek Drive: *Lowland riparian ecosystems* are well developed along Lefthand Creek. The dense native cottonwoods and willows are interrupted by introduced tree species such as Russian olive and locust.
4.8 mi., and west to 20.0 mi.	West along Lefthand Creek Drive: Ecosystems change dramatically as altitude and slope exposure change. *Ponderosa pine forests* and *Douglas fir forests* dominate mountain forests from the foothills to a few miles east of Ward. Ponderosa pine cover dry, sunny hillsides north of the road, and Douglas fir grow on moist, cool slopes south of the road. Ecosystems vary from open parklands to closed forests, depending on their age, site characteristics, and history of human use. As altitude increases, ponderosa decrease their dominance on both slopes, and forests become denser. Most trees in this canyon are young and small, but broad, flat tops of mature ponderosa pine and semirounded crowns of mature Douglas fir are occasionally outlined against the skyline.
10.1 mi. (6334')	Junction of James and Lefthand Canyons. Turn left and continue along Lefthand Canyon Drive. *Mountain riparian ecosystems* border Lefthand Creek. Notice how they change in width, density, and species composition as the road curves uphill. Cottonwoods decrease as altitude increases, and Colorado blue spruce grow only at mid-elevations. In places, species from hillside ecosystems mix with riparian species, while at the junction of James and Lefthand Canyons, riparian ecosystems disappeared when the creek was rerouted to accommodate the road. At 16.8 miles, old beaver cuts and dams are visible from the road.
*20.6 mi. (8800')	*Successional mountain meadows* cover hillsides on both sides of the road. A forest covered the hillsides in the past—notice the stumps that remain. Conifers, successional aspen, and dry shrubs are invading the meadows.

21.4 mi.   Stop sign at the intersection in the town of Ward.
(9253')   Take the right fork.

21.9 mi.   Junction with Colorado 72. Turn right.

22.0 mi.   Turn left at the entrance to the Brainard Lake Recreation Area.

*24.6 mi.   Brainard Lake Recreation Area, at the turnoff to Left-
(10,075')   hand Reservoir: Dense *Engelmann spruce–subalpine fir forests* such as these form most of our high-mountain forests. The spired tree shapes reduce the load that could collect from the 100 to 300 inches of snow that fall here each winter. Trees with very horizontal branches and upright cones are fir, while trees with hanging cones are spruce.

*25.0 mi.   Red Rock Lake: A well-developed *limber pine wood-
(10,160')   land* covers the moraine north of the road. Limber pine are better able to survive on such rocky, wind exposed sites than are other tree species. Red Rock Lake, south of the road, is one of the few lakes in this region that has water lily pads. The western and southern sides of the lake show well-developed succession from lake, to bog, to forest.

Just down the hill along the road is a large subalpine fen—another type of *mountain riparian ecosystem*. The shrubs are willow and bog birch. Spruce are invading on soil hummocks.

*27.4 mi.   Brainard Lake: From this vantage you can see four
(10,350')   ecosystem types. A *subalpine fen* is just south of the lake, which was formed by glaciers and enlarged by a dam. *Spruce–fir forests* cover hillsides up to *krummholz ecosystems*, groups of dwarfed trees forming dark green stripes along the forest edge. Flag trees, carved by strong downslope winter winds, also grow just east of Brainard Lake.

Tundra ecosystems stretch above krummholz to the mountain peaks. To get a closer look at the tundra and krummholz in this part of the state, you must hike up from one of the nearby trailheads or drive up Trail Ridge Road in Rocky Mountain National Park (US 34). Drive back to Colorado 72.

33.0 mi., and south to 50.8 mi. Colorado 72, south through Nederland, then turn left onto Magnolia Drive: The Peak-to-Peak Highway is flanked by successional *aspen groves* and *lodgepole pine forests*, which form a distinct belt between the *spruce–fir forests* above and *ponderosa pine* and *Douglas fir forests* below. The belt was burned in many fires between 1890 and 1910. Yellow-green lodgepole foliage contrasts with the light green aspen leaves and dark green needles of other conifers.

The pointed, scantily forested hill to the east, at approximately 34.8 miles, is called Potato Hill because the meadow was enlarged and planted with potatoes around the turn of the century. Today it is used as a challenge to jeepers, who have left the scars of tracks on the western hillside. Notice the multiple-topped, wind-distorted limber pine on the top of Potato Hill.

*37.7 mi. (9150′) Just north of the Rainbow Lakes access road, west of the Peak-to-Peak Highway: *Lodgepole pine forests* contrast with ecosystems described previously because the lodgepole are even-sized and all the same age. They will be replaced by spruce–fir or Douglas fir ecosystems. Because little light reaches the forest floor, few understory plants grow here.

*38.5 mi. (9100′) 0.7 miles south of the Rainbow Lakes access road: *Aspen forests* fill the valley west of the road, but a closer look at these groves will reveal that conifer seedlings are replacing the aspen. Differences in leaf colors, especially distinctive in June and October, outline aspen clones—groups of genetically identical trees that are interconnected by roots.

45.0 mi. (8234′)	Junction with Colorado 119 in the town of Neder-land. Turn right, staying on Colorado 72.
46.9 mi.	Turn left onto Magnolia Drive.
*48.9 mi. (8500′)	*Natural mountain meadows* fill the valley just south of the road. Each of the variously colored bands encircling the pond is dominated by a different kind of herb. Those closest to the edge of the pond are sedges in wet meadows. The higher, drier areas farther from the pond are dry meadows, with a variety of grasses and forbs. The thin band of aspen between the meadow and conifers on the far side of the meadow is typical of mountain meadow ecosystems.
*49.6 mi.	One of the few *climax aspen ecosystems* in this part of the state is just north of the road. In contrast to successional aspen, trees here are of many sizes and ages, and aspen reproduction is healthy. The lush, diverse understory is typical of aspen on moist, rich soil.
49.6 mi., and east, to Boulder	Magnolia Drive crosses a broad, gently rolling surface where ponderosa parklands are interrupted by rocky outcrops vegetated with members of *montane shrub ecosystems*. Many large, natural meadows were homesteaded, and the settlers' buildings still remain. As you drop down into Boulder Canyon, typical foothills forests appear again. Douglas fir cover the hillsides south of the road, and ponderosa pine cloak those north of the road. Lush *lowland riparian ecosystems* greet your return into Boulder.

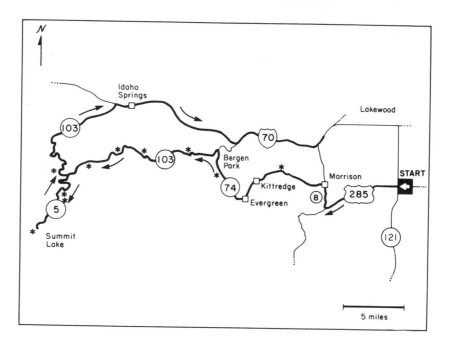

TOUR NO. 2: SUMMIT LAKE LOOP

This tour begins at the intersection of Colorado 121 (Wadsworth Blvd.) and US 285 (Hampden Ave.) west of Englewood. Length of tour is approximately 100 miles.

Start: 0.0 miles, (5600′) and east to 6.0 mi.	Driving west on US 285 toward the foothills, you pass through remnants of *plains grasslands*. Although fragmented by agriculture and urbanization, a mixture of grassland plant communities has survived. Drier areas are favored by short grasses such as buffalograss and blue grama. Little bluestem and taller grasses prefer moister sites.
4.8 mi. (5900′)	Just past the Soda Lakes Road exit, you will drive through a narrow opening in the hogback. Here, on both sides of the road, a good example of *montane shrubland* marks the transition from grassland to the east and higher-elevation forests to the west. Mountain mahogany, Gambel oak, skunkbrush, and rabbitbrush grow here, all adapted to the rocky, poorly developed soils on the eroding hogbacks.

At this location Gambel oak is only a few miles from its northern limit of distribution on the Eastern Slope of the Rocky Mountains.

6.0 mi., and north to 8.0 mi.

Take the Evergreen-Colorado 8 exit to Morrison. As you drive north notice the pattern of ecosystems to the left along the base of the foothills. Grasses predominate on the lower portions of the hills and on the drier south-facing slopes. On the moister north-facing slopes, shrubs are numerous. Farther up the slopes shrubs give way to forests of ponderosa pine, Rocky Mountain juniper and Douglas fir, an indication of the increase in soil moisture at higher elevations. Note that trees extend farther down the mountains on moist, north-facing slopes and shadowed ravines. A portion of the forest extends down to the highway, and here the trees are almost all juniper, easily recognized by their small size, dense crown, and manicured appearance.

As you approach Morrison, notice the thick stands of mountain mahogany on the hogbacks to the east. This shrub gives the foothills shrub zone its grayish color.

8.0 mi., (5800') and west to 42.1 mi.

Turn left toward Kittredge and Evergreen on Colorado 74. Here in Morrison *lowland riparian ecosystems* border Bear Creek. These riverside forests are composed of plains cottonwoods, peach-leaved willow, and box-elder trees, as well as introduced trees such as green ash.

As you drive up Bear Creek Canyon, shrublands on the sides of the canyon give way to forest ecosystems. The east-west orientation of the canyon provides a good opportunity to see the dramatic contrast between north-facing and south-facing slopes. The cool, moist, north-facing slopes on the left are occupied by *Douglas fir forests* while the sunny, drier south-facing slopes on the right are covered by *ponderosa pine forests*.

In the bottom of the canyon, the creekside plains riparian ecosystems gradually become *mountain riparian ecosystems*. Plains cottonwood is replaced by narrowleaf cottonwood, and Colorado blue spruce appears.

*14.3 mi.
(6700′)

The roadside picnic grounds provide a good opportunity to get out of your car and look at some mountain ecosystems close at hand.

Typical *ponderosa pine forests* occupy the sides of the valley on the north (right) side of the road. Ponderosa pine can be recognized by its very long (3″–7″) needles and open, rounded crown. Trees are widely spaced and interspersed by grassy meadows.

A foot bridge on the south side of the road will take you across Bear Creek to the north-facing side of the canyon where you can walk among the Douglas fir with their short, flat, soft needles. Here the forest is dense, and only a few small plants grow on the forest floor. The larger shrubs growing beneath the trees are mountain maple.

Near the picnic grounds you may notice the rounded crowns of the peach-leaved willow, and several Colorado blue spruce along the creek. The spruce can be distinguished from the Douglas fir by the very stiff, sharply pointed needles. You will also see several shrubs typical of *mountain riparian ecosystems* at this elevation, including chokecherry, alder, and a few varieties of shrubby willows.

18.2 mi.
(7000′)

The mountain town of Evergreen. Stay on Colorado 74.

*21.9 mi.
(7500′)

A good example of a *mountain meadow* is on your left. Larger meadows such as this are called parks, and this one is Bergen Park. Here you will find Kentucky bluegrass, Junegrass, needle-and-thread, and blue grama. Wild iris blooms in moist areas during late spring, and by mid-summer the showy blossoms of blanket flower appear in the meadow. Mountain bluebirds nest here; and kestrels, hovering on rapidly beating wings, hunt for prey in the summertime.

23.9 mi.
(7800′)

In Bergen Park turn left onto Colorado 103. After passing through a grove of large ponderosa pine, you have a good view of the park and can see *aspen groves* encroaching on the south side of the meadow (to your left).

*26.2 mi.
(8200′)

The appearance of *lodgepole pine forests* here indicates a past fire in the original montane forest. Look for the yellow-green color of lodgepole needles and the many old cones that remain even on dead trees. The sparse understory beneath includes buffaloberry, common juniper, snowberry, kinnikinnik, and wild geranium.

*31.1 mi.
(9200′)

Here at the junction with County Road 475 is a good opportunity to see *aspen groves*. Aspen propagate mainly by suckers, or vertical shoots from the main root system. Because young saplings are connected to the parent tree, they need not compete with grasses for water and nutrients, so aspen can easily invade mountain meadows as you see happening here. Notice the abundance of herbaceous vegetation beneath the aspen, a sharp contrast to the relatively barren understory of the coniferous forests.

Stay on Colorado 103.

*34.8 mi.
(10,100′)

The narrow, tall, spire-shaped crowns of the conifers herald *Engelmann spruce–subalpine fir forests*. The dark, reddish, flaky bark of the spruce contrasts with the silvery, smoother bark of the fir. Because of the greater amounts of precipitation received at these higher elevations, the understory vegetation of spruce–fir forests is lusher than that of lower coniferous ecosystems. If you stop and listen for a few moments, you may hear the flute-like song of the hermit thrush.

*39.8 mi.
(11,100′)

The Eagle's Aerie picnic ground on the left side of the road is a good spot to examine *limber pine–bristlecone pine woodlands*. They cover the ridge top above the road. Thin, rocky soils and high winds have favored the establishment of these hardy pines. If you stop at a picnic table for a snack, you will doubtless be visited by a Clark's nutcracker, typical of these ecosystems. These large black, white, and gray birds gather the nuts of limber pines in the fall, caching them in the forest litter. This burial facilitates germination of some of the seeds not recovered by the birds. Thus this mutual relationship benefits both bird and tree.

42.1 mi.

Turn left onto Colorado 5 toward Mount Evans.

*46.0 mi.
(11,400′)

Here at the Mount Goliath Natural Area you see one of the best examples in the Front Range of a *limber pine–bristlecone pine woodland*. The crowns of the trees have been sculpted by the wind, their bark worn and their wood bleached. On the slope above the hairpin curve of the road, the spruce–fir forest has become fragmented into tree islands, or *krummholz*.

As you proceed up the road, you will quickly pass out of the uppermost remnants of the forest into the treeless *alpine tundra*.

*48.0 mi.
(12,200′)

A small parking turnoff marks the beginning (and end) of the Alpine Garden Trail, a short loop that provides an excellent opportunity to study tundra vegetation close at hand. You will find a multitude of wildflowers along the trail. You may see American pipits and horned larks flying about, and if you are lucky, a white-tailed ptarmigan, the only year-round bird resident of the alpine tundra.

If there are any thunderstorms developing nearby, stay off the trail. The terrain is exposed and the risk of lightning is very high during electrical storms.

*51.7 mi. (12,830')	At Summit Lake you can explore wet tundra meadows, where you will see wildflowers such as elephantella, king's crown, marsh marigold, and Parry's primrose among many others. Look for pikas among the boulders above the lake. These diminutive members of the rabbit family scurry from rock to rock, barking their nasal warnings to one another if an intruder approaches their domain.

Turn around and return to Colorado 103 (approximately 9.6 mi.).

61.3 mi., and north to 74. 0 mi.	Turn left onto Colorado 103, driving past Echo Lake Lodge and Echo Lake.
*62.3 mi.	The stream at the outlet of Echo Lake is bordered by shrub willows, typical of high elevation *mountain riparian ecosystems.* Here you may see Wilson's warblers and Lincoln's sparrows, two bird species that typically breed in riparian willow thickets.
74.0 mi., and east.	Turn east onto Interstate 70 to Denver.
82.9 mi.	Well-developed *ponderosa pine forests* appear along both sides of the highway. The broad, open-crowned, mature ponderosa are interspersed with dry meadows. Some of these stately giants are among the largest trees in the region.
88.5 mi.	As you continue eastward, you will begin an abrupt drop in elevation through the foothills. The large ponderosa will give way to groves of smaller Rocky Mountain juniper and to dry shrub ecosystems of mountain mahogany and skunkbrush.
92.6 mi.	By the time you reach Exit 259 (US 40, Colorado 26) on Interstate 70, you are once again at the base of the foothills and at the edge of the plains grasslands.

You may leave Interstate 70 at this exit and drive south through Morrison back to US 285, or stay on Interstate 70 to Denver.

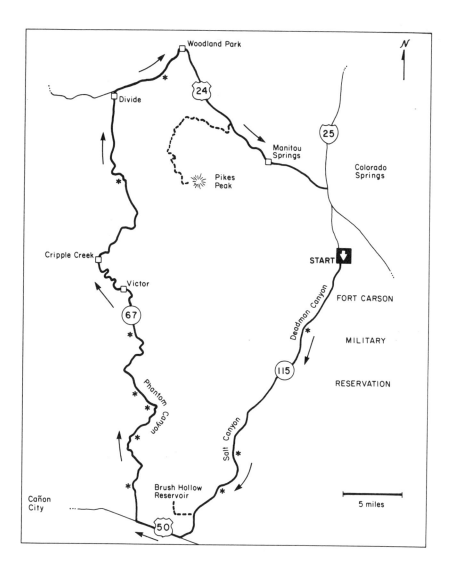

TOUR NO. 3: PHANTOM CANYON LOOP

The tour begins in south Colorado Springs opposite the main gate of the Fort Carson Military reservation on Colorado 115 (Nevada Street). (This location is approximately 5.1 miles south of the Interstate 25 overpass on Nevada Street.) Total length of the tour is approximately 106 miles.

Start: 0.0 miles (5900′) south to 26.7 mi.	Driving south on Colorado 115, you are traveling along the western edge of the *plains grasslands,* which extend eastward for hundreds of miles. Here, they meet mountain ecosystems. To the west *montane shrublands,* composed of Gambel oak, skunkbrush, and mountain mahogany, form a transitional belt between the plains grasslands and the coniferous forest. The coniferous forests that you see on the lower slopes of the foothills to the west are mainly *ponderosa pine forests.*
*4.9 mi. (6300′)	In Deadman Canyon piñon pine and one-seed juniper are mixed with ponderosa pine. The piñon and juniper trees occupy mainly the shallower rocky soils atop the Fountain and Niobrara sedimentary formations on the left side of the road. Elsewhere deep soils and soils overlying granitic rock or the hard sandstones of the Dakota and Lyons Formations have favored ponderosa establishment.
	As you continue driving south, *piñon–juniper woodlands* become more prevalent along both sides of the road.
*16.4 mi. (6200′)	Typical piñon–juniper woodlands occupy the slopes on both sides of the road as you descend through Salt Canyon. Here mountain mahogany dominates the shrub understory. Much of the bottom of Salt Canyon is covered by a *semidesert shrubland* consisting of four-winged saltbush and rabbitbrush, and a few salt cedar grow in moister areas near the creek bed. Salt Canyon is also the first opportunity to see the tall, shrublike candelabra cactus, common to southern and southeastern Colorado.
*22.1 mi. (5400′)	Here at the bridge where Beaver Creek crosses the road, you can glimpse the remnants of a *lowland riparian ecosystem* along the stream banks. Plains cottonwoods are the dominant trees, and New Mexico locust forms part of the tall shrub understory.

24.4 mi.   For an optional side trip to Brush Hollow Reservoir, turn right and follow the signs to the recreational area, about 2 miles. The area offers campsites and picnic tables for those who wish to spend more time exploring the piñon–juniper woodlands and riparian ecosystems near the reservoir. This is a good spot to look for piñon jays and plain titmice, two bird species that nest exclusively in piñon–juniper woodlands.

26.7 mi.   Junction of Colorado 115 and US 50. Turn right onto
(5272')   US 50 and proceed west.
west to
30.7 mi.   On both sides of the road, grassland ecosystems have been altered by agriculture and intensive grazing. Much of the rangeland is now covered with yucca and various cacti, species that tend to increase in numbers as a result of grazing because of their unpalatability to cattle.

*29.7 mi.   A large stand of salt cedar grows along Eight Mile Creek. This scene is typical of much of the lower Arkansas River and Rio Grande drainages, as well as most streams and rivers of western Colorado at lower elevations. This introduced Eurasian shrub has rapidly invaded stream valleys throughout the Southwest during the last century, choking watercourses and displacing native plant species.

30.7 mi.   Turn right onto Colorado 67 toward Victor and Crip-
(5457')   ple Creek. Shrublands typical of cool desert condi-
north to   tions grow to the west of the road and consist pri-
83.3 mi.   marily of rabbitbrush and shadscale. This is one of the few locations on the Eastern Slope where shadscale grows. It is also a good spot to look for roadrunners, a southwestern bird that inhabits brushlands.

*33.3 mi.   The road passes through a notch in a hogback of
(5620')   upturned erosion-resistant sedimentary formations, the most prominent being the Dakota Sandstone. This formation caps many of the hogbacks that ex-

tend northward past Denver along the eastern flank of the Front Range. Here along Colorado 67 the grassland and shrublands give way to *piñon–juniper woodlands*, which cover both sides of the hogback.

35.4 mi. (5800′)

Entering Phantom Canyon, the road parallels Eight Mile Creek. Notice the *mountain riparian ecosystem* growing alongside the creek. As you enter the canyon, plains cottonwood becomes less frequent and is replaced by narrowleaf cottonwood. Peach-leaved willow, box-elder, and hop tree also grow in the lower part of the canyon with the cottonwoods. Shrubs along the creek include wild grape, chokecherry, pin cherry, and wild plum.

Montane shrublands composed of Gambel oak, skunkbrush, and mountain mahogany grow above the cottonwoods on the sides of the canyon and are especially dense on the cooler north-facing slopes.

*37.6 mi. (6120′)

The road follows what was originally a wagon road and later the roadbed of the Florence and Cripple Creek Railroad, one of three railroads and the only narrow-gauge line serving the Cripple Creek mining district. Here at the first tunnel one can almost imagine the old steam locomotives belching smoke and cinders as they slowly chugged up Phantom Canyon, bringing supplies to the last great gold and silver bonanza in Colorado. The railroad was completed in 1894 and operated for 19 years.

41.1 mi. (6740′)

Second tunnel.

41.7 mi.

The slope to the right above the creek is covered with a dense *Douglas fir forest*, typical of north-facing slopes at intermediate elevations in the mountains. If you look carefully, you can discern the characteristic Christmas tree shape of these conifers.

On the opposite side of the canyon, above and to the left of the road, the rounded crowns of ponderosa pines are evident. *Ponderosa pine forests* are common on the warmer south-facing slopes in the upper reaches of Phantom Canyon and are more open than Douglas fir forests, harboring many species of grasses and shrubs in the understory. Here ponderosa are mixed with the smaller piñon pines and Rocky Mountain juniper. Long needles and a taller stature distinguish the ponderosa from the piñons and junipers.

42.8 mi.
(6930′)

Just beyond the bridge crossing Eight Mile Creek, you will encounter the first white fir, which are numerous in the canyon bottom for the next 12 miles. They are stately trees, with 2-inch long silvery green needles that gracefully curve skyward. During fall you may notice clusters of erect silvery cones on their uppermost branches. Phantom Canyon is near the northern limit of white fir distribution in Colorado.

43.8 mi.
(7120′)

Steel railroad trestle over creek.

*44.4 mi.
(7280′)

From this vantage point you can see large numbers of white fir in the bottom and up the north-facing slope on the opposite side of the canyon.

*46.0 mi.
(7630′)

A short distance beyond the bridge, a turnoff provides a good opportunity to more closely examine the mixed coniferous forests and *mountain riparian ecosystems* near the road.

Across the creek on the left side of the road, white fir, Douglas fir, and ponderosa pine are growing together. Here you can compare the Douglas fir with white fir and see how the cones of Douglas fir are distributed throughout the entire crown of the tree. Douglas fir needles are also shorter than those of the white fir.

On the opposite slope above the right side of the road, ponderosa, piñon pine, and Rocky Mountain juniper are intermixed, forming a more open forest. Gambel oak are also scattered about and are becoming more prevalent on the south-facing slopes because of more favorable moisture conditions as the elevation increases.

The riparian ecosystem along the creek still contains a few narrowleaf cottonwood but for the most part is dominated by numerous shrubs including willows, alder, mountain maple, wild rose, thimbleberry, and currants.

52.9 mi. (9090')   The abrupt switchback in the road here marks a point of historical interest, for at this location the old railroad right-of-way, climbing a four-percent grade, carried the tracks in a complete loop over a high trestle.

53.7 mi. (9200')   An extensive *aspen grove* on the opposite side of the valley occupies ground that was once coniferous forest that was logged or burned around the turn of the century. Many stumps of the former conifers can still be seen. Eventually the aspen will be replaced by conifers, which are slowly becoming reestablished in the shade of the aspen.

*56.1 mi. (9450')   A *limber pine–bristlecone pine woodland* grows on both sides of the road. For the next 16 miles you will be driving through the Cripple Creek mining district, which developed as a result of the discovery of gold in 1890. During the heyday of the mining boom, the original forest of Engelmann spruce, Douglas fir, and ponderosa pine that covered much of the district was cut for mine timbers, buildings, and firewood. Many limber and bristlecone pines were spared because their twisted wood was useless for construction, and these trees served as seed sources for the successional woodlands you see in this location today. Occasional large decaying stumps are the only remnants of the original climax forest.

56.9 mi.
(9600′)

For the next several miles you will see numerous *successional mountain meadows,* again the result of extensive destruction of the original forest. These are being invaded by numerous aspen groves, which in turn will be replaced by conifers, leading to the eventual reestablishment of the climax coniferous forest. The aspen grove at 58.0 mi. is mixed with many Engelmann spruce and a few subalpine fir and is in an advanced stage of replacement by these conifers.

59.3 mi.
(9700′)

Entering Victor. Stay on Colorado 67.

65.4 mi.
(9500′)

Cripple Creek, the center of the mining district, boasted a population of 30,000 during its zenith in 1900, when $18,000,000 worth of gold was produced. Between Cripple Creek and the town of Divide, much of Colorado 67 follows the roadbed of another of the three railroads that served the district, the Colorado Midland Railroad, a standard-gauge line.

*74.4 mi.
(9700′)

As you exit the old railroad tunnel, notice the large Engelmann spruce trees in the gulch to the left of the road. You are at the lower edge of the distribution of *Engelmann spruce–subalpine fir forests,* although in the Pike's Peak region, subalpine fir are not as common as they are elsewhere. Look for large numbers of small reddish brown cones hanging near the tops of the spruces. If you stop and listen, you may hear the song of the ruby-crowned kinglet, which begins with a few very high, weak notes and descends into a loud, bouncy warble. These birds are very common in lower elevation spruce–fir forests.

83.3 mi.
(9165′)

Junction of Colorado 67 with US 24 at Divide. Turn right onto US 24 and proceed east. Divide was named for the fact that the town is located on the divide between the South Platte and Arkansas River drainages.

*87.4 mi. (8900′)	Ponderosa pine parklands occupy the land on both sides of the highway. Here the pines form a very open forest, interspersed with large grassy meadows of blue grama, needle-and-thread, and Junegrass. You may also notice islands of Engelmann spruce.
89.6 mi. (8465′)	Entering Woodland Park. Here you begin to descend through the Fountain Creek valley. As you drive down the valley, once again notice the *ponderosa pine forests* growing on the warm south-facing slopes, often mixed with *montane shrublands* consisting of mountain mahogany and Gambel oak. *Douglas fir forests* can be seen on the north-facing slopes on the opposite side of the valley across the creek. Peach-leaved willow, narrowleaf cottonwood and many stands of large Colorado blue spruce grow along the creek (some of the spruce have been planted).
98.4 mi. (7400′)	To get a look at *alpine tundra*, you can take a side trip up the Pikes Peak toll road. While many plant communities present elsewhere in Colorado tundra are not well represented here, Pikes Peak nevertheless is the location nearest Colorado Springs where one may easily gain access to land above timberline. Many tundra plant species are present, and you can examine the effects of the rigorous climatic conditions.
101.8 mi. (6600′)	As you approach Manitou Springs, the granite gives way to sedimentary rocks of the Fountain Formation, and the forest abruptly changes from ponderosa to *piñon–juniper woodlands*. The woodlands meet remnants of the *plains grasslands* at the foot of the mountains. Continue driving eastward on US 24 to return to Colorado Springs.

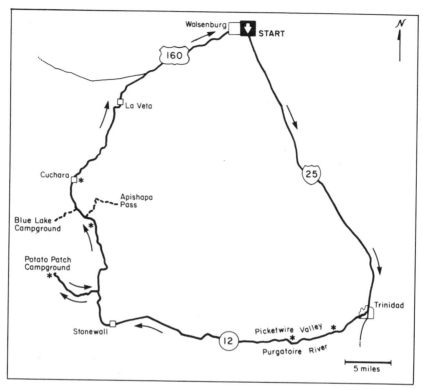

TOUR NO. 4: SPANISH PEAKS LOOP

The tour begins on southbound Interstate 25 at Exit 50 (Walsenburg). Total length of the tour is approximately 130 miles. Stay on Interstate 25, proceeding toward Trinidad.

Start:
0.0 miles,
(6200′)
and south
to 37.1 mi.

The vegetation to your left is characteristic of the *plains grasslands.* This area is dry, receiving approximately fifteen inches of precipitation annually. In its natural state it is dominated by blue grama and buffalograss: perennial, sod-forming grasses with short, curly leaves. These are interspersed with taller perennial bunchgrasses. Most of the shrubs you see are rabbitbrush, which turn bright yellow when in bloom in late summer. Also visible are yuccas with their distinctive bayonet-shaped leaves, and the tall, greenish gray candelabra cactus, whose extensively branched stems reach upward several feet and bear bright red flowers. Piñon pines and one-seed junipers are visible at slightly higher elevations to your right.

9.2 mi. (6350′) Approximately 200 yards before Exit 41, the valley bottom to the right is occupied by a *semidesert shrubland*. The taller shrubs with bright green succulent leaves are greasewood, which is interspersed with four-winged saltbush and winterfat. The latter shrub resembles a white, wooly sagebrush. Greasewood grows where soils are alkaline and fine-grained with a high water table. When soils are more alkaline than they are here, greasewood is often the only shrub present in bottomlands, while better-drained soils on surrounding slopes are covered with saltbush. The saltbush may give way to dense rabbitbrush stands as soil alkalinity decreases.

30.8 mi. (6200′) As the highway crosses the railroad tracks, it enters a *piñon–juniper woodland,* the lowest elevation forest in the foothills of this part of Colorado. Junipers are distinguished by their compact, pointed shape and, upon closer inspection, by their berries. Piñon pines, in contrast, have more open crowns and bear small cones with large seeds. The trees are widely spaced with a sparse understory of herbs and shrubs.

37.1 mi., (6000′) and east to 75.1 mi. At Trinidad take the Colorado 12 exit, traveling through Trinidad and entering the Picketwire valley.

Trinidad lies along the Purgatoire River, which supports an impressive *lowland riparian ecosystem.* Large plains cottonwoods, massive, broad-crowned trees with large, heart-shaped leaves, and peach-leaved willows dominate this ecosystem in its natural state. At Trinidad many cultivated species of deciduous trees have been introduced and mix with the native species.

*40.4 mi.
(6200')
At the top of the grade adjacent to Trinidad Lake, a well-developed *piñon–juniper woodland* lies on the right side of the road. Interspersed among the trees are Gambel oak, prickly pear cactus, mountain mahogany, skunkbrush, rabbitbrush, and wax currant. The thin topsoil of the woodland floor supports blue grama in places but elsewhere gives way to bare, rocky sandstone. The shoulder of the road just bordering the woodland is dominated by weeds that abound on disturbed soils but do not belong to the piñon–juniper ecosystem. You may see a noisy band of piñon jays flying from tree to tree, a common sight in these woodlands.

*49.1 mi.
(6400')
Just past Tijeras, across from old mine waste dumps, stop at the side of the road and view several different ecosystems. On the right side of the road, piñon pine and juniper are mixed with ponderosa pine, larger trees with long needles. As you proceed up the Picketwire Valley, *ponderosa pine forests* become more prevalent on the warmer south-facing slopes and are extensive and mature near Stonewall Gap.

The Purgatoire River, bordered by a *mountain riparian ecosystem,* flows through the valley. Trees and shrubs include narrow-leaved cottonwood, boxelder, numerous shrub willows, and chokecherry.

Across the far bank past the mine waste dumps, the base of the north-facing slope harbors ponderosa pine that gives way to Douglas fir and an occasional blue spruce as elevation increases. Farther up the valley, the extensive *montane shrublands* that you will see on the slope are composed predominantly of Gambel oak.

71.5 mi.,
(8000')
and north
to 118.6 mi.
As you pass through the opening in the rock formation at Stonewall Gap, you suddenly come upon *Douglas fir forests* on the nearby north-facing slopes. The Douglas fir is a dark blue-green conifer with

flat, short needles arranged singly on the twigs. Cones are distributed throughout the tree, with lobed bracts protruding from between cone scales. In contrast, ponderosa pine, still visible on the ridge tops to the east and scattered among the fir, is dull green with long needles in bunches in two or three. Its cones are huskier and have short spines on each scale.

The understory of the Douglas fir forest is sparse, and the ground is covered with fallen needles often several inches deep.

As you continue along the road from Stonewall Gap approaching Monument Lake, you begin to encounter white fir, a tall, stately tree with long silver-green needles curving upward on the twigs. Unlike Douglas fir, white fir is a true fir, its erect silvery cones found only on the uppermost branches of the tree. Although common in southern Colorado in many locations, white fir is rarely found in pure stands. Along this road you will see it mixed with Douglas fir, ponderosa pine, Engelmann spruce, and other conifers.

77.9 mi. (8600')   Turn left to Potato Patch (Purgatoire) Campground. The road follows the North Fork of the Purgatoire River. Dense *spruce–fir forests* on the north-facing slope (to the left) and open *limber pine–bristlecone pine woodlands* on the south-facing slope (to the right) overlook the *mountain riparian ecosystem* along the riverbank.

The *spruce–fir ecosystem,* distinguished by the tall, spire-shaped trees, consists of Engelmann spruce and corkbark fir with some white fir at lower elevations. The forest is dense and humid, and little direct sunlight reaches the forest floor. The understory contains relatively few plants. However, seedlings of spruce and fir are present, showing that this is a climax ecosystem which will retain its present characteristics through time.

The *limber pine–bristlecone pine woodland* near the road is a successional ecosystem. A fire has removed the original spruce-fir forest, and because of its dry southerly exposure, these pines have become established. In time they probably will be replaced by Douglas fir, Engelmann spruce, and corkbark fir. Near the top of the slope, where soils are thinner and trees are more exposed to wind, the limber and bristlecone pine ecosystem may persist in a climax state.

*82.6 mi.   Potato Patch Campground is located within a mixed
(9600')   *Engelmann spruce–corkbark fir* and *quaking aspen ecosystem.*

Aspen groves are successional, invading disturbed sites and improving the soil with leaf and branch litter. As aspen stands mature, the soil improvement hastens the establishment of the spruce–fir ecosystems. The area around the campground is still dominated by groves of aspen that are moderately spaced, covering the slopes together with younger spruce and fir. Upon examination the soil appears dark and rich with organic matter. It supports large aspen and a lush variety of forbs and shrubs on the forest floor. The ground surface is covered by several layers of leaves and litter. In this cool shady environment, spruce and fir seedlings grow well, and already many young Engelmann spruce are beginning to displace the aspen.

Drive back to Colorado 12.

87.3 mi.   Rejoin Colorado 12 and continue northward to Cucharas Pass.

94.0 mi.   From North Lake to Cucharas Pass, you will see a
(9200')   mosaic of different ecosystems. North-facing slopes of surrounding hills are covered by stands of mixed fir and spruce with small groves of aspen; occasionally ponderosa pine dot the base of the hills. South-

facing slopes are covered with stands of Gambel oak, limber pine, and bristlecone pine. Much of the forest that originally dominated this region was removed by fire and logging, producing the mixture of ecosystems along this section of the road.

*95.5 mi. (9700′)   A large *successional dry meadow* lies on the left side of the road. Aspen are encroaching along its margins, and occasionally elk can be seen here during twilight hours.

96.2 mi. (9994′)   Here at Cucharas Pass you may take a side trip to Apishapa Pass (Cordova Pass), about 12 miles round trip. You will pass through mixed forests of aspen, Engelmann spruce and corkbark fir, and bristlecone and limber pine. Some of the bristlecone are very large and probably very old, and are being replaced by a spruce–fir forest. While at Apishapa Pass, you may wish to follow a hiking trail to West Spanish Peak to examine *alpine tundra ecosystems*. The trail is approximately two miles long.

Continue north on Colorado 12 to the town of Cuchara.

Approximately two miles past Cucharas Pass, you may wish to turn left and follow a road to Cuchara, Bear Lake, and Blue Lake Campgrounds. Scenic Bear Lake is located in a climax *spruce–fir ecosystem*. Nearby at the Blue Lake Campground, a two-mile (relatively steep) trail ascends the west side of Trinchera Peak and provides another opportunity to view *alpine tundra ecosystems*.

*101.4 mi. (8500′)   The town of Cuchara: To the right of the road, along the Cucharas River, notice the *mountain riparian ecosystem*. Looking upward to treeline, note that once again Gambel oak mix with the *Douglas fir forest* that dominates both slopes of the valley. Just north of Cuchara, New Mexican locust trees begin to appear along the side of the road. These small trees or shrubs stand eight to fifteen feet tall and are Colorado's only native locust. When in bloom, they produce showy clusters of pink or lavender flowers.

Descending from Cuchara into La Veta, the road follows the Cucharas River down out of the montane forest into *piñon–juniper woodlands* that characterize the foothills. Both landscape and vegetation are very similar to those immediately to the west of Trinidad at the beginning of the Picketwire Valley. Beyond La Veta the foothills open into a parkland consisting of *mountain grassland* and shrublands. Blue grama and needle-and-thread grasses grow here, as well as introduced species such as crested wheatgrass. The latter species probably was established to improve range conditions since this area has a long history of intensive cattle grazing. Shrubs consist of a mixture of rabbitbrush, four-winged saltbush, and snakeweed.

118.6 mi., (6800′) and east.
Turn right at the junction of Colorado 12 and US 160 and proceed eastward on US 160 to Walsenburg. The tour ends in Walsenburg, where you rejoin Interstate 25.

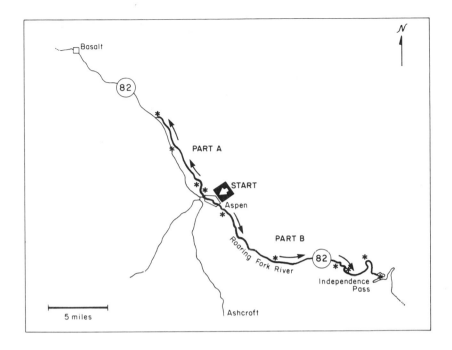

TOUR NO. 5: ROARING FORK RIVER VALLEY TO INDEPENDENCE PASS

This tour is in two parts. The first part starts in Aspen and proceeds down valley to the west. The second part also starts in Aspen and follows the Roaring Fork River eastward up the valley to Independence Pass. Both parts totaling 30.5 miles can be accomplished in a day. The routes and roadside stops conform to the similar self-guided tours on the geology of the Aspen region in *Aspen High Country: The Geology* by Laing and Lampiris, published by Thunder River Press.

Part A: Woody Creek Road

Start: 0.0 miles (7907')	From the Jerome Hotel at the intersection of Main and Mill streets in Aspen, drive west on Colorado 82 (Main Street).
0.9 mi.	Bridge over Castle Creek.
1.0 mi.	Turn right at stoplight onto Cemetery Lane.

1.6 mi.   Pause just before a right bend in the road. The prominent ridge ahead is Red Butte. Its southwest side is covered with a dense *montane shrubland* consisting of Gambel oak and serviceberry. This oak-dominated shrubland, sometimes called "petran," is extensive on south-facing slopes in the vicinity of Aspen. Farther west toward Basalt, where the climate is warmer and drier, it hugs the north-facing slopes. There the south-facing hillsides are occupied by woodlands of piñon pine and juniper, species more tolerant of warmer and drier conditions. Dense oak–serviceberry shrublands are good places to look for lazuli buntings, blue-gray gnatcatchers, green-tailed towhees, and scrub jays.

On the northeastern side of Red Butte, cool and moister conditions have permitted the establishment of a few Douglas fir mixed with Gambel oak and service-berry. As you proceed down the road and behind Red Butte, you will have a better view of these conifers.

*2.2 mi.   Parking lot to the left of the road, just past the
(7716′)   bridge over the Roaring Fork River. This is a convenient place to park if you wish to explore on foot the shrubland on the northeast side of the Butte. Near the parking area several large Colorado blue spruce grow along the river. This is the state tree of Colorado and is characteristic of mountain riparian ecosystems from elevations of 7000 to 9500 feet.

3.6 mi.   As you drive through this portion of the Roaring
to 10.0 mi.   Fork Valley, notice the *sagebrush shrublands* that occupy the deep, fine-grained soils of lower hillsides and valley terraces. Much of the shrubland has been replaced by irrigated hay meadows on the flat terrace surfaces. Elsewhere, mountain big sagebrush mixed with serviceberry, rabbitbrush, bitterbrush, and snowberry dominates the valley bottom. If you stop near one of these sagebrush stands in late spring or early summer, you are sure to hear green-tailed towhees singing from the taller shrubs.

*6.4 mi.
(7420′)

Pullout on right at bottom of hill just before an inter-section. A *mountain riparian ecosystem* dominated by narrowleaf cottonwood and blue spruce forms a narrow band of forest along the river. The tall trees and a dense understory of shrubby willows, hawthorn, serviceberry, snowberry, currant, wild rose, and other shrubs provide numerous nesting, denning, and feeding sites for many birds and other animals. The lively songs of yellow warblers hidden in the treetops are clearly audible above the river, and song sparrows and cordilleran flycatchers sing from shrub thickets.

*10.0 mi.
(7200′)

Stay right at the fork in the road and park at the base of a steep slope on the right.

A *piñon pine–juniper woodland* grows on the south-facing hillside above the road. Limited moisture and hot summer temperatures, coupled with intensive cattle grazing in the past, have produced sparse understory in these woodlands. Steep slopes and unstable, well-drained soils make it difficult for seedling establishment once plant cover is removed. The soils are relatively sterile and low in organic matter, because the dry conditions slow decomposition and retard the subsequent release of nutrients from dead plant material. Soil development is slow and meager in strong contrast to the rich, dark soils that have formed under the oak shrublands on the opposite side of the valley. Shrub understory consists mainly of mountain mahogany, skunkbrush, rabbitbrush, and a few serviceberry shrubs in less exposed sites. Pasture sage, Indian ricegrass, and cheatgrass are widespread. The latter species is a good indicator of soil disturbance and overgrazing in dry western climates.

Look for Colorado chipmunks and Nuttall's cottontails, and you should see golden-mantled ground squirrels at the base of the slope. You may hear mountain chickadees scolding from nearby conifers. Piñon jays and plain titmice are other birds characteristic of piñon–juniper woodlands.

Part B: Independence Pass Road

Start:
0.0 miles

From the Jerome Hotel at the intersection of Main and Mill streets, drive east on Colorado 82 (Main Street).

*2.0 miles
(8030′)

Pullout on right at entrance to Northstar Nature Preserve. Much of the preserve occupies the flat floodplain of the Roaring Fork River. Before ranching took place in the valley, this floodplain was probably covered with shrubby willows, typical of wet soils along mountain streams and rivers. Willows were removed by ranchers, and the floodplain was converted to the hay meadow that you see today. Willows are slowly invading the meadow and if unchecked might eventually fill the valley again.

The abundant grasses provide an ideal home for the montane and meadow voles, small mouselike rodents that construct little runways through the grass. They are active in the daytime, and you may catch a brief glimpse of one scurrying down its runway as you walk through the grass. They provide food for hawks, weasels, and other predators that hunt by day. Deer mice and least chipmunks live on drier ground at the forest edge along the margin of the floodplain. Common snipes occasionally nest in the marshy areas, and in late spring you might hear the hollow whinnying sound they produce during their aerial courtship displays high above the preserve.

The opposite side of the valley is covered with a dense *Douglas fir forest* interspersed with patches of aspen. On the warmer south-facing hillside above the road, Douglas fir and aspen are mixed with Gambel oak and ponderosa pine. The large numbers of aspen in this vicinity are a result in part of the extensive disturbance of the original coniferous forest during the mining era. Much of the forest was logged and other parts burned, allowing the establishment of aspen, which are now slowly being replaced by the original conifer species.

The low hills at the west end of the preserve are the remnants of a glacial moraine that once dammed the river, producing a lake on the site of the present meadow. Sediments and organic material eventually filled the lake. The coarse, well-drained soils of the moraine support ponderosa pine and other conifers that are unable to grow in the wetter, fine-grained soils of the floodplain. The ponderosa are distinguished by their broad, open crowns, and three- to seven-inch-long needles, the longest of any Colorado conifer. In this area ponderosa exist only as scattered individuals, but elsewhere in the state they form extensive forests.

*8.7 mi. (9350′)   Parking area on right for Weller Lake trailhead; Weller Lake Campground on left. The Weller Lake Campground is located in a typical moist *aspen grove,* with a dense understory of herbaceous vegetation: Fendler meadowrue, Gray's lousewort, white geranium, American vetch, and common lupine. Colorado columbine, the state flower, also grows here.

Several bird species are typically found in aspen groves in the valley. Warbling vireos are an inconspicuous but common resident, and their persistent rambling song is heard throughout aspen forests in the region. The red-naped sapsucker is a woodpecker that nests almost exclusively in aspen and excavates cavities that are used later by other birds, including violet-green and tree swallows and house wrens. Look for small mounds of freshly overturned soil, for this is a sure sign that northern pocket gophers have been tunneling under the surface.

Visit the *mountain riparian ecosystem* by taking the Weller Lake Trail down to the river. River birch, alder, and shrubby willows are conspicuous shrubs, typical of riparian sites at mid-elevations. Here you are likely to spot a Wilson's warbler, a small yellow bird with a black cap. The trail crosses the Roaring Fork via a bridge, which is a good spot to watch for American dippers as they fly along the river just a few feet above the water.

You may wish to continue up the trail to Weller Lake, about a quarter of a mile. The trail passes through a mixed coniferous forest of Douglas fir, Engelmann spruce, and subalpine fir. Understory vegetation is sparse compared to that of the aspen grove; heart-leaved arnica, huckleberry, and mountain lover are among the more common plants on the forest floor.

Weller Lake is of interest because of a forest fire that occurred on the west and south sides of the lake during the summer of 1980. It is a good place to see the early stages of forest succession. Since the fire many lodgepole pine seedlings have appeared, and aspen have sprouted from preexisting root systems that survived the fire.

8.7 mi. to 14.6 mi.   The forest on the mountainside above and to the left of the road is mainly a mixture of Douglas fir and aspen, but as you continue up the valley, there are many stands of lodgepole pine. Look for the yellowish green coloration of the lodgepole, their straight trunks, and old, persistent cones on the branches. If you explore any of these stands, look for burned stumps or pieces of charcoal on the forest floor, remnants of the earlier forest. The south-facing forest in the vicinity of Lost Man Campground consists almost entirely of lodgepole and aspen.

Across the river on the opposite side of the valley, the forest consists mostly of Engelmann spruce and subalpine fir. On cool, north-facing slopes, aspen and lodgepole are generally absent above 10,500 feet. Above this elevation, forest invasion of burned areas is accomplished by direct reestablishment of Engelmann spruce and subalpine fir.

*14.6 mi. Lost Man Campground on the right.
(10,500')

The Roaring Fork River can be crossed at the campground when the water is not too high, and this provides an opportunity to walk through the *Engelmann spruce–subalpine fir* forest on the south side of the valley. Broom huckleberry, heart-leaved arnica, Jacob's ladder, and curled lousewort cover mosses on the forest floor. Dark-eyed juncos and ruby-crowned and golden-crowned kinglets can often be heard singing from the trees.

*15.1 mi. Pullout on right.
(10,700')

Most of the trees on the hillside above and below the road are lodgepole pine. Many were planted during a reforestation project, as this area was severely burned and logged during the mining era in the late 1800s. Because the forest is relatively uncrowded and there is abundant light and moisture, understory vegetation is diverse. Look for Wooton's senecio, ballhead sandwort, and the purple Whipple's penstemon.

15.8 mi. Notice the treeless avalanche path that extends down through the forest on the opposite side of the valley. Periodic snow avalanches keep the track clear of trees and allow the development of a lush community of shrubs and herbaceous vegetation.

16.3 mi.   Independence Townsite.
(10,880′)

The Independence lode was discovered on July 4, 1879, and like many other mining towns Independence appeared almost overnight. The town was active for nearly twenty years and at its peak had a population of nearly 2000. The town was abandoned when the ore body was depleted.

17.7 mi.   A *natural meadow* covers the valley below the highway and is the result of a high water table and deep, fine-grained soils that discourage tree growth. The wetter areas are covered by dense communities of shrubby willows. Notice a few islands of spruce in the meadow. These occupy mounds of glacial moraine that have coarser and better-drained soils.

*18.6 mi.   Pullout on the right at the hairpin turn.
(11,506′)

Cross the road and hike a short distance up the trail where you can examine the wind-sculptured *krummholz* tree islands of Engelmann spruce and subalpine fir. Here in the forest-tundra ecotone, conifers approach their environmental limits of growth. Most of each tree island is covered by snow during the wintertime. Branches and twigs that project above the surface of the snowdrift are exposed to drying winds. Ice crystals carried by the wind create a sandblasting effect that kills the twigs and needles on the windward side of the island. This is especially noticeable on larger trunks where only the leeward branches have survived, creating "flag trees."

Extensive willow thickets occupy much of the valley in this area. They are a sign that snow covers the valley floor to a depth of a few feet throughout the winter. In order for the willows to survive the cold temperatures, they must be covered by a protective blanket of snow. The snow must not be too deep, for then it would take too long to melt, and there would be insufficient time during the short growing season to produce and store enough nutrients to survive the following winter. Tree islands and timberline willow thickets are the preferred nesting habitat for the white-crowned sparrow. These birds are abundant and can be recognized by white and black stripes on their heads. If you listen carefully, you may also hear the flutelike song of the hermit thrush from some of the taller spruce-fir forest stands nearby.

*20.5 mi. Parking area to the right at Independence Pass.
(12,095')

Alpine tundra ecosystems such as these on Independence Pass are characterized by a cold, windy climate. The average annual temperature is below freezing, and the growing season is only a few weeks long. Substantial amounts of precipitation, thirty or more inches per year, fall on the tundra, although much of the winter snow is blown away by the wind. Because of the wind, some areas are snow-free most of the winter, while nearby places may be covered by moderate amounts of snow or by deep drifts. Differences in winter snow depths, soil rockiness, and exposure create a mosaic of distinct tundra plant communities.

Except for willow shrubs, tundra plants are characterized by short stature. They live close to the ground where wind speeds are lower and air temperatures are higher. Because of the short growing season, many plants bloom within a few days following snow melt, thus allowing maximum time for development of fruits and seeds. During June and July, tundra meadows offer some of the most spectacular floral displays in the mountains. Almost all plants in the alpine tundra are perennials, and some may live for many decades. Most have large root systems that serve as food reserves during unusually poor growing seasons.

Here on Independence Pass you can see many common Rocky Mountain alpine plants. Look for alpine forget-me-not, American bistort, moss pink, alpine sandwort, and alpine wallflower. Stay on the designated trail, for these delicate alpine plants are very susceptible to trampling, and once disturbed may take decades or centuries to recover. For a close look at other alpine plant communities, you may wish to take the hiking trails to either Lincoln Lake or Independence Lake, which start at the previous roadside stop. (You should allow at least a half day for either of these hikes.) Two of the most common tundra mammals, yellow-bellied marmots and pikas, live in rock fields near Independence Lake.

While at Independence Pass, look for American pipits and horned larks, two birds that breed on the tundra. You might spot rosy finches feeding on late lying snowbanks, and if you are lucky, you could see white-tailed ptarmigan, the only year-round tundra bird resident.

Key to Common Native Tree Species

The ability to recognize dominant tree species is essential if one wishes to distinguish among the various types of forested ecosystems. Fortunately the Southern Rocky Mountain region has relatively few tree species compared to many other areas, and the identification of these species can be mastered easily by anyone willing to take the time to look closely at the trees. As one's experience grows, so does the ability to recognize the trees at a distance. The benefits are numerous. One may begin to "read" the landscape. The trees tell us something of the climate and soils in a particular location. Some indicate past disturbance to the ecosystem. Tree recognition is an excellent tool enabling one to anticipate what kinds of birds, mammals, and wildflowers are likely to be seen in a given location.

Information on the characteristics of each tree species has been organized here into a dichotomous key. A dichotomous key consists of contrasting groups of characteristics arranged in couplets. By closely examining the characteristics of the tree you wish to identify, you must choose which part of the couplet, (a) or (b), best describes the tree. Always read both parts of the couplet. Once you have decided which part of the couplet best fits your tree, that part either will tell you the name of the tree or will refer you to the number of another couplet farther down in the key.

Go directly to that couplet, bypassing all others in between. Proceed as before, deciding which of the groups of characteristics in each part of the new couplet best describes the tree you wish to identify. If possible look at several trees of the kind you are trying to identify, so that you will have a better feeling for the tree's typical appearance. As you proceed through the key, also look at several leaves, needles, berries, etc., from your tree to determine its usual characteristics at a greater level of detail.

This key includes only tree species native to Colorado. In locations where there are many introduced species, such as in *lowland riparian ecosystems,* one of the published guides on North American trees will be more useful to you.

la. Trees with broad leaves that die and fall to the ground each winter (deciduous) . . . . . go to (2).

lb. Trees with leaves consisting of needles or overlapping scales that stay green through winter and remain on the tree; cones or berries usually present on the twigs . . . . . go to (9).

2a. One leaf on each stem (petiole), leaves with wavy or finely toothed edges; fruits and flowers tiny and numerous, arranged around a central stalk, the entire structure (catkin) only a few inches long; tiny seeds, with cottony tufts . . . . . go to (3).

2b. Three to five lobed leaves on each stem (petiole), or if single leaf on each stem, the leaves with 3 to 5 deep lobes; fruits occur in hanging clusters, and within each cluster, the fruits arranged in twos, each with a papery wing attached (samaras). MAPLES . . . . . go to (8).

3a. Twigs on branches smooth and noticeably bright orange to reddish brown; the buds on each twig are covered by only one caplike scale (look closely here); leaves are 2-5 inches long and narrow, with tiny teeth along their edges; underside of leaves a pale blue color; found in riparian areas on the plains and in the foothills. PEACH-LEAVED WILLOW (*Salix amygdaloides*).

3b. Twigs on branches gray or greenish, with buds covered by 2 or more overlapping scales . . . . . go to (4).

4a. Bark smooth, white or light green but sometimes light orange, usually with black or gray scars; trunk usually straight and vertical; leaves roundish, small 1½-3 inches in diameter; usually a small- or medium-sized tree with small narrow branches; the only deciduous tree commonly found outside of riparian areas in the montane and subalpine forests. QUAKING ASPEN (*Populus tremuloides*), see illustration page 143.

4b. Older bark thickly furrowed and yellowish green to gray, especially near base of tree; trunk seldom straight, usually with several large branches; trees of riparian areas . . . . . go to (5).

5a. Leaves broad, usually a little or no longer than they are wide; leaves roughly triangular in shape, with wavy margins; trees often very large; trees of the plains or at the mouths of foothill canyons. PLAINS COTTONWOOD (*Populus deltoidea* ssp. *occidentalis*), see illustration page 61. In some southern and western Colorado locations, the plains cottonwood is replaced by the VALLEY COTTONWOOD (*Populus deltoidea* ssp. *wislizenii*), which is of similar appearance.

5b. Leaves elongate, usually at least a third longer than they are wide; smaller trees of mountain riparian areas . . . . . go to (6).

6a. Leaves ovate (egg-shaped), broadest at their base, and having a sharply pointed tip, often large, 3-6 inches long and 2-4 inches wide; develops inch-long terminal buds in the winter, which are sticky and very fragrant when crushed; uncommon, occurring in scattered locations in central and northern Colorado. BALSAM POPLAR (*Populus balsamifera*).

6b. Leaves smaller than above, 2-4 inches long; terminal buds on twigs ¾-inch long or less . . . . . go to (7).

7a. Leaves narrowly elongate, lance-shaped, tapering toward the tip, bright yellow-green above and paler underneath; leaves ½-1½ inches wide; terminal buds slightly fragrant, covered by 5 overlapping scales. NARROWLEAF COTTON-WOOD (*Populus angustifolia*). This is the common cotton-wood along mountain streams up to 10,000 ft. elevation.

7b. Leaves somewhat wider than those of the narrowleaf cottonwood, ¾-2 inches wide, dark green on top and dull green underneath; terminal buds covered by 6-7 scales and not fragrant. LANCELEAF COTTONWOOD (*Populus X acuminata*). This species is regarded as a hybrid between the narrowleaf cottonwood and the plains or valley cotton-wood. It occurs along with the narrowleaf cottonwood in the foothills, and sometimes it is difficult to distinguish be-tween the two.

8a. Three to five leaves on each stem (petiole), each leaf with several teeth or lobes, lower leaves on the petiole attached opposite each other; twigs stout, with grayish color; small tree of riversides on plains or in foothill canyons. BOX-ELDER (*Negundo aceroides*).

8b. One lobed leaf on each stem (petiole), 3 to 5 lobes; twigs slender with a reddish color; small tree in canyons of Utah and extreme southwestern Colorado. BIG-TOOTH MAPLE (*Acer grandidentatum*). ROCKY MOUNTAIN MAPLE (*Acer glabrum*) a large, common shrub of moist montane slopes and riparian zones, or rarely, a small tree, will also key to here. Its leaves are occasionally so deeply lobed as to be di-vided into three separate leaflets; the leaves of Rocky Moun-tain maple also are commonly infected with galls that ap-pear as crimson, velvety blotches.

9a. Leaves very tiny, scalelike, overlapping one another like shingles, not needlelike; fruit berrylike at maturity. JUNIPERS . . . . . go to (10).

9b. Leaves long, needlelike, attached singly or in bunches to the twig; fruits developing into woody cones. PINES, SPRUCES, FIRS, and DOUGLAS FIR . . . . . go to (12).

10a. Trees usually gray-green in color; the smallest branches or twigs (branchlets) usually very slender and long; the margins of the tiny leaves without minute serrations or teeth when viewed under a hand lens; berry with 1-3 seeds, usually two. ROCKY MOUNTAIN JUNIPER (*Sabina scopulorum*). Found at intermediate elevations throughout Colorado mountains. This is the only tree juniper found north of the Arkansas Divide on the Eastern Slope.

10b. Tree usually dark green; branchlets usually short and stout; numerous tiny teeth along the leaf margins can be seen with a hand lens; berry with 1-2 seeds, usually one . . . . . go to (11).

11a. Berries pea-sized, copper-colored to blue, and succulent when fresh; the larger branches usually leave the main trunk below ground level and appear as several trunks, giving the tree a shrubby character. ONE-SEED JUNIPER (*Sabina monosperma*), see illustration page 109. This is the common associate with piñon pine from Colorado Springs southward and also occurs in the western third of the state.

11b. Berries marble-sized, reddish brown or bluish with a powdery coating, and mealy or fibrous when fresh; the larger branches usually leave the main trunk above ground level. UTAH JUNIPER (*Sabina osteosperma*). In the western third of Colorado, associated with piñon pine and often intermingled with one-seed juniper.

12a. Needles attached to twig in bundles containing two or more needles; base of each bundle wrapped in a fibrous sheath; scales of the cones thick and woody, swollen at the tip. PINES . . . . . go to (13).

12b. Needles attached to the twig separately, without a fibrous sheath at their base; scales of cones usually thin or papery, or if woody, papery bracts protruding from between the cone scales. SPRUCES, FIRS, and DOUGLAS FIR . . . . . go to (17).

13a. Bundles typically containing 4 or 5 needles . . . . . go to (14).

13b. Bundles containing 2 or 3 needles . . . . . go to (15).

14a. Needles usually less than 1½ inches long and sparsely covered with white granules of pitch; cone scales with sharp spines or bristles. BRISTLECONE PINE (*Pinus aristata*), see illustration page 163.

14b. Needles usually longer than 1½ inches, granules of pitch absent from the needles; cone scales without bristles; a small tree usually with crooked trunk. LIMBER PINE (*Pinus flexilis*), see illustration page 162. MEXICAN WHITE PINE (*Pinus strobiformis*), a tall tree with a straight trunk, of southwestern Colorado, is a closely related species that will also key to here.

15a. Needles 4-7 inches long, occurring 2-3 to a bundle, cones 2½-5 inches long. PONDEROSA PINE (*Pinus ponderosa*), see illustration page 121.

15b. Needles less than 3 inches long, usually 2 to a bundle; cones shorter than 2½ inches . . . . . go to (16).

16a. A tall slender tree; scales of cones tipped with short bristles; cones usually persistent on branches long after maturity; a common tree in burned-over areas above 8,000 ft. elevation. LODGEPOLE PINE (*Pinus contorta*), see illustration page 156.

16b. A low, bushy tree; cone scales without bristles; cones falling at maturity; occurs from 4,000-9,000 ft. elevation. PIÑON PINE (*Pinus edulis*), see illustration page 108.

17a. Needles with 4 sides; older twigs rough with the persistent stumps of fallen needles. SPRUCES . . . . . go to (18).

17b. Needles 2-sided, flattened; older twigs smooth. TRUE FIRS and DOUGLAS FIR . . . . . go to (19).

18a. Needles very rigid and sharp; cones longer than 2½ inches; bark gray and scaly; trees often bluish in color; trees of stream sides and steep slopes from 7,000-9,500 ft. COLORADO BLUE SPRUCE (*Picea pungens*), see illustration page 74.

18b. Needles moderately flexible, pointed, but not as sharp as Colorado blue spruce; bark on larger trees in thin, reddish plates which is easily picked off in flakes; cones shorter than 2½ inches; trees of high elevations 8,500 ft.-12,000 ft.; often hybridizes in lower elevations with blue spruce, producing trees of intermediate characteristics. ENGELMANN SPRUCE (*Picea engelmannii*), see illustration page 170.

19a. Needles on very short stalks; buds at the tips of the branches sharp-pointed; cones hanging from the branches and falling from the tree in one piece; three-toothed papery bracts protruding from between the cone scales; cones distributed on branches throughout the tree crown; bark on older trees very thick and deeply furrowed. DOUGLAS FIR (*Pseudotsuga menziesii*), see illustration page 135.

19b. Needles without short stalks; buds at the tips of the branches blunt; cones erect on the uppermost branches, disintegrating in place, rarely falling from the tree in one piece; bracts do not protrude from cone scales . . . . . go to (20).

20a. Cones dark brown to purplish, 2-4 inches long, often glistening with globules of pitch; bark on young trees silvery gray and smooth; on older trees, grayish brown and shallowly fissured; a tree of higher elevations, 8,500-12,000 ft., often with an extremely narrow and spire-like crown having a deep blue-green color. SUBALPINE FIR (*Abies bifolia*), see illustration page 171. In southern Colorado, a similar species called CORKBARK FIR (*Abies arizonica*) occurs and is distinguished by soft, corky, cream-colored to gray bark, and by longer cones.

20b. Cones usually grayish green, 3-5 inches long; needles on lower branches often 2-3 inches long, which is longer than those on subalpine fir, although this characteristic not always dependable; bark of young trees smooth and gray; on older trees ashy gray and deeply furrowed; develops into a large tree with a broad, conical crown with a silver-blue to silver-green color; grows at intermediate elevations, 7,500-10,000 ft. WHITE FIR (*Abies concolor*).

Glossary

Alluvium, n. (**Alluvial**, adj.): Water-rounded sands and gravels, transported and deposited by running water.

Alpine: Treeless region on mountaintops and high ridges above upper treeline.

Arkansas Divide: High ground separating the South Platte and Arkansas River drainages. Also known as Palmer Divide.

Bedrock: Solid rock, often overlain by unconsolidated rock and soil.

Carnivore: Flesh-eating animal.

Chinook: Unusually warm, dry, westerly wind in the winter on the Eastern Slope.

Cirque: A deep, steep-walled bowl at the upper end of a mountain valley, formed by glacial erosion.

Climax ecosystem: Ecosystem that maintains its overall characteristics from century to century, providing that major geological, climatic, and human generated changes are excluded.

Community: Living part of an ecosystem that includes all of the plants and animals.

Competition: Rivalry among organisms for a common resource in relatively short supply.

Conifer: Tree or shrub with needlelike or scalelike leaves, often evergreen, that bears its seeds in cones.

Continental climate: Climate that is characteristic of the interior of a large land mass, having large daily and annual variations in temperature, and light to moderate rainfall.

Continental Divide: High ground along the Rocky Mountain chain that separates the waters flowing eastward toward the Atlantic Ocean from waters flowing westward toward the Pacific Ocean.

Convective storms: Storms generated by rising warm air circulation due to the heating effects of nearby land surfaces; these storms are usually accompanied by lightning and thunder.

Crown: Upper part of a tree, including the leaves and branches.

Deciduous: Plant that sheds its leaves each fall.

Dominant: Most characteristic plant species of an ecosystem; the species that governs the numbers and kinds of other plants and the flow of energy in the ecosystem.

Ecology: Branch of science dealing with interrelations among organisms and between organisms and the non-living environment.

Ecosystem: All the living organisms, plus the whole complex of physical factors that form the organisms' environment, in a particular time and place. The term denotes a system whereby all of the living and non-living components function as a single interacting unit.

Ecotone: Transition zone between ecosystems; has species of each ecosystem as well as characteristics of its own.

Fauna: All animals in one area at one time.

Foothills: Low mountain zone between approximately 5500 and 8000 feet elevation.

Forb: Broad-leaved, non-woody plant.

Herb: Plant without persistent above-ground parts.

Herbivore: Plant-eating animal.

Hogback: Ridge of steeply tipped sedimentary rock at base of mountains.

Invasion: Entry and establishment of an organism in an ecosystem not previously occupied by that species.

Krummholz: Transition zone between the continuous subalpine coniferous forest and the treeless alpine tundra above.

Layering: Sprouting of roots and vertical shoots from tree branches that have been partially covered by litter.

Litter: Undecomposed and partially decomposed organic debris covering the soil.

Metamorphic rocks: Formed from older rocks that have been subjected to great heat and pressure or to chemical changes.

Microtine: Native mouse or vole of the genus *Microtus*, with short ears, a stout body, and a blunt nose.

Middens: Large piles of cones and cone parts that are collected by squirrels.

Montane: Low- to mid-elevation zone of forested mountains, between approximately 5600 and 9500 feet. The portion of this zone below 8000 feet is also known as the lower montane or foothills zone.

Moraine: An accumulation of gravel, boulders, and other rock material, deposited by glaciers.

Orographic precipitation: Associated with air masses that are forced to rise and cool as they are pushed over mountains by prevailing winds.

Palmer Divide: *See* Arkansas Divide.

Park: Large meadow or mountain grassland surrounded by forest.

Patterned ground: Rock polygons, circles, stripes, and other patterns caused by frost action in the ground.

Perennial: Plant that lives year after year.

Physiographic province: A geographical region of similar geological structure and landform appearance.

Pioneer species: First organisms to invade an area devoid of life.

Plains: Low elevation region east of the Rocky Mountains composed chiefly of grasslands and, along streams and rivers, narrow belts of deciduous riparian forest; also, open areas of flat topography, covered with relatively short grasses.

Prairie: An area of open, often rolling grassland.

Rhizome: Horizontal underground stem.

Riparian: Adjacent to water.

Sediment, n. (**Sedimentary**, adj.): Loose or unconsolidated material overlying bedrock that is deposited by water, wind, or downslope movement by gravity, and includes soils, sandy or muddy river deposits, landslide deposits, etc.

Sedimentary Rock: Layered rock, formed of consolidated sedimentary material.

Semiarid: Characterized by light annual rainfall and capable of sustaining only short grasses and shrubs.

Semidesert: An arid or semiarid region often located between desert and grassland or woodland, usually characterized by sparse shrubby vegetation.

Shrub: A woody plant of relatively low height and usually having several stems rather than a central trunk.

Site characteristic: Non-living ecosystem component such as climate, soil, or geological feature.

Species: Smallest commonly used unit of organism classification; a group of organisms able to interbreed among themselves but not with members of other species.

Subalpine: Highest zone of forested mountains, between approximately 9500 and 11,500 feet elevation.

Succession n. (**Successional**, adj.): Natural change from one type of ecosystem to another type with significantly different characteristics.

Sucker: A vertical shoot produced from a network of shallow, interconnected lateral roots of certain species of trees and shrubs; especially characteristic of aspen and cottonwood.

Timberline: The upper elevational limit of continuous subalpine forests of upright trees.

Treeline: Altitudinal limit of tree growth regardless of size or shape; in the Front Range, upper treeline is at approximately 11,400 feet, and lower treeline is at 5600 feet.

Tundra: Treeless ecosystems of extremely high latitudes or above timberline in the mountains.

Understory: Layer of underlying vegetation; the shrubs and herbs of a forest, or the herbs in a shrubby area.

Windthrow: Overthrowing of trees by wind.

Suggested Reading List

There are many field guides and other publications that will help to develop an understanding of the ecology of Colorado and surrounding states. This list is not intended to be exhaustive, but it does include books that we have found to be particularly useful.

Field Identification Guides

Borror, D.J., and R.E. White. 1970. *A Field Guide to Insects of America North of Mexico.* Peterson Field Guide Series, Houghton Mifflin Co., Boston.

Burt, W.H., and R.P. Grossenheider. 1976. *A Field Guide to the Mammals.* Peterson Field Guide Series, Houghton Mifflin Co., Boston.

Carter, Jack L. 1988. *Trees and Shrubs of Colorado.* Dist. by Johnson Books, Boulder, Colorado.
Easy-to-follow botanical keys to the more common trees and shrubs of the state, with lots of good drawings.

Elmore, Francis H. 1976. *Shrubs and Trees of the Southwest Uplands.* Southwest Parks and Monuments Association, Globe, Arizona.
A nontechnical guide useful in southwestern Colorado. Many excellent illustrations.

Farrand, John Jr. (ed.). 1983. *The Audubon Society Master Guide to Birding.* Alfred A. Knopf, New York.

Designed for the experienced birder but useful to the novice as well. Excellent photographs and illustrations. Multiple volumes limit the usefulness of this guide in the field, but the more extensive discussion of each bird species compared to other guides makes this set a good reference.

Halfpenny, James. 1986. *A Field Guide to Mammal Tracking in North America.* Johnson Books, Boulder, Colorado.

Hammerson, G.A. 1982. *Amphibians and Reptiles in Colorado.* Colorado Division of Wildlife, Denver.
A well-done reference containing excellent photographs and much interesting information on each species. Small size makes this guide convenient for use in the field.

Little, E.L. 1980. *The Audubon Society Field Guide to North American Trees: Western Region.* Alfred A. Knopf, New York.

Murie, O.J. 1974. *A Field Guide to Animal Tracks.* Peterson Field Guide Series, Houghton Mifflin Co., Boston.

Nelson, R.A. 1979. *Handbook of Rocky Mountain Plants.* Skyland Publishers, Estes Park, Colorado.
One of the best nontechnical plant guides for the Rocky Mountains in Colorado. Many illustrations, some color photographs, and easy-to-follow keys to plant families and important genera.

Peterson, R.T. 1990. *A Field Guide to Western Birds.* 3d ed. Peterson Field Guide Series, Houghton Mifflin Co., Boston.
A classic, this is the most popular bird identification guide for the West.

Preston, R.J., Jr. 1975. *North American Trees.* M.I.T. Press, Cambridge, Massachusetts.
A semitechnical guide with many good illustrations. Includes keys for the major genera.

Robbins, C.S., B. Bruun, and H.S. Zim. 1983. *Birds of North America.* Golden Press, New York.
One of the most popular bird field guides on the market.

Scott, S.L. (ed.). 1983. *Field Guide to the Birds of North America.* National Geographic Society.
Excellent color illustrations.

Stebbins, R.C. 1966. *A Field Guide to Western Reptiles and Amphibians.* Peterson Field Guide Series, Houghton Mifflin Co., Boston.

Taylor, R.J., and R.W. Valum. 1974. *Wildflowers 2: Sagebrush Country.* Touchstone Press, Beaverton, Oregon.
A nontechnical guide to shrubs and wildflowers of the sagebrush shrublands. Many excellent photographs. Especially useful in northeastern Colorado.

Udvardy, Miklos D.F. 1977. *The Audubon Society Field Guide to North American Birds. Western Region.* Alfred A. Knopf, New York.

Weber, William A. 1990. *Colorado Flora: Eastern Slope.* University Press of Colorado, Boulder.
This and the next two books are technical keys to vascular plants, and recommended for the serious enthusiast. All have many excellent illustrations, and together they comprise the most complete and up-to-date taxonomic guide to the plants of the Southern Rocky Mountain region.

Weber, William A. 1987. *Colorado Flora: Western Slope.* Colorado Associated University Press, Boulder.

Weber, William A. 1976. *Rocky Mountain Flora,* 5th ed. Colorado Associated University Press, Boulder.
A technical key to vascular plants of the Front Range vicinity but also applicable in surrounding areas.

Whitaker, John O., Jr. 1980. *The Audubon Society Field Guide to North American Mammals.* Alfred A. Knopf, New York.

Young, R.G. and J.W. Young. 1977. *Colorado West, Land of Geology and Wildflowers.* Wheelwright Press, Ltd. Grand Junction, Colorado.
Nontechnical guide to the geology and wildflowers of the Western Slope. Many photographs.

Other Publications

Armstrong, D.M. 1972. *Distribution of Mammals in Colorado.* Monograph of the Museum of Natural History, the University of Kansas, Number 3. University of Kansas Printing Service, Lawrence.
A comprehensive technical text offering distribution maps, records of occurrence, and information on the natural history of Colorado mammals.

Armstrong, D.M. 1987. *Rocky Mountain Mammals.* Colorado Associated University Press, Boulder.

A nontechnical guide to the mammals of the Rocky Mountain National Park and vicinity.

Bailey, A.M., and R.J. Niedrach. 1965. *Birds of Colorado,* 2 vols. Denver Museum of Natural History.
A large text on the natural history and distribution of Colorado birds. Many photographs and illustrations.

Benedict, Audrey DeLella. 1991. *A Sierra Club Naturalists Guide: The Southern Rockies: The Rocky Mountain Regions of Southern Wyoming, Colorado, and Northern New Mexico.* Sierra Club Books, San Francisco.
Good summary of the ecology, geology, and climate of the Southern Rocky Mountain region.

Bissell, S.J., and M.B. Dillon. 1982. *Colorado Mammal Distribution Latilong Study.* Colorado Division of Wildlife, Denver.
Summarizes present knowledge of distribution, abundance, and habitat preferences of the mammals of Colorado.

Chase, C.A. III, S.J. Bissell, H.E. Kingery, and W.D. Graul (eds.). 1982. *Colorado Bird Distribution Latilong Study.* Colorado Field Ornithologists (available from Colorado Division of Wildlife, Denver).
Summarizes present knowledge of distribution, abundance, and habitat preferences of the birds of Colorado.

Chronic, H. 1980. *Roadside Geology of Colorado.* Mountain Press Publishing Co., Missoula, Montana.
A useful nontechnical guide that explains many areas of geological interest along Colorado's highways.

Chronic, J., and H. Chronic. 1972. *Prairie Peak and Plateau: A Guide to the Geology of Colorado.* Colorado Geological Survey Bulletin 32, Colorado Geological Survey, Denver.
A small handbook that provides an excellent nontechnical overview of Colorado geology.

Costello, D.F. 1969. *The Prairie World.* University of Minnesota Press, Minneapolis.
A very readable text on grassland ecosystems of North America.

DeByle, Norbert V., and Robert P. Winokur (eds.). 1985. *Aspen: Ecology and Management in the Western United States.* U.S.D.A. Forest Service General Technical Report RM-119, Rocky Mountain Forest and Range Experiment Station, Fort Collins, Colorado.

One of the most complete summaries of the ecology, physiology, management, and other aspects of aspen.

Gregg, R.E. 1965. *The Ants of Colorado*. University of Colorado Press, Boulder.
Provides an excellent synopsis of Colorado ecology, as well as a complete technical treatment of Colorado ants.

Halfpenny, James C., and Roy Douglas Ozanne. 1989. *Winter: An Ecological Handbook*. Johnson Books, Boulder, Colorado.
More than just an ecological handbook, this has lots of interesting information on snow and ice, the physiological response of humans to cold, and field experiments for outdoor classes.

Hammerson, G.A., and D. Langlois. 1981. *Colorado Reptile and Amphibian Distribution Latilong Study*. Colorado Division of Wildlife, Denver.
Summarizes present knowledge of distribution, abundance, and habitat preferences of the reptiles and amphibians of Colorado.

Hansen, W.R., J. Chronic, and J. Matelock. 1978. *Climatography of the Front Range Urban Corridor and Vicinity, Colorado*. Geological Survey Professional Paper 1019. United States Government Printing Office, Washington, D.C.

Harrington, H.D. 1964. *Manual of the Plants of Colorado*. Swallow Press, Chicago.
A comprehensive though dated book on the identification of the flowering plants of Colorado. Technical keys and species descriptions, no illustrations or photographs.

Lane, J.A., and H.R. Holt. 1979. *A Birder's Guide to Eastern Colorado*. L and P Press, Denver.
Numerous self-guided tours to bird finding in eastern Colorado.

Lanner, R.M. 1981. *The Piñon Pine: A Natural and Cultural History*. University of Nevada Press, Reno.
A fascinating book that covers many aspects of the ecology of piñon pines.

Lechleitner, R.R., 1969. *Wild Mammals of Colorado: Their Appearance, Habits, Distribution and Abundance*. Pruett Publishing Company, Boulder, Colorado.
A semitechnical text that offers a wealth of interesting facts about the natural history of Colorado mammals. Out of print but available in many libraries.

Moenke, H. 1971. *Ecology of Colorado Mountains to Arizona Deserts*. Denver Museum of Natural History.

Richmond, G.M. 1974. *Raising the Roof of the Rockies*. Rocky Mountain Nature Association, Inc.
A geological history of the Front Range in Rocky Mountain National Park.

Siemer, E.G. 1977. *Colorado Climate*. Colorado Experiment Station, Colorado State University, Fort Collins.
A comprehensive summary of climatic data reported by numerous weather stations across the state.

Ward, J.V., and B.C. Kondratieff. 1992. *An Illustrated Guide to the Mountain Stream Insects of Colorado*. University Press of Colorado, Niwot, Colorado.

Willard, B.E., and S.Q. Foster. 1990. *A Roadside Guide to Rocky Mountain National Park*. Johnson Books, Boulder.
A complete and easy-to-use guide to the geology, wildlife, plant life, ecology, history and prehistory of the park.

Windell, J.T., B.E. Willard, D.J. Cooper, S.Q. Foster, C.F. Knud-Hansen, L.P. Rink, and G.N. Kiladis. 1986. *An Ecological Characterization of Rocky Mountain Montane and Subalpine Wetlands*. U.S. Fish and Wildlife Service, Biological Report 86(11).
A good summary of what is known about the many different types of wetlands in the Rocky Mountains.

Zwinger, A.H. 1981. *Beyond the Aspen Grove*. Harper and Row, New York.
A naturalist's look at many aspects of Colorado ecology. Immensely readable.

Zwinger, A.H., and B.E. Willard. 1972. *Land Above the Trees. A Guide to American Alpine Tundra*. Harper and Row, New York.
A well-written guide to alpine tundra ecology, with many excellent drawings of tundra plants.

If you are interested in preserving natural ecosystems . . .

Because of continually increasing pressures which disturb and destroy the region's natural ecosystems, certain governmental and private organizations have dedicated their efforts to the preservation of a sampling of ecosystems in their virgin condition. Notable among these organizations are the Colorado Natural Areas Program, administered by the Colorado Division of Parks and Outdoor Recreation, and the Nature Conservancy, a private nonprofit organization.

The Natural Areas Program identifies, evaluates, and protects sites on public and private lands having ecological or geological value of state or national significance. Protection occurs through designation of sites as Colorado Natural Areas. These preserves can contain relatively undisturbed, good representatives of any natural ecosystem or plant association, or they can be sites with special natural features (such as endangered species of plants or animals, or exemplary geological formations).

The Nature Conservancy purchases land with these same types of features and places the land in a nationwide set of preserves. The Nature Conservancy also has undertaken an ongoing program called the Natural Heritage Inventory to identify remaining undisturbed regional ecosystems and other special natural features. The two organizations are working against time to assure that examples of remaining natural ecosystems, rare species and geological features remain in perpetuity. For further information, contact:

Colorado Natural Areas Program
Division of Parks and Outdoor Recreation
Colorado Department of Natural Resources
1313 Sherman Street, Room 618
Denver, Colorado 80203

The Nature Conservancy
1244 Pine Street
Boulder, Colorado 80302

Index

Page numbers in **boldface type** indicate illustrations.

Abert's squirrel. *See* Squirrel, Abert's

Acid precipitation, effect on ecosystems, 217, 222

Agricultural use. *See* Cultivation; Grazing

Alder, 73, 75, **75**, 76, 78, 83, 148, 238, 247, 262

Algae, 206, 210, 218

Alpine tundra ecosystem. *See* Tundra ecosystem

Animal characteristics, 23-25. *See also* individual animal species and ecosystems

Apishapa Pass, 255

Aquatic ecosystems, 17, 59, 205-226

Arkansas Divide, 4, 5, 13, 271-274

Arkansas River, 4, 5, 61-62, 89, 95, 109, 244, 248, 275

Aspen (town), 142, 257

Aspen forest ecosystem, quaking, 21, 50, 51-52, 78, **140**, 141-152, 153, 169, 205, 234-235, 239, 254, 261

Aspen, quaking, 14, 21, 71, 76, 78, 83, 121, 123, 134, **140**, 141-152, **143**, 150, 165, 169, 171, 174, 182, 184, 227, 232, 235, 239, 247, 254-255, 260-261, 262, 269, 284

Avens, alpine, 193-194, **195**, 199, 202

Balsam poplar, 74, 83, 269

Battlement Mesa, 6

Beaver, 25, 69, 78, **81**, 84, 148, 210

Beetle, mountain pine, 123-124, 155

Bergen Park, 45, 239

Berthoud Pass, 163, 171, 182

Birch, 50, 56, 73, 77, 83, 182-183, 233

Bison, 27, 36, 39, 42, 52, 64

Bistort, alpine, reproduction of, 193, 194, 202

Blackbrush, 88, 89, 91, 103

Bluebird, mountain, **51**, 54, 57, 117, 125, 130, 149, 151, 239

Blue grama, 30, 31-34, 41, 50, 52, 56, 91, 101, 104, 111, 112, 116, 120, 130, 231, 236, 238, 249, 250-252, 256

Blue spruce. *See* Colorado blue spruce

Bluestem, 31-33, 41, 236

Boulder, **7**, 12, 81, 171, 231, 235

Boulder County loop tour, **231**, 231-235

Brainard Lake Recreation Area, 77, 172, 233

Bristlecone pine, **160, 163,** 161-166, 169, 174, 182, 185-186, 247, 253, 254, 272

Bristlecone pine woodland ecosystem, 21, **160**, 161-168, 240, 247

Buffalograss, **31**, 31-32, 34, 41, 236, 250

Cacti, 31, 41, 116, 130, 243, 244, 251-252

Caddisfly, 211, 212, **214**, 224. *See also* Insects, aquatic

Caloplaca, 102

Canada goose. *See* Goose, Canada

Canon City, 90

Cattle. *See* Grazing

Chaining, effect on ecosystems, 112

Chickaree. *See* Squirrel, pine

Chinook, 12, 275

Chipmunk, Colorado, 57, 101, 105, 117, **122**, 131, 139, 259

Clark's nutcracker. *See* Nutcracker, Clark's

Climate, 8-13, **20-21**. *See also* individual ecosystems

Continental, 275

Clone, aspen, 234

Cold air drainage, 9, **13, 20-21,** 48, 60

Colorado blue spruce, 73, **74**, 76, 81, 83, 232, 238, 249, 252, 253, 259, 273

Colorado National Monument, 109, **111**

Colorado Plateau Province, 2, 6-7, **8**, 17, 87, 88, 91, 142, 208

Colorado River, 1, 4, 6, 7, 62, 89, 213, **219**

Colorado Springs, 5, 13, 109, 227, 242, 249, 271

Columbine, Colorado blue, 144, **145**, 150, 178, 261

Comanche National Grasslands, 28

Continental Divide, 1, 4-6, **7**, 10, 12, 95, 108-109, 276

Corkbark fir, 170, 178, 253, 255, 273

Cottontail, Nuttall's, 23, **24**, **54**, 57, 84, 96, 117, 126, 131, 139, 151, 159, 167, 179, 259

Cottonwood, 27, 59, 60, **61**, 61, 62, 63, 64, 65-66, 67, 73, 74-76, 83, 148, 231-232, 238, 243, 245, 247, 249, 252, 259, 269-270

Crested Butte, 142

Cripple Creek, 244, 245, 248

Cucharas Pass, 255

Cultivation, effect on ecosystems, 27, 35, 39-40, 54, 92-93, 103, 128, 206, 244

Currant. *See* Wax currant

Current, effect on ecosystems, 205, 206-207, 208, 210, 211, 218

Cushion plants, 191, 192, 193, 197
Cushion trees, 181

Deer, mule, 25, 36, 42, 52, 54, 57, 64, 69,
    92, 96, 102-103, 105, 113, 117, 126,
    126, 128, 131, 139, 146, 147, 151, 156,
    159, 176, 187, 199, 203; white-tailed,
    63, 64, 69
Denver, 1, 4, 5, 13, 77, 120, 241, 245
Detritus, 209, 210, 211, 212, **215**
Dinosaur National Monument, 109
Dipper, American, 25, 65, 79, **82**, 84, 262
Douglas fir, 14, **20-21**, **22**, 81, 107, 121,
    123, 125, 133-134, 135, **135**, 138, 147,
    150, 154, 155, 165, 169, 232, 237-238,
    246-247, 252-254, 258, 260-262, 271-
    273
Douglas fir forest ecosystem, **20-21**, 21, 99,
    133, 133-140, 142, 232, 234, 235, 237,
    245, 249, 252-253, 255-256, 260
Dragonflies, 79-80, **215, 216,** 224. *See also*
    Insects, aquatic
Drought, 14, 35, 40, 48, 122
Durango, 99, 120, 142

Elk, 25, 36-37, 42, 49, 52, 54, 57, 64, 113,
    117, 126, 128, 131, 139, 146, 147, 148,
    151, 155, 156, 176, 179, 187, 199, 203,
    255
Engelmann spruce, 14, 76, 147, 150, 155,
    165, 169-170, **170**, 178, 182, 184, 186,
    247-248, 254-255, 262, 264, 273
Engelmann spruce–subalpine fir forest
    ecosystem, **20-21**, 21, 133, 154, 169-
    180
Estes Park, 45
Eutrophication, 217
Evergreen, 237-238

Fens, 45, 46, 47-48, 49-50, 55, 73, 76-77
Fire, effect on ecosystems, 31, 35, 81, 96,
    101, 112, 123, 136, 154, 164-165, 166,
    172, **173**, 174, 176, 177, 182, 186, 187,
    228, 234, 247, 254-255, 261-263
Fish, 206, 207, 210, 212-213, 216-217, 218,
    220, 222-223
Flag trees, **180**, 181, 184, 233, 264
Flooding, 60, 65, 72, 73, 78, 208-209, 222,
    223
Florissant Fossil Beds, 227
Foothills zone, **19**, 120
Fountain Creek Valley, 249
Four-winged saltbush, *See* Saltbush
Forest-tundra transition, **20-21**, 72, 170-
    171, 181-188, 190, 194, 234, 240, 264,
    276
Freeze-thaw processes, 4, 190, 194
Frog, wood, distribution of, 79, **219**
Front Range, 4, **7**, 9, 12, 14, **22**, 27, 47,
    135, 163, **191**, 240, 245, 278, 283

Gambel oak, 17, **87**, 98, 99, **100,** 100, 101,
    103, 107, 116, 123, 129, 236-237, 243,
    245-247, 249, 252, 255, 258, 260
Glaciers, 4, 76, 191, 213, 233, 277
Goose, Canada, 39, 64, **68**
Grand Junction, 7, 21
Grand Mesa, 6
Grand Valley, 93
Grasslands ecosystems. *See* Mountain
    grasslands; Plains grasslands
Grazing, effect on ecosystems, 27, 30, 35,
    40, 50-51, 52, 81, 92-93, 96, 103, 111,
    112, 115, 124, 128, 149, 199, 200, 228,
    244, 259
Greasewood, 17, 88, **89**, 89, 90-91, 92, 93,
    95, 103, 111, 251
Great Basin, 17, 23, 90, 94-95, 97
Great Plains, 1, 2, 4-6, **6**, 14, 23, 28
Great Plains Province, 6
Great Sand Dunes National Monument, 12,
    111
Greeley, 63
Ground squirrel, golden mantled, **53**, 53-
    54, 57, 97, 101, 105, 117, 126, 131,
    139, 151, 159, 167, 179, 203, 259

Hare, snowshoe, 23, 151, 167, **175**, 175,
    179, 199, 203
Human use of ecosystems, 206. *See also*
    Chaining; Cultivation; Fire; Grazing;
    Individual ecosystems; Logging; Min-
    ing; Recreational use; Urbanization

Ice ages, 4, 227
Indian paintbrush, 96, 104
Indians, 27, 110, 115, 158, 162, 200
Insects, aquatic, 65, **82**, 206, 207, 209, 210-
    212, **214-215**, 218, 219, 222

Jay, piñon, **114**, 114, 115, 244, 252, 260
Junegrass, 31, 32, 33, 34, 41, 50, 56, 96,
    104, 111, 112, 116, 130, 144, 150, 164,
    167
Juniper, **22**, 108, **109**, 109, 110, 111, 112,
    113, 116, 120, 121, 123, 129, 135, 138,
    144, 150, 154, 158, 166, 239, 243, 246,
    251, 252, 270-271

Kobresia, 184, 193, 200-201, **202**
Krummholz ecosystems. *See* Forest-tundra

Lakes, 71, 72, 76, 77, 205, 206, 213-221,
    224
La Veta, 256
Layering, 173, 185, 276
Limberpine, 123, 133, 161-168, **162**, 169,
    174, 182, 184, 233, 240, 247, 255, 272
Limberpine woodland ecosystem, 21, 133,
    161-168, 233, 240, 247, 253-254
Lizard, short-horned, 38, 42, **94**, 104, 116,
    126, 130

Lodgepole pine, 50, 51, 121, 123, 125, 146, 152, **156**, 158, 165, 169, 171, 174, 182, 234, 239, 262-263, 272
Lodgepole pine forest ecosystem, 14, 21, 136, **152**, 153-160, 171, 234, 239
Logging, effect on ecosystems, 65, 121, 128-129, 136, 164-165, 166, 174, 176, 228, 247, 255, 261, 263
Long's Peak, 12
Lowland riparian ecosystem, 17, 59-70, 72, 73, 74, 83, 232, 235, 243, 251, 268
Lumbering. *See* Logging

Marmot, 57, 101-102, 105, 126, 131, 139, 151, 159, 167, 179, **186**, 198, 203, 266
Marten, pine, 136, 139, 156, **157**, 159, 167, 175, 179, 203
Mesa Verde National Park, 109
Middle Park, 9, 45, 46, 95
Middle Rocky Mountain Province, 2
Migration, animal, 23-24, 64, 72, 79, 126, 198, 227; plant, 14, 205
Mining, effect on ecosystems, 65, 82, 128, 137, 142, 158, 176-177, 187, 212, 222, 247, 261
Mistletoe, 124, 128, 130, 155, 158
Monarch Pass, 171
Monsoon flow, 10
Montane forests, 16, 17-18, 50, 72, 75, 83, 98, 125, 133, 136, 142, 153, 155, 163
Monument Lake, 253
Moose, reintroduction of, 78-79, **84**
Morrison, 99, 237, 241
Mountain grassland and meadow ecosystems, 16, **44**, 45-57, 72, 76, 121, 122-123, 134, 174, 232-233, 235, 238, 248, 255, 256, 264
Mountain mahogany, 17, 98-99, 100, 101, **102**, 102-103, 111, 113, 116, 123, 129, 236-237, 241, 243, 245, 249, 252, 259
Mountain riparian ecosystem, 17, 46, 50, 52, 60, **70**, 71-86, 141, 147, 232, 233, 238, 241, 245, 246, 252, 253, 259, 262
Mount Elbert, 4
Mount Evans, 163, 200, 240
Mount Goliath Natural Area, 163, 240

Nederland, 234
Niwot Ridge, 185, **191**
North Park, 9, 45, 46, 95, **219**
Nutcracker, Clark's, 115, 136, 138, 158, 159, **164**, 165, 167, 176, 178

Oak. *See* Gambel oak
Otter, river, reintroduction of, 79
Ouray, 142
Overgrazing. *See* Grazing
Overturn, lake, 217
Owl, burrowing, 34, 38, 42; western screech, 68, **80**, 84
Owl Canyon, 110

Pagosa Springs, 120
Paintbrush. *See* Indian paintbrush
Palmer Divide. *See* Arkansas Divide
Patterned ground, 190-191, **191**, 193, 196, 277
Pawnee Buttes, **6**, 162
Pawnee National Grassland, 28
Periphyton, 210, 211-212
Permafrost, 191, 194
Phantom Canyon loop tour, **242**, 242-249
Physiographic provinces, defined, **3**, 2-7
Pika, **198**, 198, 203
Pike, Zebulon, 63
Pike's Peak, 2, 4, 8, 170, 249
Pine beetle. *See* Beetle, mountain pine
Pink, moss, **192**, 193-194, 202
Piñon jay. *See* Jay, piñon
Piñon pine, 14, 89, **108**, 108, 110, 112, 162, 243, 246-247, 251, 252, 271, 272, 283
Piñon pine–juniper woodland ecosystem, 2, 16, 17, **20-21**, 28, 95, 99, **106**, 107-118, **111**, 120, 142, 165, 243-244, 249, 251, 256, 259
Plains grasslands ecosystem, 14, 16, **20-21**, 27-44, **26**, 49, 94, 98, 231, 236, 243, 249, 250
Plains life zone, 16, **19**, 268
Plankton, 218, 220
Plant characteristics. *See* individual plant species and ecosystems
Plant distribution, changes with altitude, **19**, 14-23, 46-47, 72, 110-111, 120, 142, 174, 181; changes with exposure, **19**, **22**, 22, 134, 136, 142, 182, 237; correlation with environment, 14-23. *See also* individual ecosystems and species
Pocket gopher, northern, 35, 52-53, 57, 128, 147, 148, 151, 195-197, 199, 203, 261
Pollution, water, effect on ecosystems, 82, 206, 212, 222, 228
Poncha Pass, 95
Ponderosa pine, 14, **22**, 46, 47, 48, 50, 51, 54, 99, 107, **121, 125, 129,** 134, 135, 136, 142, 154, 155, 165, 231-232, 237, 238, 241, 243, 247, 252-254, 260, 272
Ponderosa pine forest ecosystem, 17-21, **20-21**, 28, 101, 119-132, **133**, 134, 142, 232, 234-235, 237-238, 241, 243, 246, 249, 252
Ponds, 62, **64**, 65, 71, 72, 76, 77, 78, 79, 83, 205, 206, 207, 213-221, 224
Poplar. *See* Balsam poplar
Porcupine, 117, 127, 139, 151, 159, 165, 167, 179
Prairie, 1, 2, 27-44, 189, 277
Prairie dog, black-tailed, 35, 36, 37-38, **38**
Precipitation, acid; change with elevation, 9-10, **11**, 13, **20-21**, 208; convective, 10, **11**, 276; orographic, 9, **11**, 277; upslope, 10, **11**. *See also* acid precipitation

Pronghorn, 27, **28**, 36, 38, 43, 52, 64, 92, 96, 105, 113
Ptarmigan, white-tailed, 187, **196, 197**, 198, 203
Pueblo, 90
Purgatoire River, 5, 110, 251-253

Rattlesnake, western, 37, 42, **97**, 104, 115, 116, 130
Rabbitbrush, 34, 41, 90, 95-96, 101, 103, 111, 116, 236, 243-244, 250-252, 256, 258-259
Recreational use, effect on ecosystems, 81, 187, 200-201, 218
Red Mountain Pass, 142
Red Rocks Lake, 77
Reservoir, 65, 205, 213, 218, 220-221, 222
Riffles, **207**, 207, 208, 210
Rifle, 7, **106**
Rio Grande River, 4
Riparian ecosystems. *See* Lowland, mountain riparian ecosystems
Rivers, 59, 60, 64, 65, 81, 205, 206-213, 224
Roan Plateau, 6
Roaring Fork River, 257-260, 262-263
Roaring Fork River Valley to Independence Pass tour, **257**, 257-266
Rocky Mountains, 1, 2-4, 14, 16, 23, 64, 65, 79, 133, 148, 186
Rocky Mountain National Park, 4, 12, **44**, 95, 122, 183, 200, 212, 234

Sagebrush, 17, **33**, 34, 35, 41, 87-88, 90, 91, 93, 93-97, 103, 111, 116, 142, 258
Salamander, tiger, 57, 65, 68, 79, 84, 220-221, 225, 226
Saltbush, four-winged, 17, 34, 41, 88-91, 93, 95, 103, 111, 116, 243, 251, 256
Salt cedar, 61-62, 67, 243-244
Sand dunes, 12, 91
Sandhills, **33**, 34-35
Sangre de Cristos Range, 12
San Juan Mountains, 5, 142
San Luis Valley, 9, 12, 17, 47, 48, 89, 93, 95, 110
Shadscale, 17, 88, 89-90, 91, 95, 103, 111, 116, 244
Sheep, bighorn, 57, 131, **199**, 199, 203
Shrubland ecosystems, 17, 28, 87-106; sagebrush, 17, **19**, 87, 93-97, 258; semidesert, 17, **19**, **20-21**, 88-93, 243, 251; mountain, 17, **19**, 48, 71, 98-103, 121, 123, 134, 231, 235, 236, 243, 249, 258
Snowshoe hare. *See* Hare, snowshoe
Soils, 236, 240, 243, 251, 254, 258-261, 264. *See also* individual ecosystems
Southern Rocky Mountain Province, 2-6, **3, 5, 18**, 23, 25, 119, 120, 134, 136, 142, 147, 163, 165
South Park, 9, 45, 46, 55, 163

South Platte River, 4, 5, 60-63, 248, 275
Spanish Peaks, 5, 255
Spanish Peaks loop tour, **250**, 250-256
Sparrow, white-crowned, 54, 79, 84, **187**, 187, 198, 203, 265
Spruce-fir ecosystems. *See* Engelmann spruce–subalpine fir ecosystems
Squirrel, Abert's, 115, 125, **127**, 127-128, 131; pine, 136, **137**, 139, 155, 156, 159, 165, 167, 176, 179
Stonewall Gap, 252
Streams, 59, 60, 61-62, 65, 66, 71, 72, 75, 76, **77**, 79, 81, **82**, 82, 205, 206-213, **207**, 218, 219, 221, 224
Subalpine fir, 14, 21, 133, 147, 150, 155, 165, 169-180, **171**, 178, 182, 184, **185**, 248, 262, 264, 273
Subalpine forests, 16, **20-21**, 21, 50, 72, 75, 142, 153, 163, 174, 188, 190
Suckers, aspen, 52, 144-145, 146, 239, 278
Summit Lake loop tour, **236**, 236-241

Temperature, change with elevation, 9, **20-21**; water, effect on ecosystems, 205, 217
Timberline, 16, 49, 52, 162, 166, 182, 216, 249, 278
Tree island, 181, 184-186, **185**, 240, 264-265
Treeline, 14, 142, 154, 170, 174, 177, 182, **183**, 186, 190, 227, 231, 255, 275, 278
Trinidad, 5, 99, 250-251, 256
Trout, **209**, 210, 212, 213, 220, 220-221, 226
Tundra ecosystem, alpine, 1, 9-10, 12, 14, 16-17, **20-21**, 21-22, 72, 87, 166, 181, **188**, 189-204, 216, 234, 240, 249, 255-256, 265, 278
Turbidity, water, effect on ecosystems, 205, 208, 210, 212

Uncompahgre Plateau, 6
Upper Sonoran life zone, 19
Urbanization, effect on ecosystems, 27, 38-39, 228

Walsenburg, 89, 110, 250, 256
Wax currant, 51, 56, 67, 120, 123, 129, 252
Western red cedar. *See* Juniper
Wet Mountain Valley, 46-47, **47**
White fir, 21, 73, 76, 83, 133-134, 246, 253, 274
Willow, 27, 49-50, 56, 60-62, 67, **72**, 73, 74-79, **77**, 80-81, 83, 183-184, 194, 198, 202, 207, 232-233, 237, 238, 241, 245-247, 249, 252, 259-260, 264-265, 268
Wind, change with elevation, 12; valley, 12, **13**. *See also* Chinook
Wolf Creek Pass, 171
Woodrat, distribution of, 113; Mexican, **98**, 102, 105, 113, 117, 131
Wyoming Basin Province, 17